THE IMMIGRATION AND NATIONALITY ACT OF 1965

THE IMMIGRATION AND NATIONALITY ACT OF 1965

A REFERENCE GUIDE

Michael C. LeMay

Guides to Historic Events in America
Randall M. Miller, Series Editor

ABC-CLIO®

An Imprint of ABC-CLIO, LLC
Santa Barbara, California • Denver, Colorado

Library of Congress Cataloging-in-Publication Data

Names: LeMay, Michael C., 1941- author.
Title: The Immigration and Nationality Act of 1965 : a reference guide / Michael C. LeMay.
Description: First edition. | Santa Barbara : ABC-CLIO, 2020. | Series: Guides to historic events in America | Includes bibliographical references and index.
Identifiers: LCCN 2019053844 (print) | LCCN 2019053845 (ebook) | ISBN 9781440868979 (cloth) | ISBN 9781440868986 (ebook)
Subjects: LCSH: Emigration and immigration law—United States. | United States. Immigration and Nationality Act Amendments of 1965. | United States—Emigration and immigration—Government policy—History. | Emigration and immigration law—United States—History.
Classification: LCC KF4819 .L46 2020 (print) | LCC KF4819 (ebook) | DDC 342.7308/2–dc23
LC record available at https://lccn.loc.gov/2019053844
LC ebook record available at https://lccn.loc.gov/2019053845

ISBN: 978–1–4408–6897–9 (print)
      978–1–4408–6898–6 (ebook)

24 23 22 21 20   1 2 3 4 5

This book is also available as an eBook.

ABC-CLIO
An Imprint of ABC-CLIO, LLC

ABC-CLIO, LLC
147 Castilian Drive
Santa Barbara, California 93117
www.abc-clio.com

This book is printed on acid-free paper. ∞
Manufactured in the United States of America

CONTENTS

LIST OF TABLES

SERIES FOREWORD

P erhaps no people have been more difficult to comprehend than the Americans. As J. Hector St. Jean de Crèvecoeur asked during the American Revolution, countless others have echoed ever after—"What then is this American, this new man?" What, indeed? Americans then and after have been, and remain, a people in the process of becoming. They have been, and are, a people in motion, whether coming from a distant shore, crossing the mighty Mississippi, or packing off to the suburbs, and all the while following the promise of an American dream of realizing life, liberty, and happiness. The directions of such movement have changed, and sometimes the trajectory has taken a downward arc in terms of civil war and economic depression, but always the process has continued.

Making sense of that American experience demands attention to critical moments—events—that reflected and affected American ideas and identities. Although Americans have constructed an almost linear narrative of progress from the days of George Washington to today in relating their common history, they also have marked that history by recognizing particular events as pivotal in explaining who and why they believed and acted as they did at particular times and over time. Such events have forced Americans to consider closely their true interests. They also have challenged their commitment to professed beliefs of freedom and liberty, equality and opportunity, tolerance and generosity. Whether fighting for independence or empire, drafting and implementing a frame of government, reconstructing a nation divided by civil war, struggling for basic rights and the franchise, creating a mass-mediated culture, standing up for capitalism and democracy and against communism, to name several critical developments, Americans have understood that historic events are more than just moments. They are processes of change made clear through particular events but not bound to a single moment or instance. Such thinking about the character and consequence of American history informs this new series of *Guides to Historic Events in America*.

Drawing on the latest and best literature, and bringing together narrative overviews and critical chapters of important historic events, the books in the series function as both reference guides and informed analyses to critical events that have shaped American life, culture, society, economy, and politics and fixed America's place in the world. The books do not promise a comprehensive reading and rendering of American history. Such is not yet, if ever, possible for any single work or series. Nor do they chart a single interpretive line, though they share common concerns and methods of inquiry. Each book stands alone, resting on the expertise of the author and the strength of the evidence. At the same time, taken together the books in this new series will provide a dynamic portrait of that on-going work-in-progress, America itself.

Each book follows a common format, with a chronology, historical overview, topical chapters on aspects of the historical event under examination, a set of biographies of key figures, selected essential primary documents, and an annotated bibliography. As such, each book holds many uses for students, teachers, and the general public wanting and needing to know the principal issues and the pertinent arguments and evidence on significant events in American history. The combination of historical description and analysis, biographies, and primary documents also moves readers to approach each critical event from multiple perspectives and with a critical eye. Each book in its structure and content invites students and teachers, in and out of the classroom, to consider and debate the character and consequence(s) of the historic event in question. Such debate invariably will bring readers back to that most critical and never-ending question of what was/is "the American" and what does, and must, "America" mean.

Randall M. Miller
Saint Joseph's University, Philadelphia

PREFACE

T his book is a narrative history and analysis of fundamental law of U.S. immigration policy: the forces that shaped it; both its short-term and long-term impact on the flow of immigration to the United States since it was enacted in 1965; how and why major changes were made to it; which organizations and actors have played and play important roles in determining immigration policy; its transformative impact on American culture, economics, politics, and society; and where immigration is likely headed in the future. It is also about the dynamic ethnicity of America. Immigration is an extraordinarily complex process. Crafting immigration policy is likewise complex, often contentious, and for many observers of American politics and policymaking, at times obtuse and frustrating.

The impact of immigration is enormous and filled with dramatic human interest. America has absorbed a diverse array of ethno-religious groups that have profoundly shaped and re-shaped the country. A host of interest groups developed within the American political scene to advocate for or against immigration reform measures. Organized labor, as exemplified by the American Federation of Labor–Congress of Industrial Organizations (AFL-CIO), long advocated to restrict immigration, but then essentially flipped their position on the matter after enactment of the 1965 act. Church groups, such as the Catholic Legal Immigration Network and the Church World Service, have for some decades strongly supported comprehensive immigration reform measures. Ethnic groups, like the League of Latin American Citizens, used the federal courts to adjudicate on the issue of immigration and on the impact of immigration policy on their members.

A group of unauthorized migrants brought to the United States as children, commonly known as the Dreamers, formed an advocacy group—United We Dream—to get President Barack Obama's DACA program enacted into a law to give them a more secure, legal foundation for being in the United States and to protect against deportation. Think tanks, such as the Center for Immigration Studies, the Center for Migration Studies, and the Pew Hispanic Center, developed to study problems associated with the immigration flow and to issue scholarly reports on the topic. Progressive advocacy groups such as the American Civil Liberties Union took positions on pro-immigration reforms and battled with such conservative advocacy groups as the American Immigration Control Foundation, Americans for Legal Immigration PAC, and the Federation of American Immigration Reform that took essentially opposite positions. The huge wave of refugees after the Vietnam War and passage of the 1965 act generated groups like the National Network for Immigration Refugee Rights to advocate for them.

In short, immigration has been and continues to be a transformative force on America, to the delight of some and the chagrin of others. Since 1965, immigration and immigration law can be said to have significantly remade America. As detailed in this book, the cultural, demographic, economic, political, and social impacts have been profound, and Congress has been struggling with the issue of comprehensive immigration reform for more than the past decade. It is an important and timely topic, perennially impacting American politics. The stalemate over solutions to the immigration policy problem between pro- and anti-immigration forces in American politics have made it a public policy conundrum.[1]

The book is structured as follows: an introductory essay that puts immigration law into a broader U.S. and world historical context, a Chronology presenting the most critically important events in immigration lawmaking from 1820 to the present; three chapters that review U.S. immigration policy from the precursor laws—especially the national-origins acts of the 1920s, to the enactment of the Immigration and Nationality Act of 1965—and detail its elaborate system of preferences, and then assess its long-term impact on immigration policymaking from the 1970s to today. The chapter on the 1965 law and its aftermath emphasizes the transformative impact of immigration law. The analysis of U.S. immigration law over its 200-year history suggests to the reader insights into the advantages and disadvantages as well as some likely anticipated and unanticipated consequences of major revisions to U.S. immigration law, policy, and politics. The chapters are followed by 15 analytical and biographical essays that profile five organizations and 10 individuals that illustrate the impact of the many stakeholders involved in immigration policymaking and in proposing or opposing changes to immigration law. A primary documents section presents excerpts of public laws, presidential statements or executive orders, and court rulings on immigration law and policy. An annotated bibliography of some major print sources covers important works on immigration and immigration law and provides useful guides for future research. A glossary of key terms and a detailed subject index comprise the backmatter of the book.

NOTE

1. Michael Barone, *Shaping Our Nation: How Surges of Migration Transformed America and Its Politics* (New York: Crown Forum, 2013); Patrick J. Hayes, ed., *The Making of Modern Immigration: An Encyclopedia of People and Ideas* (Santa Barbara, CA: ABC-CLIO, 2012); Hiroshi Motomura, *Immigration Outside the Law* (New York: Oxford University Press, 2014); and Aristide Zolberg, *A Nation by Design: Immigration Policy in the Fashioning of America* (Cambridge, MA: Russell Sage Foundation at Harvard University Press, 2008).

CHRONOLOGY

1790   Congress establishes uniform rule of naturalization, imposing a two-year residency for aliens who are "free white persons of good moral character."

1802   Congress revises 1790 Act to require a five-year residency and that naturalizing citizens renounce allegiance and fidelity to foreign powers.

1819   Congress requires shipmasters to deliver a manifest enumerating all aliens transported for immigration and requiring secretary of state to inform Congress of the numbers. For the first time, an official count of legal immigrants is kept.

1848   Treaty of Guadalupe Hidalgo guarantees citizenship to Mexicans remaining in the territory ceded by Mexico to the United States. Treaty sets the first base for the flow of Mexicans to the United States and provides base for future legal and undocumented immigration forging the first link in "chain migration" from Mexico.

1855   Castle Garden becomes New York's port of entry for legal immigration. The volume of immigration sets the stage for later development of "visa overstayers" who remain because such extensive numbers overwhelms the ability of immigration authorities to keep track of them.

1862   Congress passes Homestead Act, granting acres of free land to settlers who develop land in frontier regions and remain on it for five years, spurring high levels of immigration.

1868   The Fourteenth Amendment is ratified, guaranteeing that all persons born or naturalized are citizens and that no state may abridge their rights without due process or deny them equal protection under the law, ensuring citizenship rights to former slaves and ending "free white persons" phrase of citizenship. It establishes supremacy of federal law over acts by state governments in matters pertaining to citizenship, naturalization, and immigration.

1870   Congress enacts law granting citizenship to persons of African descent.

1882   Congress passes Chinese Exclusion Act barring immigration of Chinese laborers for 10 years and denying them eligibility for naturalization. Its harsh provisions induce many Chinese immigrants to get around the law by using false documents—such as paper sons and daughters—setting the precedent for using fraudulent documents by illegal aliens used to the present day.

1885   Congress enacts law banning laborers to immigrate under a contract with a U.S. employer who in any manner prepays passage of the laborer.

1886   *Yick Wo v. Hopkins* overturns a San Francisco ordinance against Chinese laundry workers as discriminatory and unconstitutional under the Fourteenth Amendment on grounds of depriving any person, even a noncitizen, of life, liberty, or property without due process.

1888   Congress passes the Scott Act, expanding the Chinese Exclusion Act by rescinding reentry permits for Chinese laborers and prohibiting their return.

1889   In *Chae Chan Ping v. United States,* the Supreme Court upholds the right of Congress to repeal the certificate of reentry as in the 1888 Scott Act, thereby excluding ex post facto certain Chinese immigrants previously entered legally.

1891	Congress expands the classes of individuals excluded from admission, forbids soliciting immigrants, and creates the office of superintendent of immigration.
1892	Ellis Island is opened as the leading port of entry.
1894	Congress extends the Chinese Exclusion Act and establishes the Bureau of Immigration within the Treasury Department.
1897	A federal district court decides the case *In re Rodriquez*, affirming the citizenship rights of Mexican based on the 1848 Treaty of Guadalupe Hidalgo notwithstanding that such persons may not be considered "white."
1898	In the case of *United States v. Wong Kim Ark* the Supreme Court rules a native-born son of Asian descent is indeed a citizen of the United States despite the fact that his parents may have been ineligible for citizenship.
1903	Congress enacts moves immigration responsibility to the Department of Commerce and Labor.
1906	The Basic Law of Naturalization codifies a uniform law for naturalization, that with some amendments and supplements, forms the basic naturalization law thereafter.
1907	Congress adds regulations about issuing passports and about the expatriation and marriage of U.S. women to foreigners that is not repealed until 1922. President Theodore Roosevelt issues the executive order known as the Gentleman's Agreement by which Japan agrees to restrict emigration of laborers from Japan and Korea, then under Japanese jurisdiction. Picture brides are permitted emigration. Congress passes the White-Slave Traffic Act forbidding importation of any woman or girl for the purpose of prostitution or similar immoral purposes.
1911	The Dillingham Commission issues its report, the recommendations of which form the basis for the quota acts of the 1920s.

1915   The Americanization/100 Percent campaign begins supported by government and private enterprises. These social movements are the first attempt at "forced assimilation" and the adoption of the English language and social customs. After World War I, its perceived failures set the stage for the quota acts of the 1920s.

1917   The United States enters World War I in April. Congress enacts a literacy test and bars all immigration from a specified area known as the Asian barred zone. The Departments of State and Labor issue a joint order requiring issuance of visas by U.S. consular officers in the country of origin rather than seeking permission to enter the United States when arriving at the port of entry. Puerto Ricans are granted U.S. citizenship.

1918   Congress grants the president sweeping power to disallow entrance or departure of aliens during time of war, similarly used in virtually all periods of war thereafter.

1919   Congress grants honorably discharged Native Americans citizenship for their service in World War I. In the summer, the Red Scare following the Bolshevik Revolution in Russia leads to summary deportation of certain specified "radical" aliens deemed a threat to national security, serving as a precursor to the USA Patriot Act in that respect.

1921   Congress passes the first Quota Act basing immigration from a particular country at 3 percent of the foreign-born population from that country as enumerated in the 1910 census.

1922   Congress enacts the Cable Act stating that the right of any woman to become a naturalized citizen shall not be abridged because of her sex or because she is wed to an alien ineligible for citizenship.

1923   In *United States v. Bhagat Singh Thind*, the Supreme Court rules that "white person" means those persons who appear and would be commonly viewed as white. East Asian Indians, although Caucasians, are not "white" and are therefore ineligible for citizenship through naturalization.

1924   Congress passes the Johnson-Reed Act setting the national origin quota for a particular country at 2 percent of the foreign-born population from that country as of the 1890 census, drastically shifting immigration from southern, central, and eastern Europe to northwestern Europe. It bars the admission of most Asians, classified as "aliens ineligible for citizenship." Congress passes an act granting citizenship to those Native Americans who had not previously received it by the 1887 Dawes Act or by military service during World War I.

1925   Congress establishes the Border Patrol to police the U.S. borders against undocumented entrants. The Border Patrol is charged with finding and deporting unauthorized aliens from the interior who had eluded apprehension at the border.

1929   President Herbert Hoover proclaims new and permanent quotas in which national-origin quotas for European immigrants are based on the proportion of those nationalities in the total population using the 1920 census and fixing the total number to be admitted at just over 150,000.

1929 to 1939   U.S. immigration levels slow dramatically in response to the worldwide Great Depression.

1940   Congress passes the Registration Law requiring noncitizens to register their addresses every year. The process remains in effect until 1980. Millions of those forms are backlogged and "lost" in INS warehouses. The failure of this program contributes to the push in the 1980s to crack down on illegal immigrants and visa overstayers through enhanced capability of the INS, which is never achieved.

1941   President Franklin D. Roosevelt issues a proclamation to control persons entering or leaving the United States based on the first War Powers Act.

1942   The United States and Mexico allow migrant farm-workers to enter the United States as temporary labor to satisfy wartime labor shortages in agriculture in what becomes known as the Bracero Program.

1943   The Supreme Court rules, in *Hirabayashi v. United States*, that the executive orders for curfews and evacuation programs are constitutional, based on "military necessity."

1944   On December 18, in *Korematsu v. United States*, the Supreme Court again affirms the constitutionality of the executive orders excluding Japanese Americans from remaining in certain "excluded zones." The court rules in *ex parte Mitsuye Endo* that the internment program is an unconstitutional violation of the habeas corpus rights of U.S. citizens—namely the *nisei.*

1945   Congress passes the War Brides Act to admit alien spouses and alien children of citizen members of the U.S. armed forces.

1949   Congress passes the Agriculture Act with provisions to recruit temporary farmworkers from Mexico, establishing by law the Bracero Program.

1956   President Dwight Eisenhower establishes a "parole" system for Hungarian Freedom Fighters. Two years later, Congress endorses the procedures by an act to admit Hungarian refugees.

1959   Congress amends the Immigration and Nationality Act of 1952 to provide for unmarried sons and daughters of U.S. citizens to enter as "nonquota" immigrants.

1960   On July 14, Congress enacts a program to assist resettlement of refugees from communist countries who are paroled by the attorney general, mostly Cubans. On

November 8, John F. Kennedy is elected president of the United States.

1963   On November 22, John F. Kennedy is assassinated in Dallas, Texas.

1964   The Bracero Program ends. On November 3, Lyndon B. Johnson is elected president of the United States.

1965   On October 3, Congress passes the Immigration and Nationality Act, amending the 1954 act, ending the quota system, and establishing a preference system emphasizing family reunification and meeting certain skill goals, standardizing admission procedures, and setting per country limits of 20,000 for Eastern Hemisphere nations, with a total of 170,000, and setting the first ceiling on Western Hemisphere immigration at 120,000.

1966   Congress amends the 1965 act to adjust the status of Cuban refugees setting up the distinction between refugees based on anticommunist U.S. foreign policy goals and those based on economic refugee status.

1967   The UN Convention and Protocol on Refugees is established; 130 nations sign the protocol accords. Refugees entering under its provisions, such as Cuban refugees, are given resettlement assistance, whereas those entering as economic refugees, such as the Haitians, are excluded.

1968   The Bilingual Education Act is passed. President Johnson issues a proclamation on the UN Protocols on the Status of Refugees endorsing the U.S. commitment to the multinational protocols.

1972   The U.S. House of Representative passes, but the Senate kills, a bill that would have made it illegal to knowingly hire an illegal alien, becoming the first attempts prior to 1986 to impose what becomes known as "employer sanctions" for hiring illegal aliens.

1975	The fall of Saigon and Vietnam, along with Cambodia and Laos, precipitates a massive flight of refugees to the United States from the Indochina region. As refugees from communist countries, Vietnamese, Cambodians, and Laotians are assisted in resettlement and aided by assimilation-assistance programs, many conducted by church-based organizations assisting immigrants. President Jimmy Carter later establishes, and Congress funds, the Indochinese Resettlement Program. Soviet Jews flee in large numbers. A civil war in El Salvador causes their refugee movement, and Haitians continue arriving in large numbers.
1976	Congress amends the 1965 act extending the per-country limits of visa applications on a first-come, first-served bases to Western Hemisphere nations as regulated by the preference system. The Supreme Court rules, in *Matthews v. Diaz*, that an alien has no right to Social Security or Medicare benefits into which that they paid.
1978	President Jimmy Carter and Congress establish the Select Commission on Immigration and Refugee Policy (SCIRP).
1979	SCIRP begins its work. An influx of boat people from Vietnam and Southeast Asia arrives.
1980	Congress passes the Refugee Act to systematize refugee policy, incorporating the UN definition of refugee into U.S. law; and accepting 50,000 persons annually who have a "well-founded fear" of persecution based on race, religion, nationality, or membership in a social or political movement, and providing for the admission of 5,000 "asylum seekers."
1981	An economic recession begins. On March 1, SCIRP issues its final report recommending changes in policy that form the basis for the Immigration Reform and Control Act of 1986 and subsequent reform acts

underlying proposed reforms even after 2001. President Ronald Reagan creates a Task Force on Immigration and Refugee Policy.

1982   A federal district judge rules the incarceration of Haitians unconstitutional; orders the release of 1,900 detainees. A major bill to amend the Immigration and Nationality Act of 1965 is introduced into Congress.

1983   Another immigration reform bill is introduced into Congress. The Supreme Court rules, in *Chadha et al.*, that the use of the legislative veto to overturn certain INS deportation proceedings, rules and regulations by the House of Representatives is unconstitutional.

1984   Immigration reform bills pass in different versions in both chambers of Congress but die in conference committee.

1985   Senator Alan Simpson (R-WY) reintroduces what is known as the Simpson/Mazzoli/Rodino bill to reform U.S. immigration law with a focus on illegal immigration.

1986   The Supreme Court rules, in *Jean v. Nelson*, that the INS denial of parole to certain undocumented aliens (Haitians) is unconstitutional. Congress enacts the Immigration Reform and Control Act (IRCA) that imposes employer sanctions and establishes a legalization program granting amnesty to about 1.5 million illegal aliens and more than 1 million special agricultural workers.

1987   In *INS v. Cardoza-Fonseca*, the Supreme Court decides that the government must relax its standards for deciding whether aliens who insist they would be persecuted if they returned to their homeland are eligible for asylum.

1988   The Senate passes, but the House kills, the Kennedy-Simpson bill in what becomes the 1990 act. The U.S.-

Canada Free Trade Implementation Act is signed into law. Congress amends the 1965 Immigration Act regarding H-1 category use by nurses.

1989   The International Conference for Central American Refugees is held.

1990   Congress passes IMMACT, a major reform of legal immigration that sets new ceilings for worldwide immigration, redefines the preference system for family reunification and for employment-based preference, and establishes a category called "the diversity immigrants." It enacts special provisions regarding Central American refugees, Filipino veterans, and persons fleeing Hong Kong, and providing for revisions to the naturalization process.

1993   Congress ratifies the North American Free Trade Agreement (NAFTA). Donald Huddle issues his report, "The Cost of Immigration," beginning a decades-long debate over the relative costs and benefits of legal and illegal immigration.

1994   California passes Proposition 187, the "Save Our State" initiative. Congress passes the Violence Against Women Act granting special status through cancellation of removal and self-petitioning provisions.

1995   A federal district court rules, in *LULAC et al. v. Wilson et al.*, many of the provisions of Proposition 187 unconstitutional. The Government Accountability Office issues its first major report on the costs of illegal aliens to governments and to the overall economy. A Human Rights Watch report is highly critical of the INS and alleged abuses.

1996   In June, the Board of Immigration Appeals grants for the first time asylum to a woman on the basis of gender persecution (female genital mutilation). Congress passes the Personal Responsibility and Work Opportunity

Act with numerous immigration-related provisions that essentially enact aspects of Proposition 187 regarding welfare and other public benefits that had been overturned by the *LULAC v. Wilson* decision. Congress passes the Illegal Immigration Reform and Immigrant Responsibility Act (IIRIRA) with more than 60 provisions of the omnibus spending bill removing welfare and economic benefits to illegal aliens and to some legal resident aliens. The Anti-Terrorism and Effective Death Penalty Act passes, giving INS inspectors the power to make "on-the-spot credible fear" determinations involving asylum. The Central American Regional Conference on Migration is held in Puebla, Mexico. The Border Patrol records 1.6 million apprehensions at U.S. borders, and Congress authorizes the addition of 1,000 new Border Patrol agents annually.

1997   The Jordan Commission on Immigration Reform recommends restructuring the INS. Expedited Enforcement Rules of the IIRIRA take effect at U.S. land borders, international airports, and seaports to issue and enforce expulsion orders, and 4,500 INS officers are added at 300 ports of entry. The Government Accountability Office issues its *Report on the Fiscal Impact of Newest Americans.*

1998   President Clinton sends a bill to Congress to restructure the INS, but it dies in committee when the Judiciary Committee begins impeachment hearings. The Agriculture Job Opportunity Benefits and Security Act creates a pilot program for 20,000 to 25,000 farmworkers. The Social Security Board documents the effects of immigration on the Trust Fund and on the long-term SSF crisis as the U.S. population ages and fewer active workers support ever-growing numbers of retirees. Congress passes the American Competitiveness and Workforce Improvement Act expanding the H-1B category to include the computer industry. California voters approve

Proposition 227, ending bilingual education in state schools. The Children of Immigrants Longitudinal Study is issued.

1999   The Carnegie Endowment for International Peace presents its International Migration Policy Program. Twenty-one nongovernmental organizations involved in immigration policy call for INS restructuring, the separation of enforcement from visa and naturalization functions, and sending some of its functions to the Department of Labor and to Health and Human Services. INS provides Border Patrol adjudication. In *INS v. Aguirre-Aguirre*, a unanimous Supreme Court rules that aliens who have committed serious nonpolitical crimes are ineligible to seek asylum regardless of the risk of persecution when returned to their country of origin. The Trafficking Victims Protection Act is passed. With a restored economy, President Clinton restores some of the benefits stripped away from legal immigrants by the 1996 IIRIRA act. On November 22, Elian Gonzalez is rescued off the Florida coast. UNHCR issues guidelines related to detention of asylum seekers in Geneva, Italy. The Trafficking Victims Protection Act is passed.

2000   Negotiations on the Elian Gonzalez case begin Attorney General Reno approves a DOJ raid on the Miami home to return Gonzalez to his father in Cuba. On June 1, in *Gonzales v. Reno*, a circuit court rules that only the father of Elian Gonzalez can speak for the boy.

2001   September 11, terrorists attack the World Trade Center's towers in New York City and the Pentagon in Washington, D.C. Immediate calls for a crackdown on terrorists begin. On October 24, Congress passes the USA Patriot Act granting the AG, the FBI, and DOJ sweeping authority to detain "enemy combatants" involved in or suspected of terrorism. The "Dream Act" is introduced for the first time.

2002   The INS issues notice to several of the, by then, dead hijackers' permission to enroll in U.S. flight training programs. This results in immediate calls to restructure the INS and to remove its Border Patrol functions. In November, Congress creates a cabinet-level Department of Homeland Security (DHS), giving the attorney general (AG) sweeping new powers for expedited removal. The INS is abolished, and immigration policy is moved to the DHS. The UN issues its Protocols on Human Trafficking and Immigrant Smuggling, signed by 141 countries.

2003   In January, the Terrorist Threat Integration Center is created.

2004   The 9/11 Commission issues its report. Congress passes the Intelligence Reform and Terrorism Prevention Act with a director of National Intelligence. A National Counterterrorism Center is created, largely housed and staffed in the CIA. Unauthorized immigrants in the U.S. reach an estimated record 11 million. ICE reports 1.1 million apprehensions at U.S. borders.

2005   The Real ID Act is passed. Nine states pass anti-human trafficking laws.

2006   Congress extends the USA Patriot Act, and passes the Secure Fence Act authorizing construction of a 700-mile bollard-type fence on the Southwest border.

2008   President Obama's administration begins a surge in use of expedited removals to deport unauthorized immigrants under the Trafficking Victims Protection Reauthorization Act.

2009   President Obama uses executive action to mitigate certain aspects of IIRIRA. Arizona enacts law mandating state and local police demand anyone suspected of being illegal to show documents to prove their legal status.

2010   In *Arizona v. U.S.*, the Supreme Court rules the Arizona measure unconstitutional.

2012   President Obama issues the DACA executive order granting temporary, legal status to "Dreamer" children.

2013   Senate passes S.744, a comprehensive immigration reform measure that is blocked in the House of Representatives and dies. Senator David Vitter (R-LA) and Rep. Steve King (R-IA) introduce a bill to end birthright citizenship to persons born in the United States to parents in illegal status. President Obama issues DAPA order.

2014   A surge in arrivals of children unaccompanied by adults from El Salvador, Guatemala, and Honduras arrives; President Obama grants temporary protected status to 5,000 such children deemed unsafe to return to their country of origin.

2015   House Republicans introduce the Secure Our Borders First Act of 2015. President Obama issues DAPA order.

2016   U.S. District Judge Andrew Hanen places injunction on the Obama administration's implementation of the DAPA order. In November, President Donald Trump is elected.

2017   President Trump appoints John Kelly secretary of DHS. President Trump issues executive order to start a pilot program to build a wall, issues an executive order against sanctuary cities, and issues a Muslim travel ban. He fires Acting AG Sally Yates for refusing to defend the travel ban. Former senator Jeff Sessions is sworn in as AG. The DOJ issues a crackdown on sanctuary cities order. President Trump orders DHS to establish a Victims of Immigration Crime Enforcement program.

HISTORICAL OVERVIEW

Measured in total numbers, the United States leads the world as an immigrant-receiving nation. Since 1820, when the federal government first started counting immigrants, approximately 80 million individuals have immigrated to the United States as legal permanent residents (LPRs). Other high-level immigration-receiving countries, such as Australia, Canada, and Israel, to name but three, may have comparable immigration flows when measured as a percentage of their total populations, but none has experienced immigration from so many and such varied nations of origin, nor of such diverse populations—ethnic, racial, religious—as has the United States. According to the 2010 census, the United States was then home to a significant number of residents born in about 170 countries from around the globe. Estimates of worldwide migration, not counting refugees, suggest that approximately two-thirds of people immigrating do so to the United States.

Total immigration to the United States between 1792 and 1819 has been estimated to have been just over 369,000.[1] Since then, the total number of immigrants who have come for permanent resettlement likely approaches 90 million persons if one includes the estimated number of unauthorized, and therefore uncounted, immigrants, commonly referred to as "illegal aliens" or "undocumented immigrants." The Census Bureau, in its 2014 American Community Survey, projected that in 2060 the number of immigrants who will reside in the United States and their percentage of the total U.S. population will grow from the current 48 million and 14.3 percent of the population to an estimated more than 78 million immigrants comprising just under 19 percent of the total U.S. population.[2]

In 1819, the first immigration law was enacted—a "manifest law" that simply enumerated immigrants arriving for permanent resettlement (Act of March 2, 3 Stat. 489). In the 2010 census, the foreign-born residing in the United States numbered about 40 million and comprised 12.9 percent of the total population.

The impact of receiving so many individuals from so many and such varied nations of origin has had a profound impact on the economy, culture, and politics of American society. It may be a cliché, but it is nonetheless true that the United States is "a nation of nations." A student of American history, as well as the general reader, can better understand that history by paying attention to the transformative role of the immigration process and its periodic overhauls.

Immigration and its policymaking are inherently interesting subjects. How the United States absorbed so many millions of immigrants, why and how they came to America literally from across the globe, and how they mixed and mingled in American society is a compelling story. It gives life to the nation's motto: *E Pluribus Unum* (from many, one).

The impact of immigration on the United States has been revolutionary. To cite one example: in studying the voting behavior of ethno-religious group affiliation and their percentage of Democratic versus percentage of Republican Party voters, political scientists distinguished the behavior of numerous such ethno-religious groups: Irish Catholics, all Catholics, Confessional German Lutherans, German Reformed, French Canadian Catholics, less Confessional German Lutherans, English Canadians, British stock, German Sectarians, Norwegian Lutherans, Swedish Lutherans, Haugean Norwegians, Quakers, Free Will Baptists, Congregational, Methodists, Regular Baptists, Blacks, Presbyterians, Episcopalians, Disciples, Southern Baptists, and Southern Methodists, and others—all of these groups were heavily influenced by, if not mainly comprised of, immigrants coming to the United States with particular ethno-religious affiliations.[3]

Of course, the intended results of a change in immigration law are not always achieved, nor do they persist for a very long time. In 1986, for example, Congress passed the Immigration Reform and Control Act (IRCA, 100 Stat. 3360), which imposed employer sanctions provisions to reduce the flow of illegal immigration by "de-magnetizing" the draw of the U.S. economy through law by making it illegal to hire an illegal immigrant (then principally aimed at undocumented immigration from Mexico). IRCA imposed fines on employers who did so. For less than two years it reduced the flow of illegal immigration, at least as measured by apprehensions at the southern U.S. border, but the flow resumed to equal and then to exceed the pre-IRCA level.[4] An unanticipated conse-quence of IRCA was simply to be a spur to the fraudulent documents industry. The "law of unintended consequences" often applied to immigra-tion policies, as this book will show.

Immigration policymaking is an excellent lens through which to view the interaction of the branches and levels of government in the American federal system. Studying immigration policymaking enables one to see in action the checks-and-balances system established by the U.S. Constitution. The legislative branch—both the U.S. Congress and state legislatures—view problems, issues, and often proposed solutions to immi-gration as domestic policy matters—i.e., how will *my* district be affected? Legislators, representing smaller geographic areas typically with fairly eth-nically homogeneous populations, respond to a few vested interest groups important to their district. The majority of legislators come from "safe" dis-tricts in terms of political party competition.[5] They do not have to con-sider how their position on an immigration bill will impact their party's chances in national electoral politics, so they see an immigration "prob-lem" differently than does the executive.

Presidents, meanwhile, have largely viewed those same matters through the prism of foreign policy—i.e., how will immigration policy-making affect the relations of the United States with other countries, or impact ongoing treaty negotiations, or impact the overall economy? At the same time, whenever immigration concerns became domestic political issues, presidents have responded by staking out their own positions, whether for reasons of principle, policy, or partisanship. The president, as the only elected official of all the people residing in the United States (that is, citizens and noncitizens alike), responds to a far wider array of interest groups than do legislators. The president, as the titular head of a political party, must consider how immigration policymaking will influence the electoral prospects of the party. Presidents of both political parties have had, rather frequently, adversarial relations with Congress over immigration policymaking, on occasion even with congressional members of their own political party. Presidents have exercised executive powers—for example, the veto, proclamations, executive agreements, executive actions, execu-tive authority over the regulations and procedures of administrative departments and bureaus, establishing presidential study commissions—to promote their position on immigration policy matters. A recent and obvious example is President Donald Trump's various iterations of a travel ban to limit or even foreclose immigration from predominantly Muslim countries or countries designated as posing a national security risk to the United States.

Factors other than laws can have a more profound impact on the total number of immigrants coming to the United States than do laws specifically designed to do so. Wars, depressions, recessions, epidemic disease outbreaks, and violent social upheavals all profoundly influence people's decisions on whether or not to emigrate. So, too, do disruptions in the means of moving from country to country. Total legal immigration to the United States dipped markedly, for example, during World War I, the Great Depression years, and World War II, without a significant change in the law.

Using a long-term historical analysis helps an attentive observer to identify a number of commonalities in how immigration policy achieves a consensus for a time, then how and why that consensus changes in response to events in the political environment that precipitate a reassessment to the weight given four basic elements involved in all immigration policymaking: (1) national security concerns (which in earlier years was called "ensuring domestic tranquility"), (2) economic needs and considerations, (3) racism, and (4) the collective sense of national identity or "people-hood."

During the 1920s, nativist and restrictionist fervor reached its peak, following concerns about immigrant loyalties during World War I and goaded on by the xenophobia of the revived Ku Klux Klan that grew in membership and influence. A 1924 statement by the Grand Dragon of the Ku Klux Klan advocated even stricter national origin quotas than were provided for in the act of May 19, 1921, the so-called "Emergency Immigration Quota Act" (42 Stat. 5, 8 U.S.C. 229). Both the Democratic and Republican Party platforms also called for limits on immigration in their 1920 and 1924 platforms.

Dramatic changes in the composition of the immigrant populations are associated with extensive and dramatic changes in immigration law. A change from Protestants from northwestern Europe to Catholics, Orthodox, and Jews largely from southern, central, and eastern Europe led to the enactment of the quota system to limit and redress that change in the composition of the flow of immigrants. The need to deal with the refugee crisis after World War II and the coming of the Cold War in U.S. foreign policy was reflected in the Immigration Act of 1952 (a.k.a. the McCarran-Walter Act, 66 Stat. 163, June 27) that compelled another substantial change in policy. Responding to civil rights concerns, a changing economy, an emphasis on "family values," and continued Cold War pressures, Congress shifted to a new preference system with the 1965 immigration law that is the central focus of this book. The current and massive immigration flow is shifting away from northern and western Europe toward Mexico, Central and South America, and Asia. That shift has led to the new demands to "control the borders," and to protect the United States from a perceived danger of international terrorist cells entering the nation amidst a wave of undocumented immigrants, or a wave of displaced refugees from the Middle East. The proposed or implemented restrictive immigration procedures and practices of the Trump administration both reflected and directed the xenophobia of the 2010s.

Major shifts in U.S. immigration policy came after one or both of the major political parties in American politics decided to advocate such change as an important plank in their party platform. Likewise, major shifts seen herein followed the formation of specific ad hoc interest groups who became major stakeholders advocating or opposing such change: for example, the Asian Exclusion League of the 1880s and 1890s, the Ku Klux Klan in the 1920s, the Federation for American Immigration Reform and Zero Population Growth of the 1990s, and the Tea Party and the Heritage Foundation of the past decade. These interest groups formed coalitions to advocate the need for fundamental change in immigration policy. After the 1920 depression, business interests that previously had been strong advocates of keeping the immigration door relatively open to ensure a supply of cheap labor either remained silent or shifted to a restrictionist stance.

Many in Congress began to refer to massive immigration (in the decade prior to 1920, legal immigration had reached more than one million a year entering the United States) by such terms as an alien flood, a barbarian horde, and the foreign tide. Restrictionist forces turned to the U.S. Congress Joint Immigration Commission (1907–1911), more commonly known as the Dillingham Commission, after its chairman, Senator

William P. Dillingham (R-VT), to justify a drastic reduction in immigration to the United States. Senator Dillingham was but one of the restriction advocates serving on the commission. Senator Henry Cabot Lodge (R-MA) and Cornell University economist Jeremiah Jenks had a strong impact on the commission's findings that supported a dramatic reduction in immigration and a policy that embraced then-popular ethnic and racial ideas and was specifically designed to change the flow of legal immigration from south, central, and eastern European nations back to the pre-1880s flow that was predominated by northern and western Europeans.

In terms of both absolute numbers and as the foreign-born percentage of the total population, the decade from 1900 to 1910 showed the largest immigration flow in American history, averaging just under one million per year for the decade. When the literacy test, enacted in 1917, failed to stem the immigrant flow, Congress moved to enact the quota acts. Those national origin quotas had their desired effect, shifting a much reduced flow from southern, central, and eastern Europe to northern and western Europe. The National Origin Acts (of 1921, 1924, and 1929) plus the impact of the Great Depression resulted in the decade of 1930 to 1939 having a negative decennial net migration as a percentage of population growth in which emigration from the United States exceeded immigration to the United States by 85,000. Indeed, the 1930–1939 decade had the lowest average annual immigration in American history, measured by both absolute numbers and as a percentage of the total U.S. population.[6]

Restrictionist forces in Congress (members and committee staff) were gaining not only in numbers, but also in their positions of influence. Among the more prominent advocates for strict restrictionist policy were such notable Republican senators as Hiram Johnson and Samuel Shortridge of California and Henry Cabot Lodge of Massachusetts. Arch restrictionist William Dillingham chaired the powerful Immigration Committee in the Senate, and Representative Albert Johnson (R-WA), also an arch restrictionist, chaired the House Committee on Immigration.[7]

The 1919 Red Scare, following the Bolshevik Revolution in Russia, coupled with the 1920 recession, led to the adoption of a pro-restrictionist position from forces one might otherwise expect to favor a more open policy. The Progressive Party voiced concern about the ability of the U.S. economy to absorb and assimilate so many aliens. The *New Republic* opined that unrestricted immigration was an element of nineteenth-century liberalism, and that a progressive society could not allow social ills evident at the time to be aggravated by excessive immigration. The American Legion, and similar nationalist groups within the Americanization movement, became a leading organization advocating for restriction.[8] As Robert Divine, a leading scholar of the movement for restriction, noted:

> Fundamentally, it was the transformation in American economic and political development that set the stage for restriction. The growth of the American economy and particularly the technological changes brought about by the industrial revolution had greatly reduced the need for the raw labor furnished by immigrants. A mature industrial system required a moderate number of trained workers, not great masses of manual labor.[9]

As the United States emerged from World War I as a true world power, it developed a more intense sense of nationalism in which citizens increasingly demanded unity and conformity. The new position of the United States on the international stage became a basis for advocating restrictionism. Demographic diversity of the population was no longer a highly valued element either in American culture or in the political calculus of immigration policymaking. The return to economic prosperity in 1921 relegated economic issues to a secondary role in the debates over passage of an immigration law. While the National Association of Manufacturers (NAM) led pro-immigration forces, the American Federation of Labor (AFL) attacked NAM as being solely interested in cheap labor. The AFL argued that there was already an adequate supply of labor in the work force.

As the economic element in immigration policymaking waned, the national identity element—a sense of peoplehood—waxed. An ethnic theory approach emerged, led by such voices as Carl Brigham, a Princeton psychologist famous for developing the IQ (Intelligence Quotient) test; William MacDougall, of Harvard University, who proposed a Nordic Race superiority theory, and Harry Laughlin, the prominent and extreme eugenicist, who was the biological expert for the House Immigration Committee and who went so far as to advocate for the sterilization of all inmates in mental institutions.[10] Their ideas were echoed in the popular press that stressed the need for national unity and conformity by defending racial and cultural homogeneity and a new sense of racial nationalism.

These racial theories were popularized, as well, by the highly influential book by Madison Grant, *The Passing of the Great Race*, published in 1916 and reissued in 1921 and 1923. Grant wrote that the nation was becoming increasingly inundated by:

> a large and increasing number of the weak and broken and mentally crippled of all races drawn from the lowest stratum of the Mediterranean basin and the Balkans, together with the hordes of the wretched, submerged population of the Polish ghettos. Our jails, insane asylums and almshouses are filled with this human flotsam and the whole tone of American life, social, moral and political, has been lowered and vulgarized by them.[11]

Grant popularized a Nordic theory that there was a three-tiered hierarchy within the white race of Mediterraneans, Alpines, and Nordics. According to Grant, white Americans were Nordics, the highest, and they should regard any mixture with the other two as a destructive process of mongrelization.

Senators Hiram Johnson and Samuel Shortridge and a number of representatives from California led others from the West Coast to advocate to restrict immigration from Asian countries, playing on a "Yellow Peril" theme, warning that Japan's overpopulation and thirst for land would lead to a future race war. Representative Carl Vinson (D-GA), speaking on behalf of the restrictive quotas of the 1924 national origins bill before the Immigration Committee, noted that:

> I would have no concern upon the problem confronting us...if, in the main, they belonged to the same branch of the Aryan race. Americans and their forebearers, the English, Scotch and Welsh, are the same people. These ancestors of the real American people were related one to the other and possessed, to a large degree, similar tastes, traits and characteristics. And in the amalgamation of these people and their transition to American life we find the persons who created and now maintain the greatest Nation on the globe. But it is the new immigrant who is restricted in emigrating to this country. The emigrants affected by this bill are those from Italy, Greece, Russia, Poland, Bulgaria, Armenia, Czechoslovakia, Yugoslavia, and Turkey. I respectfully submit, with all the power within me, that the people from these countries do not yield their national characteristics, but retain them practically unimpaired by contact with others.[12]

In the final congressional debate over the act of May 19, 1921, the Quota Act of 1921, also called the "Emergency Quota Act" (42 Stat. 5, 8 U.S.C. 229), the primary organization support in favor of the national-origins bill and its racially charged concept included the American Federation of Labor, the American Legion, the Immigration Restriction League, the National Grange, the Ku Klux Klan, and the Junior Order of the United American Mechanics, as well as such patriotic and nationalist associations as the Sons of the American Revolution and the Daughters of the American Revolution. The primary opposition to the proposed law included the Anti-National Origins Clause League, a New York taxpayers association, several industrial and employer organizations (chiefly the National Association of Manufacturers, the American Mining Congress, the Associated General Contractors, the National Industrial Conference Board, and the U.S. Chamber of Commerce), some farm organizations concerned that agriculture would be denied sufficient manpower, and spokesmen for various Jewish, foreign-language, and other "ethnic groups" whose compatriots would be adversely affected by the use of 1890 as a base year to calculate the quotas, such as the Vasa Order of America (Swedish), the Steuben Society, the Danish Brotherhood of America, the Sons of Norway, and the German American Citizens League.[13]

The long-term historical narrative of American immigration highlights recurrent arguments, like variations on a symphonic theme, from advocates for immigration policy change. Time and again, concern is expressed over the impact of immigration on jobs, wages, and working conditions. Over and over, advocates for change in immigration policy voice xenophobic attitudes toward the newcomers, whom they argue cannot, will not, or should not be allowed to assimilate into American society. These social forces fear that the newcomers will damage American culture, religious freedom, social mores, and politics—in their view forever changing the very face of America in a detrimental way, putting the country on what they perceive of as the wrong track and necessitating the need "to take back America" or to "make America great again."

Legislators and stakeholders of immigration politics often seek some new *method* to "fix" the immigration problem. Advocates for change suggest some new method or device to screen immigrants. This historical narrative shows how such devices varied over time from the use of excluded categories, to a literacy test, to a quota system, to an elaborate preference system, to employer sanctions, to barring immigrants from social and welfare services, to militarizing the border or amending the Constitution to deny birthright citizenship to persons born in the United States of parents who are in the country illegally, or to ban entire groups on the basis of their national affiliation based on the implementation of "extreme vetting" aimed at targeted groups, or thinly disguised religious-motivated travel bans.

Throughout American history, immigration policy advocates have formed and maintained stable coalitions of interest groups advocating more or less unrestricted immigration versus a coalition of groups advocating the need for restrictionist policy. Time and again, there is a coalition of business and ethno-religious associations favoring immigration doing battle with labor, "patriotic," or social conservative groups pushing for restrictions to "take back" the country from the influence of newcomers they deem undesirable. Time and again, these coalitions lobby and work with and through fairly stable factions in Congress. On occasion, these factions establish an informal bipartisan caucus of legislators, whose members share a common interest important to their respective electoral districts.

This book uses historical analysis to focus on those commonalities and themes evident in immigration policymaking. It focuses on the period 1920 to the present, highlighting particularly ethnic-related interest groups advocating or opposing change at any given time, and the coalition of congressional political party or congressional caucus forces that they marshal in seeking to implement or to oppose a major policy shift.

Group theory is helpful to better understand immigration policymaking. This analysis underscores the essential gatekeeping function of immigration policymaking. It demonstrates that immigration policy is one area that reflects the interest of dominant groups. As groups gain or lose power and influence, policy is altered in favor of those gaining influence at the expense of those whose influence is waning.

A review of immigration policymaking shows a constant struggle for control of the immigration process. It highlights trends in the flow of immigration—where they come from and how large and diverse is that flow. It emphasizes periodic attempts to achieve a politically acceptable consensus about procedural justice in the matter of regulating the entrance for permanent legal residency of individuals and groups. It shows that the disparities in power among competing groups seeking to influence that balance or consensus is the key to one's understanding of immigration policy. The interplay among groups is central to understanding the shifts in policymaking and the periodic review and revisions in policy and procedures designed to arrive at a new consensus as to how open or closed the door to America will be at any given time.

NOTES

1. Bureau of the Census, *Historical Statistics of the United States* (Washington, DC: U.S. Department of Commerce, 2006).

2. Decentennial censuses for 1900 to 2000, American Community Survey for 2014, Census Bureau population projections, March 2015, Number and Percent of Immigrants in the United States, 1900–2014; Plus Census Bureau Projections to 2060, Figure 1.

3. Paul Kleppner et al., *The Evolution of the American Electoral System* (Westport, CT: Greenwood Press, 1981).

4. Keith Crane et al., *The Effects of Employer Sanctions on the Flow of Undocumented Immigrants to the United States* (Santa Monica, CA: The Rand Corporation Press, and the Urban Institute Press, 1990); Michael LeMay, *Anatomy of a Public Policy: The Reform of Contemporary Immigration Law* (Westport, CT: Praeger Press, 1994), 112–16; and M. J. White, F. D. Bean, and T. J. Espanshade, *The U.S. Immigration Reform Act and Undocumented Migration to the U.S.* (Washington, DC: The Urban Institute, 1989).

5. Michael C. LeMay, *The American Political Party System: A Reference Handbook* (Santa Barbara, CA: ABC-CLIO, 2017), 105–8.

6. Select Commission on Immigration and Refugee Policy, *Staff Report* (Washington, DC: U.S. Government Printing Office, 1981), 28; and Michael LeMay, *From Open Door to Dutch Door* (New York: Praeger Press, 1987), 74.

7. LeMay, *From Open Door to Dutch Door*, 77.

8. John Higham, *Strangers in the Land* (New Brunswick: Rutgers University Press, 1955), 302.

9. Robert A. Divine, *American Immigration Policy, 1924–1952* (New Haven, CT: Yale University Press, 1957), 9.

10. William Bernard, ed., *Immigration Policy: A Reappraisal* (New York: Harper Brothers, 1950), 29.

11. Madison Grant, *The Passing of the Great Race* (1916: reprint ed. New York: Arno Press, 1916), 89–90.

12. Cited in Marion Bennett, *American Immigration Policies: A History* (Washington, DC: Public Affairs Press, 1963), 48.

13. Ibid., 52–53; and Divine, *American Immigration Policy*, 33–37.

CHAPTER 1

PRECURSOR LAWS OF AMERICAN IMMIGRATION POLICY

INTRODUCTION: IMMIGRATION FLOWS AND PRIOR POLICY

Current immigration law for the United States was established by the Immigration and Nationality Act of 1965, which abolished the national origin quota system and enacted a system based on a seven-point preference system favoring family reunification and attracting skilled labor to the United States. Also known as the Hart-Celler Act (H.R. 2580, Pub. L. 89-236, 79 Stat. 911), it can reasonably be claimed that the law transformed America, spurring total immigration dramatically over that occurring over the previous four decades, and shifting the source of that vastly expanded immigration flow from northwestern European countries to those coming from Asia, Africa, and Latin America.

Since 1819, when the United States first began keeping count of immigration, more than 80 million persons have immigrated and have been admitted for permanent legal resident status (commonly referred to as legal immigrants). According to data in the American Community Survey Reports of the U.S. Census Bureau, as of the 2010 census, the foreign-born totaled 39,956,000, or 12.9 percent of the total population of 309,350,000.

Within the United States, the foreign born are widely dispersed, residing in every state, ranging in terms of their percentage of the state's population from a low of 1 percent in West Virginia to a high of 27 percent in California. Despite that wide dispersal, immigrants are concentrated in 10 states, which collectively are home to 74 percent of all the foreign born. The top 10 states and their percentage of the total foreign

born are: California, 25.4 percent; New York, 10.8 percent; Texas, 10.4 percent, Florida, 9.2 percent; New Jersey, 4.6 percent; Illinois, 4.4 percent;
Massachusetts, 2.5 percent; Georgia, 2.4 percent; Virginia, 2.3 percent, and
Washington, 2.2 percent. The top four states in terms of the foreign born
are also the top four states in terms of their total populations: California,
with 37.3 million; Texas, with 25.3 million; New York, with 19.4 million;
and Florida, with 18.8 million. Collectively, these four states represent
33 percent of the total U.S. population. Immigration, and the higher birth
rates of children of immigrant parents compared to the birth rates
among native-born parents, is the most important factor determining U.S.
population growth.

Census data show that immigrants come to work. The percentage of the
population 16 years old and older who are in the labor force is 64.4 percent
when counting both sexes, but among the native born, 63.8 percent are in
the labor force whereas 67.7 percent of the foreign born are in the labor
force. Among men, 69.8 percent of all men of working-age are in the labor
force; but where 68.1 percent of the native born men are working, 79.9 percent of the foreign born men are in the labor force. Only among women
are native born employed at a higher percentage than foreign-born
women. For all women, 59.3 percent are in the labor force; 59.7 percent
of the native born, and 57 percent among the foreign-born women.

The flow of immigration is determined by what social scientists distin-
guish as "push and pull" factors. Push factors can be defined as events that
compel large numbers of persons to emigrate—that is, to leave their nation
of birth or adoption for work or permanent resettlement elsewhere. Pull
factors are aspects of the receiving nation that draw immigrants to the
country for permanent resettlement. An important pull factor drawing
immigrants to America's shores has been and still is its politically open
society, attracting those escaping political repression. Another pull factor
is the reputation of the United States as a land of nearly boundless opportunity which draws those fleeing dire economic deprivation and sometimes
starvation conditions in their homelands, for example, the Irish fleeing
famine from 1847 to 1852. Freedom of religion guaranteed by the U.S.
Constitution has been another major pull factor throughout American
history. Since its inception, the United States prided itself on being a land
of asylum, and throughout much of its history it accepted waves of refugees. Between 1975 and 1980, for example, the United States led by far

all nations of the world in accepting refugees—677,000. The next nearest nation receiving refugees was China, with 265,000.[1]

Since the 1860s, but especially since 1900, U.S. cities grew rapidly, sometimes exponentially. Chicago, for example, grew from 4,000 when it was incorporated in 1937 to 1,690,000 by 1900. Such dramatic urban growth was another powerful pull factor because it required a massive unskilled labor force to build the infrastructure, especially in the case of really large cites. As we have said elsewhere, ironically, many immigrants were drawn to the United States as "the land where the streets were paved with gold" only to discover those streets were often unpaved, and they would comprise the bulk of those doing the paving—in brick and cobblestone rather than gold.[2] Rapid industrialization (in the United States, from around 1850 to 1900) was largely made possible by the cheap labor supplied by immigrants. This kept wages down and enabled the accumulation of the vast sums of capital necessary to industrialize. Mass immigration provided the United States with a large pool of unskilled labor precisely at the time it was most needed.

THE WAVES OF IMMIGRATION

The surging and ebbing of immigrant arrivals to the shores of the United States suggest a wave metaphor to characterize the flow. The distinctions among the waves are based on the size and the composition (numbers arriving from certain nations of origin) of the flow that comprised each successive wave.

The first wave, from 1820 to 1880, was comprised of slightly more than 10 million immigrants entering the United States for permanent resettlement. They came when U.S. immigration policy was to provide an open door. Not only were there few restrictions on immigration, but prior to 1885, the law even allowed for the actual recruitment of immigrants. European nations sent from 80 to 90 percent of the first-wave immigrants, with those coming from northwestern Europe predominating throughout the period, on average totaling about 80 percent of the total. From 1820 to 1860, for example, northwestern Europeans made up 85 percent, with 3 percent coming from North America (Canada), and 2 percent from southern and eastern Europe. Immigrants who came during this open-door era are commonly referred to as the "old" immigrants. The wave marked a sudden and dramatic increase in total immigration to the United States. From the end of the Revolutionary War to 1819, an estimated 125,000 immigrants entered as legal immigrants. Their numbers have to be estimated because a formal count was neither kept nor mandated by law. Most were Protestants from the British Isles and northern Europe. That composition began to change after the 1830s. Irish and German peasants came by the millions after the potato famines and the economic depressions of the 1840s and a failed attempt at revolution in 1848 broke out in several European nations, most notably, for American immigration, in Germany. The vast majority of immigrants coming from Ireland, as well as those coming from southern Germany, were Catholics. This sudden influx of Catholics led to the first anti-Catholic, anti-immigrant reaction. The most important pre-Civil War group advocating restriction of immigration was the American Party (better and more commonly known as the Know Nothing Party). It was distinctly anti-immigrant and notoriously and often violently anti-Catholic.

The second major wave, commonly referred to as the "new" immigrants, occurred from 1880 to 1920. During this wave nearly 23.5 million immigrants arrived in the United States in what was perceived by the native stock as a "flood" of immigration. These new immigrants were predominantly from southern, central, and eastern Europe (SCE). They were more visibly different from the native stock than were those of the first wave. Alarming to many Protestant Christians in the native stock, they were overwhelmingly Catholic, Greek or Eastern Orthodox, and Jewish. This religious diversity set off a xenophobic reaction that culminated in the restrictive immigration law marking the end of the second wave—the three quota laws passed in 1921, 1924, and 1929.

The third wave lasted from 1920 to 1965. Its size was a dramatic drop from that of the second wave: from about 23.5 million to just over 5.5 million. This wave of immigrants is marked by several changes in the composition of the influx. Europeans comprised roughly 60 percent of the wave, with immigrants from northwestern Europe gradually rising from just more than 30 percent in the 1920s to nearly 50 percent by the 1960s. Immigrants from the Western Hemisphere rose to around 30 to 35 percent of the total. Immigrants, in total number and as a percentage of the U.S. population also declined in each decennial census between 1920 and 1970: in 1920, 13.9 million immigrants comprised 13.2 percent of the population;

in 1930, 14.2 million were 11.6 percent of the population; in 1940, 11.6 million immigrants made up 8.8 percent of the population; in 1950, 10.3 million immigrants comprised 6.9 percent of the total population; in 1960, 9.7 million immigrants were only 5.4 percent of the population; and by 1970, 9.6 million immigrants totaled the lowest percentage of the population, at 4.7 percent. After 1970, the number and percentage of immigrants rose each decade, from 14.1 million at 6.2 percent in 1980 to 31.1 million and 11.1 percent by 2000.[3]

During the fourth wave, from 1965 to 1985, total immigration nearly doubled. Immigrants coming from the Western Hemisphere dominated this wave, rising to half of the total. A dramatic increase in Asian immigration also distinguishes this wave, especially post-1970.

U.S. immigration law reflects the perceived needs of the nation as those needs shift over time in response to changing domestic cultural, economic, political, and social conditions, and in reaction to the changing nature and composition of the immigrant waves. Various Cold War, economic, ethnic, foreign policy, and religious issues played key roles in the debates over immigration law during the fourth wave as they do in the current debates over reforming immigration law.

Shifts in immigration law reflect conflicting value perspectives that tug and pull at one another, resulting in a sort of oscillation in policymaking among them. On the one hand is the perspective that values immigrants as a source of industry and renewed vigor, a desirable infusion of new blood into the American body politic, enriching the national heritage and spurring new economic growth. This perspective forms the traditional base for a more open immigration policy.

The other perspective calls for varying degrees of restriction. Its proponents fear the strangers who cannot or, in their view, should not be incorporated into the American polity. Opponents of mass immigration fear what they deem to be the dilution of American culture. They fear that massive immigration will destroy the economy or at least severely depress wages and working conditions. They advocate restricting immigration to avoid such dire effects. They fear what many in their ranks deplore as the "browning" of America. In their view, such unbridled and uncontrolled immigration is adversely changing the very face of the American population.

Immigration law performs a gatekeeping function: who is or is not allowed entrance into the United States for legal, permanent resettlement.

Policy shifts both reflect and result in dramatic changes in the size and composition of the waves of immigration. The gatekeeping function suggests the use of a door image to characterize immigration policy at a given point in U.S. history.

In trying to better understand the changes in immigration law over 200 years of American history, it is useful to break down that history by categorizing various phases or eras. An open-door era characterizes the period of U.S. immigration law from 1820 to 1880.[4] During this phase there were virtually no, or at most only a few, restrictions on immigration in American law. Practically all who sought entrance were allowed to do so. Indeed, government policy was to reach out and seek immigrants. Many state governments and a number of budding industries in the United States sent agents to Europe to recruit immigrants, particularly farmers and skilled laborers who had been employed in European industry, which developed there about five decades before the United States. There were only a few restrictions in the law based on diseases or morality consideration.

THE BEGINNINGS OF RESTRICTIVE IMMIGRATION LAW, 1880–1920

The second phase, what we have called elsewhere the Door Ajar era, lasted from 1880 to 1920.[5] This phase witnessed the beginning of restrictions. While the door was still open to most who sought to enter, legislators increasingly began to experiment with a number of provisions—called excluded categories—enacted into law as measures to control the immigration process.

The first intentionally restrictive immigration laws began during the Door Ajar era. As the flow of immigrants shifted markedly and dramatically from northwestern Europe to south, central, and eastern (SCE) Europe, and to a far lesser extent from China, it caused a strong xenophobic reaction. The new immigrants looked more alien—strange coloring, physiques, customs, languages, and religions—arousing fear that these strangers would be unable to assimilate. A spate of pseudoscientific studies by historians, sociologists, and biologists attacked the newcomers as biologically and racially inferior. Racist fervor led to the first blatantly restrictive immigration law, the Chinese Exclusion Act of 1882.

Nativist groups formed in the 1880s—like the American Party in 1886, the American Protective League of True Americans in 1887, the Sons of the American Revolution in 1889, and the Daughters of the American Revolution in 1890. Nativists argued that the new immigrants were racially inferior and more inherently likely to become criminals or bring with them and spread loathsome communicable diseases. Such arguments undercut the earlier tradition of welcome to "all the poor and the oppressed" famously inscribed on the base of the Statue of Liberty, America's most revered symbol of immigration. Restrictive immigration policies responded to four historical trends culminating in the 1880s and 1890s: (1) the mushrooming of cities and rapid industrialization; (2) the official closing of the frontier; (3) the persistence among the "new immigrants" to maintain their culture and traditions far longer and more visibly than did the "old immigrants"; and (4) the greater religious divergence from Protestantism among the "new immigrants," who were overwhelmingly Catholic, Jewish, or Greek and Russian Orthodox.

Immigrants who were adherents to a number of non-Christian, or non-traditional "Christian sects," as opposed to traditional Christian denominations, entered the country in fairly significant numbers, some among the "old immigrant" wave, and some among the "new immigrants." These included Buddhists from China and Japan, Daoists from China, and Shintoists from Japan. Among the nontraditional Christian sects were the Old Order Amish and Mennonite Anabaptists, Pietists like the Old German Baptist Brethren, and Moravian Brethren. Yiddish-speaking Jews, such as the Chabad/Hasidic sects, were yet another minority religious group among the "new" immigrants.[6]

The Immigration Act of August 3, 1882 (22 Stat. 214, 8 U.S.C.) barred the immigration of "lunatics, idiots, convicts, and those liable to become public charges." It added new categories of exclusion that reflected the hysteria of the nativist movement: those suffering from "loathsome or contagious diseases" and persons convicted of crimes of "moral turpitude" were denied entry. The law also provided for the medical inspection of new arrivals.

Enactment of these laws, however, failed to satisfy the forces advocating restriction. High levels of immigration continued and even increased during the 1880s. This led nativists to renew their efforts to change immigration law even more drastically. They began to focus on a proposed new device for restrictive regulation—a literacy test.

The first literacy bill was introduced into Congress in 1895, where it quickly passed both houses but was vetoed by Democratic president Grover Cleveland. In 1906, another comprehensive immigration act was proposed that included both a literacy test for admission and an English-language test for naturalization. Labor unions joined the restrictionist coalition to advocate this new approach to policy. Two national associations of labor unions formed after the Civil War: the Noble and Holy Order of the Knights of Labor, founded by Uriah Smith Stevens in 1869 and led in the 1880s by Terrance Powderly; and the American Federation of Labor, formed in 1886. The unions were increasingly wary of the economic threat to their wages and working conditions implicit in unrestricted immigration. The budding national labor union movement backed successful enactment of an 1887 law to prohibit contract labor.

The groups advocating restriction succeeded in all of their stated goals with the exception of enactment of the literacy requirement for entry or naturalization. English-language proficiency was accepted for citizenship. In 1907, Congress passed a law creating a joint congressional/presidential commission to study the impact of immigration. Begun in 1909, the Dillingham Commission, as it was known after its chairman, Senator William Dillingham (R-VT), espoused the pseudoscientific, racist theories so prevalent in the United States at the time. The commission's recommendations, published in 1911, called for a literacy test and other restrictive legislation.

Despite these efforts, opponents of immigration were striving against an immigration tide. War in Europe was generating economic growth and labor demands in the United States, both of which ran counter to restrictive policy. The growing political influence of the new immigrant groups, coupled with the demand of business enterprises for new labor, preserved the more "free-entry" policy. In 1912, Congress again passed a literacy test bill, only to have it vetoed by Republican president William Howard Taft. In 1915, when yet another literacy bill was passed by the Congress, again it was vetoed, this time by Democratic president Woodrow Wilson.

The United States entered World War I in 1917. Congress passed another literacy bill, and this time finally overrode yet another veto by President Wilson. The 1917 law made literacy an entrance requirement.

It codified a list of aliens to be excluded and effectively banned all immigration from Asia (Act of February 5, 1917, 39 Stat. 874, 8 U.S.C.). The xenophobic reaction during the World War I years contributed significantly to the success of the restrictionist forces in the movement to "educate" the foreign born into U.S. language and customs. An Americanization movement began in 1910. Between 1919 and 1921, 27 states passed laws creating Americanization programs. Many groups participated in the Americanization movement: prominent businesses including the Ford Motor Company and the National Chamber of Commerce; labor unions, such as the United Mine Workers of America; patriotic groups like the Sons of the American Revolution and the Daughters of the American Revolution, the Colonial Dames of America, and the National Security League; civic groups including the Young Men's Christian Association and the Young Women's Christian Association; and church-based groups such as the Knights of Columbus, the National Catholic War Council, and the National Council of Jewish Women.

For the first time ever, even industry joined the movement to restrict immigration. This resulted in a new phase of immigration policy, what we have called elsewhere the Pet Door era, which enacted a series of laws that established the national origins quota system.[7] A frenzy of anti-German activity culminated in this "Americanization" movement.

The first target of the movement to restrict immigration by law, and the first success in securing national legislation, took aim at the Chinese. Anti-Chinese political agitation began in California in the early 1850s. Violent crimes against the Chinese immigrants took place in the mine fields (which opened with the California Gold Rush in 1848). Such violence went unpunished because, by 1849, a Know Nothing judge serving on the California Supreme Court ruled that the Chinese were forbidden to testify against white men. Until the 1890s, the federal government had not yet asserted its primacy in immigration law. The California legislature erected various legal barriers against the Chinese in the 1850s. It passed the Foreign Miners tax in 1855, imposing a four-dollar-per-month tax that increased each year the foreign miner did not become a citizen. Since the Chinese were by law forbidden naturalization, the tax effectively expelled them from the mine fields. California also banned their entry into public schools and denied their right to testify in courts against whites. Miscegenation laws forbade them from marrying whites (miscegenation is defined as a mixture of races, especially marriage, cohabitation, or sexual intercourse between a white person and a member of another race). By 1865 calls for the outright banning of Chinese immigration began. In 1867, the Democratic Party swept the offices of California by running on an anti-Chinese platform. The Panic of 1873 (a severe recession or depression in today's parlance) aroused fears of the "Yellow Peril." In 1867, the Workingmen's Party won control of San Francisco, calling for an end to all Chinese immigration. The Workingmen's Party was first established in Philadelphia in 1828 and in New York in 1829, but its virulently anti-Chinese group was formed in California in 1877, led by Dennis Kearney. By the 1870s, anti-Chinese sentiment was so strong on the West Coast that it was virtual political suicide to take the side of the Chinese immigrants.

Violence against the Chinese was also used to deter their immigration or internal migration. In 1871, a riot in Los Angeles killed 21 Chinese immigrants. In 1876, in Truckee, a town in Nevada County, California, located by the Truckee River, a violent raid perpetrated by whites burned down a Chinese home and shot the inhabitants as they fled the flames. The whites tried for the crime were acquitted. In 1876, in California, the Supreme Order of Caucasians formed, advocating the elimination of Chinese in the United States by driving them out of the country through violence. It quickly grew to 64 chapters (called "camps") statewide and claimed a membership of 5,000. Mobs killing Chinese and driving them from their homes were not restricted to California. Such tactics were also used in Denver, Colorado, in Tacoma and Seattle, Washington, and in Oregon City, Oregon.

The Teamsters, the Workingmen's Convention, the People's Protective Alliance, and Dennis Kearney's Workingmen's Party led efforts for legal restriction of Chinese immigration. Sinophobia was strong enough in California that in 1878, its constitution was amended placing a host of legal restrictions on them, and West Coast politicians pushed for federal laws to restrict their immigration. In New York, the state threatened to close down Castle Garden, at the time the major reception station for immigrants entering the country, if Congress did not act. However, state and local taxes against them were declared unconstitutional by the U.S. Supreme Court in *Henderson v. Mayor of City of New York* (92 U.S. 259, 1875).

The Door-Ajar era of immigration law is well exemplified by the various Chinese Exclusion Acts of the 1880s and 1890s. Congress first passed a Chinese Exclusion Act in 1879. It was vetoed, however, by Republican president Rutherford B. Hayes on the grounds that it violated, as it clearly did, the Burlingame-Seward Treaty of 1868. President Hayes (1877–1881) was an ardent abolitionist and a former congressman and governor of Ohio. The treaty was negotiated by Anson Burlingame, a Republican representative from Massachusetts, and William Seward, a former governor of New York and the secretary of state appointed by President Abraham Lincoln. A new treaty was negotiated in 1880, ratified by the Senate in May 1881, and formally proclaimed by Republican president Chester Arthur (1881–1885). The new treaty did not use the term "exclusion." Rather, it allowed for a temporary suspension. Immediately after ratification of the new treaty, the Senate passed a new law suspending all Chinese immigration for 20 years. President Arthur vetoed that bill. Congress passed a second bill in May 1882 (22 Stat. 58). Commonly known as the Chinese Exclusion Act of 1882, it abrogated the treaty's free immigration clauses altogether. It stopped virtually all Chinese immigration for 10 years. The impact of the law was immediate and dramatic. In 1881, 12,000 Chinese entered the United States, and nearly 40,000 came in 1882 (before the law took effect). That number dropped to 8,031 in 1883 and to 23 by 1885. The law also prohibited their naturalization.[8] The 1882 law was the beginning of a sustained campaign and effort involving harsh laws to suppress the Chinese immigrants already here, targeted violence to drive them out, and increasingly restrictive laws to ban their immigration. The anti-Chinese immigration campaign has been compared to a war against them.

Anti-immigration activists in Congress pushed for an even more sweeping immigration ban. In August 1882, Congress enacted the first general immigration law with an avowedly restrictionist goal. The Immigration Act of 1882 (22 Stat. 214) excluded "any convict, lunatic, idiot, or any person unable to take care of himself or herself without becoming a public charge." The law's exclusionary categories included persons of moral turpitude, and those with certain specified "loathsome, communicable diseases." This 1882 act designated the secretary of the treasury responsible for the administration of the new law and imposed a tax of 50 cents per head on immigration. Its enforcement, however, was left to state boards or officers designated by the secretary of the treasury.

Congress passed the Alien Contract Labor Law in 1885 (23 Stat. 332), more commonly known as the Foran Act after its author, Representative Martin A. Foran (R-OH). The law was strongly advocated by the Knights of Labor, the Order of American Mechanics, and assorted patriotic, veteran, and fraternal associations. The American Protective Association, formed in 1887 in Clinton, Iowa, went on to become the largest and most powerful of the Protestant secret anti-Catholic societies adopting a strong anti-immigration stance. Social scientists began questioning the economic value or need for wide-scale immigration and advocated for a measure of the ability of groups to assimilate as a criterion for assessing their desirability or their undesirability.

It is ironic that in October 1886, at the very time this restrictionist movement was gaining political and electoral strength throughout much of the nation, the Statue of Liberty was dedicated. The anti-immigrant sentiments of the movement contrasted starkly with the words of the famous poem, "The New Colossus," written by Emma Lazarus, dedicated to the statue and later inscribed on her base:

> Not like the brazen giant of Greek fame,
> With conquering limbs astride from land to land; Here
> At our sea-washed, sunset gates shall stand
> A mighty woman with a torch, whose flame
> Is the imprisoned lightening, and her name
> Mother of Exiles. From her beacon-hand
> Glows world-wide welcome, her mild eyes command
> The air-bridged harbor that twin cities frame.
> "Keep, ancient lands, your storied pomp!" cries she
> With silent lips. "Give me your tired, your poor,
> Your huddled masses yearning to be free,
> The wretched refuse of your teeming shore.
> Send these, the homeless, tempest-tossed to me.
> I lift my lamp beside the golden door."[9]

Labor strife during the mid-1880s caused a renewed nativism in response to the Molly McGuires, a secret society of Irish-immigrant coal miners that emerged from the labor strife exacerbated by the Great Panic of 1873, who used a violent campaign against the mine owners in Pennsylvania, and to the Haymarket Riot in Chicago in 1886, in which foreign-born anarchists were accused of throwing bombs that killed policemen. That year saw the formation of the nativist political party, the American Party, in California. Congress, in 1884, amended the Chinese Exclusion Act to tighten its restrictions and require all permanent residents to acquire a "reentry certificate"—that era's version of the green card or LPR card—before traveling to China if they planned to reenter the United States. That practice was fairly common among Chinese residents who went back to China to get married, since miscegenation laws forbade their marrying white women in the United States, or to bury the remains of family members with their ancestors. Newspaper publisher Joseph Pulitzer crusaded against New York City's immigration-reception station at Castle Garden in 1888, and Congressman Melbourne Ford (R-MI) offered a resolution to investigate the administration of Castle Garden, which was officially closed in April 1890.

Congress further amended the Chinese Exclusion Act in 1888, when the Scott Act, as it was called, not only reaffirmed the ban of the original act but extended it by banning the return to the United States of any Chinese laborer who had gone back to China. The law was named after Representative William Lawrence Scott (D-PA). A former mayor of Erie, he served on the Democratic National Committee from 1876 to 1888, and as a U.S. representative from Pennsylvania from 1885 to 1889. The 1888 Chinese Exclusion Act was signed into law by Democratic president Cleveland on October 1, 1888. The Scott Act was immediately challenged before the U.S. Supreme Court, in *Chae Chan Ping v. United States* (130 U.S. 1889). Chae was a Chinese laborer who had resided in San Francisco for 12 years and had returned to China in 1887, having obtained a certificate for reentry as required by the 1884 law. The Supreme Court upheld the Scott Act. The majority opinion in the case was written by Associate Justice Stephen Johnson Field. Its obvious ex-post-facto nature was ignored, earning Justice Field, in subsequent years, the distinction of being one of the five worst justices in U.S. Supreme Court history on due process grounds. In his majority opinion, Justice Field reflected racial animus when he referred to Chinese immigrants as a "vast horde" that merely by coming to the United States represented foreign aggression and encroachment. In his opinion, Justice Field stated that it was the:

highest duty of every nation to preserve its independence, and give security against foreign aggression and encroachments ... [This was true] ... no matter in what form such aggression and encroachment come, whether from the foreign nation acting in its national character or from the vast hordes of its people crowding in upon us. The government, possessing the powers which are to be exercised for protecting its security, is clothed with authority to determine the occasion on which the powers shall be called forth; and its determination, so far as the subjects affected are concerned, are necessarily conclusive upon all its departments and officers. (130 U.S. 1889: 606)

The Court, despite the fact that long-standing resident aliens had significant property investments in the United States and had that property taken from them without due process, ruled that Congress had the right and power to make such immigration law as it saw fit. Aliens, the Court said, did not have the rights of citizens and were therefore not governed by nor protected by the due process clause. The Chinese immigrant, no matter how long that person was in the United States, had no vested right of return once leaving the country and could be barred from reentry by an act of Congress as could any first arrival.

A depression in 1891 spurred renewed efforts to restrict immigration, and an even more severe depression in 1893 led to a natural falling-off in immigration. In the decade 1891 to 1900, only 3,687,564 immigrants entered in comparison to 5,246,613 persons who came to the United States during the decade 1881–1890.[10]

In 1891, Congress created the Superintendent of Immigration Act (26 Stat. 1084). (The title of the office was changed to commissioner-general of immigration in 1895.) The 1891 act also added to excluded categories "paupers, polygamists, and those with contagious diseases, and for the first time placed the supervision of immigration wholly under the authority of the federal government."[11] Congress passed a resolution to establish an immigration depot (i.e., reception station) on Ellis Island in New York harbor in April 1890. It was signed by Republican president Benjamin Harrison (1889–1893). The 1891 law placed immigration matters under federal authority by creating the Office of Superintendent of Immigration within the Treasury Department, and a Bureau of Immigration within the department, on July 12, 1891.

Labor strife, which began in the 1870s, continued in the 1880s, exemplified by the International Harvester plant strike near Chicago in 1884. Violence that occurred during that strike was attributed to "enemy-alien anarchists." Labor strife followed recessions in 1892 and 1893–1894, such as the Homestead Steel strike and the Pullman Strike.

Organized labor blamed the Depression of 1891 on immigrants, and by 1892 Congress passed the Geary Act (Pub. L. 52-10, 27 Stat. 2) which extended the Chinese Exclusion Act for another 10 years. Named after Representative Thomas Geary (D-CA), the Geary Act has been described as the "most repressive legislation every experienced by the Chinese in America ... which violated every single one of the articles of the [Burlingame] Treaty of 1880."[12]

In 1892, Senator Henry Cabot Lodge (R-MA) advocated for the use of a literacy test to ban immigrants. In 1896, Congress passed a law imposing such a test, but it was vetoed by Democratic president Grover Cleveland.

In 1894, Congress increased the authority of the secretary of the treasury and the Treasury Department to prevent Chinese immigrants (and later, others as well) from exercising a right to redress through the federal courts.

Also in the 1890s, scholarly studies began developing a social concept of race that became increasingly accepted and held in the common culture. Racism, as it came to be understood then, supported the need for restriction of immigration. By the 1890s, SCE Europeans came to be called the Italian race, the Greek race, and even the Jewish race. General Francis A. Walker, president of MIT and incoming president of the American Economic Association, called for a sharp reduction of immigration. In 1894, John Fiske, Nathaniel Shaler, and Senator Henry Cabot Lodge organized the Immigration Restriction League. The League spearheaded the restriction movement for the next two decades, advocating for the literacy test and emphasizing the differences between the "old" and the "new" immigrants as to their capabilities to assimilate. The American Protective Association peaked in its membership in 1894. The Knights of Labor added their strength to the growing arguments against "new" immigrants, and they began to advocate for a literacy test in 1897. Violent outbreaks against Italian and eastern European immigrants became almost commonplace from the mid-1890s to the early 1900s. As William Bernard summarized the trend:

From the 1890s to the First World War, and in the succeeding decade, a large number of American scholars, journalists, and politicians devoted their talents to elaborating the doctrine of "racism" as the basis for immigration and population policy. In this country the varied and considerable literature which they produced had a profound effect in preparing the public for the National Origins Law before it passed and in creating a set of rationalizations to justify the law after it was passed. We might add that these writings not only molded American attitudes but proved extremely useful in the propaganda of the leaders of Nazi Germany in later years.[13]

The creation of a federal immigration bureaucracy was especially important since the Supreme Court so often deferred to those administrative officers all the powers granted by Congress over immigration matters. The Court ruled that Congress had sole and virtually absolute discretion in deciding whom to admit, ban, or allow to remain and under whatever administrative conditions Congress desired. In 1896, a majority opinion of the Supreme Court stated that position in racially biased and quite stark terms:

> No limits can be put by the Court upon the power of Congress to protect, by summary methods, the country from the advent of aliens whose race or habits render them undesirable as citizens, or to expel such if they have found their way into our land and unlawfully remain therein. (*Wong Wing v. United States*, 163 U.S. 228, 237, 1896)

By the mid-1890s, immigration officers could and did operate with wide latitude, and their actions, too, reflected the growing racist ideas of the era.

Another trend adding to the momentum of the movement to restrict immigration was the wave of Japanese immigration. Japan passed its first emigration law in 1855, allowing for the first time a real influx of Japanese immigrants to the United States. A small group of Japanese immigrants (148 contract workers) went to Hawaii in 1868, welcomed as an alternative to the Chinese "coolie" labor force. After an initial three-year contract, some immigrated to the U.S. mainland. In 1870, there were only 56 Japanese immigrants on the mainland. By 1890, they exceeded 24,000; by 1910, they numbered more than 72,000; and in 1920, they exceeded 111,000, at which level they stabilized because they were barred by the 1924 Johnson-Reed Act.

Japanese immigrants were very literate (98.7 percent—more so than any other immigrant group) and soon were highly successful on the mainland. Prior to World War I, for example, although Japanese immigrants (the *issei*, or first-born) farmed less than 1 percent of the agricultural land in California, and that often the most marginal land, they produced 10 percent of the state's agricultural crop. Their success and the reaction it elicited were described as follows by Thomas Sowell:

> No matter what their first jobs, most Japanese wanted to acquire a plot of land, and many accomplished this goal piecemeal through a succession of different types of tenure. By 1890, according to the Immigration Commission's estimate, throughout the West some 60,000 Japanese were farming a total area of more than 210,000 acres. The success of these farms derived in part from an unusual degree of specialization, but more fundamentally from the hard work and extraordinary efficiency of the owners or tenants. To block this advance, California enacted the first anti-Japanese land law in 1913. Even though President Wilson sent his Secretary of State to Sacramento to argue against it, the bill passed by 35 to 2 in the Senate, and by 72 to 3 in the House. Under its terms, persons ineligible for citizenship could not own agricultural land or lease it for more than three years.[14]

The rapid immigration of Japanese instigated a Supreme Court case, the ruling of which had significant impact for the power of immigration officials to allow or refuse entry into the United States. In *Nishimura Ekiu v. United States* (142 U.S. 651, 1891) the Court ruled that immigration officials had such power. Equally, if not more importantly, in *Fong Yue Ting v. United States* (149 U.S. 698, 1893) the Court upheld their power to expel an alien. Fong Yue Ting was a Chinese laborer who challenged the immigration order to expel him because he failed to have a "certificate of residence." The Court ruled that such matter was of civil law, not criminal law, and civil law operated with fewer due process restrictions, arguing that immigration policy was a matter of sovereignty, not merely commerce.

The immigration bureaucracy became increasingly important in the process of admission or denial. Boards of Special Inquiry, begun in 1893, soon heard tens of thousands of cases annually. In 1910, for example, they heard 70,829 cases.[15] Critics charged that the boards were often arbitrary, inefficient, and politically corrupt, but such criticism did not limit their authority or actions.

In 1896, following a lingering depression, the bureau used the special inquiry process to detain hundreds of Italian immigrants seeking permanent entry status by invoking the "pauper" clause. Conditions on Ellis Island became so bad that Italians seeking admission rioted. The commissioner of immigration on Ellis Island, a Dr. J. H. Senner, worked openly with Prescott Hall, Robert DeCourcey Ward, and Senator Henry Cabot Lodge of the Immigration Restriction League. Inspectors were hired on the basis of a political spoils system and throughout the decade were badly administered and politically corrupt. The money-exchange service, baggage handling, and food concessions were a source of money and an inducement to corruption. The flood of immigrants entering the United States through Ellis Island taxed the system as well, since at the time Ellis Island processed some 6,500 immigrants daily. Parts of the station were burned down in a fire in 1897, and a new main reception hall or building was constructed to process the increasingly large immigration.

In 1896, Senator Lodge sponsored a literacy bill that passed both chambers in Congress but was vetoed by President Cleveland during his last days in office. A coalition of southern senators helped maintain Cleveland's veto. They wanted the influx of cheap labor to continue to support agriculture in southern states.

Also in 1896, Terrence Powderly, leader of the Knights of Labor, became commissioner-general of immigration. Factions within the Treasury Department, which at the time housed the immigration service, developed between Powderly in Washington, D.C., and New York commissioner of immigration Thomas Fitchie, an 1897 appointee of President William McKinley. Given his labor union background, Powderly favored strict restriction, whereas Commissioner Fitchie was willing to be more flexible.

FURTHER ATTEMPTS AT RESTRICTIVE IMMIGRATION LAW IN THE 1900s

In 1902, Republican president Theodore Roosevelt attempted to clean up the worst aspects of political corruption within the bureau. The agency began to tighten administrative procedures from 1903 to 1907, when Robert Watchorn, a career immigration service officer, was selected by Roosevelt to take over Ellis Island in 1907. His administration there was highly praised for its humanitarian reforms and attempts to control rampant political corruption at Ellis Island at a time of heightened immigration.

In the early 1900s the movement to restrict immigration, led by the Immigration Restriction League, pushed several approaches. It advocated exclusion of the Japanese as well as the Chinese, extending the list of excluded groups, and the adoption of a literacy test. The League was joined in its lobbying campaigns by organized labor, a variety of patriotic groups, and some leading sociologists and biologists. Opposing them were an assortment of ethnic societies, the steamship and railroad lines, manufacturers, and the National Liberal Immigration League, formed in 1906 specifically to counter the Immigration Restriction League.

The efforts to enact a literacy law failed prior to World War I because an effective coalition developed against those bills. Business groups remained in favor of open-door policy as a means to ensure a continued supply of cheap labor. The National Union of Manufacturers and the National Association of Manufacturers helped defeat several such literacy bills.

During the period between the Spanish American War (1898) and World War I, overall nativism declined somewhat as the United States experienced a period of economic expansion and social buoyancy. An imperialistic outburst (largely during Republican Theodore Roosevelt's presidency) drained off some xenophobic impulses. At the same time, a growing number of ethnic associations fought proposals to limit immigration: the German-American Alliance, the Ancient Order of Hibernians, the B'nai B'rith, the Hebrew Immigrant Aid Society, and the Council of the Union of American Hebrew Congregations. The Republican Party platforms from 1904 through 1912 had no restriction plank, as they had had in their platforms during the 1890s. Speaker of the House Joe Cannon led the effort to strenuously and successfully defeat the literacy bills.

Two bills were passed in 1903 that signaled a slight movement in favor of restriction. One act (32 Stat. 1213) codified all existing immigration acts into a single statute and, in doing so, expanded the number of excluded category groups to include epileptics, prostitutes, and professional beggars. It added anarchists to the classes of excluded aliens, inspired no doubt by the assassination of Republican president William McKinley in 1901 by an avowed anarchist, Leon Czolgosz. In doing so, it enacted guilt by association.

A second statute (32 Stat. 828) moved the immigration service from the Treasury Department to the newly created Department of Commerce and Labor. It also strengthened the organization and structure of the administrative authority by giving the commissioner-general of Immigration enhanced control over the personnel and activities of enforcement. By 1906 the new commissioner-general took pride in claiming that his bureau was being converted into an efficient and depersonalized bureaucratic instrument of social policy. Critics of the department, however, maintained that its policy was inhumane, inequitable, and cruel in the treatment of hapless human beings. As Benjamin Ringer observed:

> Aware of their strategic role as gatekeepers, a number of these officials soon took advantage of the situation in which so much was at stake for the Chinese, particularly the merchants. They extorted bribes, and engaged in other corrupt practices. Compounding these problems ... was the fact that many of these officials were drawn from California with its pathological dislike of the Chinese. As a result, they resorted to technicalities to reject the credentials of Chinese, detained many others unnecessarily while their credentials were being checked, and demanded payoffs from still others.[16]

In the decade 1900 to 1910, the United States experienced the largest influx of immigration ever up to that time, when 8,795,386 persons entered. This renewed surge of massive immigration, coupled with heightened racial concern over Japanese immigration and the Panic of 1907 and its subsequent economic depression, fueled the fire for a renewed effort to restrict immigration.

Japanese immigrants faced hostility and violence soon after their arrival on the mainland, when anti-Chinese sentiment was extended to them. The shoemakers' union attacked Japanese cobblers in 1890, and similar attacks by cooks' and waiters' union members followed in 1892. The American Federation of Labor argued that the Japanese succeeded the Chinese as the "Yellow Peril," more threatening than their predecessor. Fears of the Yellow Peril increased markedly after the surprising victory of Japan over Russia in the Russo-Japanese War of 1905. In May 1905, a Japanese-Korean Exclusion League formed and quickly grew to 100,000 in California alone. It renamed itself the Asian Exclusion League in 1907 and by then, as Benjamin Ringer notes, was comprised of 231 affiliated groups, 84 percent of which were labor organizations.[17] San Francisco segregated Japanese students, compelling them to attend Chinese schools. Responding to labor union pressure, Republican president Theodore Roosevelt issued an executive order in 1907, known as the Gentlemen's Agreement, which lasted until 1948 and barred Japanese entry into the United States from a bordering country (Canada and Mexico) or U.S. territory (Hawaii). Even the American Socialist Party, normally pro-immigration from Europe, and especially from eastern Europe, opposed immigration of "Asiatics." Congress weighed in on the issue by enacting the Immigration Act of 1907 (34 Stat. 898). It raised the head tax on immigrants from 50 cents to four dollars; banned persons with tuberculosis, imbeciles, and "persons of moral turpitude"; and added more stringent enforcement machinery. The sheer volume of immigration taxed the ability of the immigration bureaucracy's enforcement procedures when in 1905, for example, Ellis Island alone processed 821,169 aliens, and each inspector had to examine and process 400–500 immigrants daily.[18]

The results of the Gentlemen's Agreement and the Immigration Act of 1907 were dramatic and quick. By its first full year of operation, in 1909, immigration from Japan/Korea dropped from 30,824 in 1907, to 16,418 for 1908, to 3,275 in 1909, and to fewer than 3,000 in 1911.[19] Homer Lea, California's leading publicist of the Yellow Peril, warned in 1909 that the United States was losing its "racial purity" to Asian and SCE European immigrants. The American Federation of Labor's Samuel Gompers endorsed a literacy test.

Congress passed a literacy test bill in 1909, but it was vetoed by Republican president William Howard Taft, who, with his secretary of labor, argued there was still need for immigrant labor.

Congress established the Dillingham Commission in 1907 to study immigration policy. Its members were heavily stacked in favor of restriction. It issued its massive—42 volumes—and final report in 1911. Although supposedly objective and scientific, given its membership, it recommended the adoption of a literacy test "demanded by economic, moral, and social considerations."[20] It openly included the literacy test as a device designed to decrease immigration by 25 percent:

> Among its suggested means of obtaining restrictions were the following: a literacy test, the exclusion of unskilled laborers; an increase in the amount of money which the immigrant was required to have in his possession; and

an increase in the head tax. The Commission also suggested the introduction of the principle of limiting the number of each "race" admitted during any given year, such limitation to be based on the numbers of that "race" which had entered the United States during a given period of years—a proposal which foreshadowed the quota law.[21]

The Commission accepted the Social Darwinian theories taken by the Immigration Restriction League from the writings of John Commons, Edward Ross, and especially William Ripley's *The Races of Europe* (1899). The racial overtones of the commission's report were augmented in time by Madison Grant's influential book, *The Passing of the Great Race* (1916), which warned that supposedly unassimilable dark and culturally different people were overtaking "civilization."

In California the anti-Japanese movement led to passage, in 1913, of the California Alien Land Act, known as the Webb-Heney bill, which restricted Japanese aliens from owning land, limiting their leasing land to three years, and prohibiting land already owned from being bequeathed—that is, from passing ownership from the *issei* (first-born) generation parent to their *nisei* (second-generation) children, who were native-born citizens. The law was ruled constitutional by the Supreme Court and spurred several western states to pass their own versions of the land act. California's Attorney General Ulysses S. Webb frankly described the law he coauthored with attorney Francis Heney as follows:

> The fundamental basis of all legislation . . . has been and is, race undesirability. It seeks to limit their presence by curtailing the privileges which they may enjoy here, for they will not come in large numbers and long abide with us if they may not acquire land. And it seeks to limit the numbers who will come by limiting the opportunities for their activities here when they arrive.[22]

Following the recommendations of the Dillingham Commission, Congress passed a literacy bill in 1913, which was promptly vetoed by Republican president William Howard Taft. That year Congress also moved the immigration service to the newly created Department of Labor (37 Stat. 737). The law divided the service into two bureaus, the Bureau of Immigration and the Bureau of Naturalization, placed under the secretary of labor, who promptly reduced the immigration service staff.

THE POST–WORLD WAR I YEARS

Immigration dropped off by 75 percent during the World War I years. A literacy bill passed in 1915 was vetoed by Democratic president Woodrow Wilson. His veto was sustained. He described the bill as a test of opportunity, not of intelligence. The Bolshevik Revolution in Russia renewed efforts by the forces of restriction, and they were more effective in the postwar years. The American Legion, established in 1919, the National Grange (formally the National Grange of the Order of Patrons of Husbandry, established in 1867), and the American Federation of Labor (1896) all strongly supported the literacy test bill, which was passed in 1917 and enacted over President Wilson's veto (39 Stat. 874). The new law added several categories of excluded classes—e.g., chronic alcoholics, those suffering from psychopathic inferiority—and it created an Asiatic Barred-Zone, virtually excluding all Asians except Japanese picture brides. The 1917 law also increased the head tax on immigrants from four to eight dollars.

In the post–World War I years, radicals of all types were persecuted— Wobblies (members of the International Workers of the World union), socialists, anarchists, and persons suspected of holding such views were tarred and feathered, jailed, and sometimes even lynched. During the Red Scare, in the summer of 1919, thousands of suspected "communists" were rounded up and jailed pending deportation hearings. Eventually 500 "radicals" were deported, many aboard a ship, the *Buford*, dubbed "the Soviet Ark."

In 1922, in the *Ozawa v. United States* case (260 U.S. 178), the Supreme Court upheld as constitutional the law that excluded the Japanese immigrants from naturalization. The *issei* were thereby subjected to the various state land laws and similar discriminatory local ordinances based on their being noncitizens and not eligible to become citizens.

The postwar period unleashed the darker forces of the American psyche. The Ku Klux Klan grew alarmingly, espousing radical and often violent anti-Catholic, anti-Semitic, and anti-foreign rhetoric. The phrase "100-Percent Americanism" became the order of the day. The Klan joined forces with the American Protective League and the True Americans (1887) and launched an incendiary period of anti-Catholicism.

The triumph of racist ideas provided the rationale for the restrictive immigration laws of the 1920s. "Eugenics," a pseudoscience, supposedly "proved" that certain races were endowed with a hereditary superiority or inferiority and provided the basis for the quota system acts intended to stem the expected immigrants from south, central, and Eastern Europe.

THE PET DOOR ERA BEGINS: THE IMMIGRATION ACT OF 1921

A third phase, known as the Pet Door era, lasted from 1920s to 1965.[23] During this era the national origin system formed the basis of immigration law. A highly restrictive and racially biased policy, it proved to be highly effective. It allowed in only a favored few—hence the image of the "Pet Door." By design, the national origin quota laws (of 1921, 1924, and 1929) tilted the flow of a much reduced level of immigration from those coming from southern, central, and eastern Europe back to northwestern Europe. It lasted as the fundamental immigration law for more than 40 years.

The principle of allocating quotas on the basis of those already represented by the various nationalities among the U.S. foreign-born population was first introduced by Dr. Sidney Gulick in 1914. He intended it as a liberal alternative to positions being advocated by strict restrictionists calling for a total suspension of immigration. He was a former missionary in Asia. In 1918, he formed the National Committee on Constructive Immigration Legislation, which suggested that each nationality be assigned a quota proportionate to the number of naturalized citizens and their U.S.-born children already drawn from that nationality. Annually, an immigration commission would fix a certain percentage—he suggested 10 percent—of those first- and second-generation citizens. As Gulick stated it: "The proved capacity for genuine Americanization on the part of those already here from any land should be the measure for the future immigration of that people."[24] The "percentage quota principle" would soon be the central piece of the immigration laws passed in the 1920s. What differed among them was how the quotas would be set up. After the 1921 law, the basic principle that there should be annual numerical quotas was fairly well accepted. The pivotal and basic function of the quota system was to limit immigration from Europe, and the immigration reform battles that took place throughout the decade were over how to distribute such quotas among the various nations of Europe.

In the debates leading up to enactment of the 1921 bill—and, indeed, in subsequent debates for the 1924 bill—the primary organizations in favor of the origins bill included the American Federation of Labor, the American Legion, the Immigration Restriction League (1894), the National Grange, the Ku Klux Klan, and the Junior Order of American Mechanics (1853) as well as such patriotic associations as the Sons of the American Revolution, the Patriotic Order of the Sons of America, and the Daughters of the American Revolution. The organizations who opposed the bill included: the Anti-National Origins Clause League, a taxpayers' association from New York, and several industrial and employer organizations, such as the National Association of Manufacturers (NAM), the American Mining Congress, the Associated General Contractors, the National Industrial Conference Board, and the U.S. Chamber of Commerce. Also active in opposition to the proposed law were farm associations concerned that they would have insufficient manpower, spokesmen for various Jewish, foreign-language, and other "ethnic groups" that would be adversely affected by the 1890 base year, including ones from northern and western Europe that restrictionists still wanted to encourage coming to America: the Vasa Order of America (Swedish), the Steuben Society, the Danish Brotherhood of America, the Sons of Norway, and the German-American Citizens League.

The U.S. Senate passed a measure sponsored by Senator Dillingham that limited European immigration to 5 percent of foreign-born of that nationality as present in the 1910 census, and limited total immigration to a quarter of a million. The House favored the Senate bill but reduced limits from 5 to 3 percent of the 1910 census and total immigration to 350,000, and assigned most of that to northern and western Europe. Congress adopted the House version in a conference committee, but Democratic president Woodrow Wilson killed the bill with a pocket veto during his last days in office. The pocket veto, however, was quickly to be in vain. Incoming Republican president Warren G. Harding called a special session of Congress, and when Washington State's Representative Albert Johnson, one of the leading restrictionists in Congress, supported the bill rather than his own total suspension plan, it passed the House without a recorded (roll-call) vote. In the Senate, it passed 78–1 and was signed into law in May 1921. Known as the Emergency Immigration Restriction Act(42 Stat. 5, 8 U.S.C. 229), it established the principle of the quota system. It set total immigration at 357,803. It drastically cut immigration from Asia, Africa, and Oceania, to fewer than 1,000 immigrants, northwestern Europe to 200,000, and south, central, and eastern Europe to 155,000 immigrants. It reaffirmed all the previous restricted "excluded groups" established in the 1917 act. The basis for determining each country's quota was 3 percent of the foreign-born population as present in the United States according to the 1910 Census. [25]

THE IMMIGRATION ACT OF 1924

Enactment of the 1921 law did not settle the matter. Those advocating restriction were not satisfied that the law sufficiently limited immigration. Moreover, the quota system as was temporarily established imposed some harsh injustices. Ships entering U.S. ports often carried more than the monthly quota set for a country allowed entry. Polish, Rumanian, and Italian immigrants jammed Ellis Island and steamships in the harbors of Boston and New York. The immigration service used administrative exemptions to the monthly quotas to deal with backlogs in the ports and reception stations. This simply angered the congressional forces for restriction. From 1921 to 1923, Congress was deadlocked over attempts to set up a permanent quota system. Representative Albert Johnson (R-WA) chaired the House Immigration Committee and backed the AFL and American Legion's call for total suspension. Prescott Hall, of the Immigration Restriction League, Madison Grant, Lothrop Stoddard, Kenneth Roberts, and Harry Laughlin all supported the Johnson Committee and stirred up public debate on the issue.

A prominent New York lawyer, John D. Trevor, began to work with the Johnson Committee. Restrictionist members on the committee began advocating changing the base year from 1910 to 1890, and reducing the quotas from 3 to 2 percent. The change to the 1890 census as base meant that total immigration would be less and that the continued immigration from SCE European countries would be reduced from a flood to a trickle. By 1923, the Senate Immigration Committee, at the urging of the National Association of Manufacturers, introduced a bill retaining the quota system but allowing for additional immigration in times of labor shortage. Senator David A. Reed (R-PA) sponsored a compromise bill that increased total immigration but reduced the share allotted to SCE

European countries. With various business organizations conflicting in what they advocated, the battleground shifted to various ethnic organizations pushing for or opposing quotas, as they would affect the immigration from their nations of origin. Gradually, a "Nordic theory" gained ground. Newly elected Republican president Calvin Coolidge supported restriction forces in his first inaugural address, calling for a system that would assure that "America might be kept American."[26] The Johnson Committee, relying heavily on its unofficial advisor, John Trevor, supplied what became the solution to the deadlock.

Trevor argued that the 1921 quotas, based on the 1910 census, did not reflect the "racial status quo" of the nation. He used a "racial breakdown" of the U.S. population published by Clinton Stoddard Burr in *America's Race Heritage* (1922). Trevor's analysis "proved" that as of 1920, about 12 percent of the U.S. population derived from southeastern European countries, but on the basis of the 1921 quota system, they were allocated 44 percent of total immigration quotas. If, however, the 1890 census were used, they would only have 15 percent. Johnson's committee introduced a new bill, based on Trevor's brief, and the Ku Klux Klan launched a massive campaign supporting the bill designed to "preserve" America's racial purity. Congressional members from southern states supported the bill, distinguishing between the "old" and the "new" immigrants. Representative Carl Vinson (D-GA) stated:

> But it is the "new" immigrant who is restricted in emigrating to this country. The emigrants affected by this bill are those from Italy, Greece, Russia, Poland, Bulgaria, Armenia, Czechoslovakia, Yugoslavia and Turkey. I respectfully submit, with all the power within me, that the people from these countries do not yield their national characteristics, but retain them practically unimpaired by contact with others.[27]

Congressmen from California, the West Coast, and the South especially voiced similar racial ideas and played on the Yellow Peril theme, warning that Japan's overpopulation and thirst for land would lead to a future race war.

Senator David Reed of Pennsylvania pushed through the Senate committee a proposal using quotas based on the 1890 census data, receiving valuable support from Senator Henry Cabot Lodge of Massachusetts.

The full Senate, however, adopted a version retaining the 1910 census and stipulating the quota system would not go into effect until 1927, to give the immigration service ample time to formulate exact quotas. A compromise version won Senate support, 62–5, and passed in the House, 323–71. Republican president Calvin Coolidge signed the bill into law on May 26, 1924 (43 Stat. 153, 8 U,S.C. 201). The Johnson-Reed Act, as the 1924 law became known, included a provision requiring visas as an effective regulating device, and the overseas issuing of visas charged against quotas became the most effective device to control the use of quotas and allow for administrative screening of immigrants prior to their entry into the United States. Moreover, its provision of prohibiting persons who might become public charges was used to dramatically cut total immigration during times of recession and depression by setting strict standards for economic tests to demonstrate the applicant's admissibility. The "public charge" provision, and exclusion on medical grounds (the most often used condition to bar entrance was trachoma, a highly contagious disease of the eyes) were especially effectively used at the Ellis Island station at the time, as well as sometimes the rule that the steamship lines had to assume the cost of returning any immigrant not admitted to the United States.

THE NATIONAL QUOTA ACT OF 1929

In 1928, John Trevor formed a new group, the American Coalition, comprised of a coalition of patriotic groups, such as the Sons of the American Revolution, the Patriotic Order of the Sons of America, and the Daughters of the American Revolution, which proved to be successful. Groups such as the AFL, the Junior Order of United American Mechanics, and the American Legion continued their staunch support for the quota system, as did the U.S. Chamber of Commerce. These pro-quota system groups were opposed by the Anti-National Origins Clause League, which worked with various ethnic groups favoring revisions to the quota system that would lessen its adverse impact upon their nationality group. They emphasized economic arguments that stressed the continuing need for labor, and that immigrants would do jobs that native workers were unwilling to do.

The 1924 Johnson-Reed Act had its desired impact. European immigration fell from more than 800,000 in 1921 to less than 150,000 by 1929. Still, the forces advocating a total ban on immigration, or at least much

Table 1.1   Decline in Immigration under the Quota System, Selected Years

Year	Immigrants Admitted
1914	1,218,480
1921	805,228
1922	309,556
1925	294,314
1930	241,710

Source: Author.

more severe restrictions, were not satisfied. The 1924 act exempted countries in the Western Hemisphere and the Philippine Islands (then a U.S. territory). They began targeting immigration from Mexico and Latin America.

In 1926 Representative John Box (D-TX, 1923–1931), an ardent restrictionist, led a strongly southern contingent that included Hiram Johnson of Texas and Thomas Heflin of Alabama. In the Senate, leading proponents of restriction were Senators William Harris (D-GA), Frank B. Willis (R- Ohio), and David Reed (R-PA). They began arguing that Congress needed to "close the back door to immigration."[28] When Senator Harris introduced a bill, in 1929, to amend the quota law to include a limit on Mexican immigration, President Herbert Hoover threatened to veto it. The National Origins Plan was enacted in its final form in 1929. It capped total immigration at 153,714; total from northwestern Europe at 125,853; and total from SCE Europe at 24,648, Asia a mere 1,805, Africa 1,200, and the Pacific 700.[29] Table 1.1 shows the dramatic drop in total immigration resulting from the three quota acts, presenting the number of immigrants admitted in five selected years: 1914, the year just before World War I; 1921, the full year before passage of the 1921 act; 1922, the first full year after passage; 1925, the first full year after enactment of the Johnson-Reed Act; and 1930, the first full year after President Hoover's proclamation.

THE GREAT DEPRESSION AND WORLD WAR II YEARS

No major legislation was needed during the 1930s when immigration fell off naturally, due to the Great Depression, to a million for the entire decade. The Depression and the quota system had their intended effect. Northwestern European immigration fell from over 70 percent of the total of the 1880s to 20 percent in the 1910–1920 decade, which shifted upward to 40 percent in the 1930s. SCE European immigration fell from 71 percent in the 1910–1920 decade to less than 30 percent during the 1930s. Immigration nearly ceased during the World War II years. The distribution of those who did come reflected the 1930–1940 decade. From 1940 to 1947, northwestern European immigration was 34.9 percent of the total and SCE Europe was 9.5 percent, while Canada sent 23.2 percent, Mexico 8.7 percent, and all others 23.6 percent. Net immigration during the Depression years was negative, with more emigrants departing than immigrants admitted. During the war years net immigration ranged from 18,000 to 22,000, except in 1944 –1945, when it was 30,677.[30]

THE DUTCH DOOR ERA

In 1950, a special Senate committee, authorized in 1947 under the chairmanship of Senator William Chapman Revercomb (R-WV) and continuing under Senator Patrick McCarran (D-NV), issued the most comprehensive study of immigration since the Dillingham Commission Report in 1911. Both Senator McCarran and his coauthor, Francis Walter (D-PA), were noted anti-communists. The committee's report served as the basis for the congressional debates and the resulting proposed legislation that marked the beginning of the Dutch Door Era, the McCarran-Walter Act of June 27, 1952 (66 Stat. 163).

While the act reaffirmed the restrictive policy of the national origins system, the years of President Dwight David Eisenhower's administration saw a gradual chipping away at restriction. It reflected perceived foreign policy concerns of the Cold War, as several laws were passed allowing admission for special "refugees" and "anti-communist freedom fighters." By the mid-1960s, the forces advocating relaxation of restrictions were on the political offensive, and forces trying to maintain restriction were increasingly fighting a holding action.

While it did not fully abolish the national origins quota approach (and received a veto from President Harry Truman as a result, on June 25, 1952), for the first time the McCarran-Walter Act introduced the concept of "preferences" by adding some to the quotas to be used for certain skilled labor and for relatives of U.S. citizens and permanent resident aliens. The McCarran-Walter Act increased the numerical limits for the Eastern Hemisphere (from 120,000 to 150,000) and retained the unlimited number for the Western Hemisphere. Reflecting the change in foreign policy during World War II when China became an ally of the United States, the 1952 law added a small quota for overall Asian immigration, granting a token quota to those nations in what it defined as the "Asia-Pacific Triangle." Congress overrode Truman's veto by a vote of 278–113 in the House and 57–26 in the Senate.[31]

This law, since it first broached the idea of preference categories, set the stage for the Dutch Door era that is characterized by the preferences approach to immigration policymaking enacted by the 1965 act. Just before leaving office, President Truman established a Presidential Commission on Immigration in January 1953. Among other things, it recommended abolishing the quota system in its final report, "Whom Shall We Welcome."

The McCarran-Walter Act avoided the more racist arguments characterizing the original implementation of the quota system. The Senate Immigration Committee's report on the bill did reaffirm the U.S. immigration policy should and would favor NW over SCE European countries since, in the committee's words, "the peoples who had made the greatest contribution to the development of this nation were fully justified in determining that the country was no longer a field for further colonization, and henceforth further immigration would not only be restricted but directed to admit immigrants considered to be more able to assimilate because of the similarity of their cultural background to those of the principle component of our population."[32]

Exigencies in foreign policy during the Cold War caused further erosion of the quota system policy in 1953, 1956, and 1957, when Congress enacted additional "refugee" measures outside of the quota system. The Refugee Relief Act of August 7, 1953 (67 Stat. 400), provided for entrance of refugees still in camps in Europe after World War II. Republican president Dwight D. Eisenhower favored more generous immigration policy and sent Congress a message calling on it to enact such policy in February 1953. Congress debated immigration for some time, then passed two laws: the Act of September 11, 1957, which amended the 1952 act to allow more refugee admissions (71 Stat. 639), and the Act of July 25,

1958, to allow admission for permanent residence for Hungarian refugees, known as the Hungarian Freedom Fighters, fleeing communism after their failed revolution attempt in 1956 (72 Stat. 419). A host of religious-affiliated groups, all opposed to "godless communism," supported the shift in refugee policy to allow the entry of "anti-communists." President Eisenhower initially brought in 5,000 under the Refugee Relief Act of 1953. In early 1957, Eisenhower was granted greater latitude to bring in more freedom fighters, which he did by a "special parole" that enabled 30,000 more to enter that year.[33] And in 1957, Congress cancelled the mortgage quotas of the Displaced Persons Act, marking a further breakdown in the restrictive policies of the quota system.

Late in 1959, President Eisenhower again used the parole status to admit Cuban refugees. Ultimately, some 800,000 Cuban refugees entered the United States, making it the largest long-term refugee movement in

Table 1.2   Refugees Accepted by Country, 1975–1980

Country	Number	Country	Number
United States	677,000	Austria	4,000
China	265,000	New Zealand	4,100
Israel	105,700	Belgium	3,900
Malaysia	102,100	Argentina	2,800
Canada	84,100	Norway	2.700
France	72,000	Denmark	2,300
Australia	51,000	Romania	1,200
Germany (FRG)	32,100	Spain	1,100
United Kingdom	27,600	Italy	900
Tanzania	26,000	Chile	800
Hong Kong	9,400	Japan	800
Switzerland	7,500	Cuba	700
Sweden	7,300	Mexico	700
Netherlands	4,700		

Source: 1981 World Refugee Survey, ed. Michael Sherbinin. New York: U.S. Committee for Refugees, 1981, as presented in Michael LeMay, *Anatomy of a Public Policy* (New York: Praeger, 1994), 19.

U.S. history.[34] Eisenhower also used the parole device for Chinese refugees from Communist China arriving from Hong Kong. In all, from the end of World War II until 1980, more than 1.4 million refugees from all over the world immigrated to the United States.[35] Table 1.2 details the number of refugees accepted by country between 1975 and 1980, and showing the United States to be the most refugee-receptive nation.

Congress established a category for refugees from Communist-dominated countries in Europe or from the Middle East. It expanded entrance for certain relatives of U.S. citizens and lawfully resident aliens by the Act of September 22, 1959 (73 Stat. 644) and for further resettlement of World War II refugees still in camps in Europe in 1960 (74 Stat. 504). These various acts indicated that Congress was approaching the policy position of scrapping the quota system itself as no longer a workable policy position to govern immigration, where the need so far exceeded the limits allowable under the quota acts.

Another method of getting around the inflexibility of the quota system was use of the private bill. Under this procedure, an alien sought exception from the quota system through private legislation. A member of Congress introduced a bill for his/her relief. The use of this procedure expanded during the 1950s. While the numbers of immigrants who actually entered by this method was not large, totaling only in the thousands, it further chipped away at the quota system.

In 1962, after the election of Democratic president John F. Kennedy and a somewhat more liberal U.S. Congress, Congress passed the Migration and Refugee Assistance Act. In part a response to the Cuban refugee problem, the law strengthened the role of the executive branch in the formulation and implementation of immigration policy, paving the way for the Immigration and Nationality Act of 1952. While a U.S. Senator, Kennedy (D-MA) had written an article published in the *New York Times Magazine* (1958) and subsequently published posthumously in 1964, titled *A Nation of Immigrants*, in which he showed his obvious favorable attitude towards a more open immigration policy. His election, in 1960, and the development of the civil rights movement and its campaign against overt racism in U.S. law (for example, the *de jure* segregation of blacks from whites in the southern states), further signaled the willingness of Congress to consider overhauling the immigration system. It did so when it honored the by then "martyred" President Kennedy by enacting the Immigration and Nationality Act of 1965 (commonly known as the Kennedy Immigration Act, which officially amended the 1952 act)—the Act of October 3, 1965 (79 Stat. 911).

As will be seen in greater detail in the next chapter, the 1965 act reflected the civil rights era and domestic policy concerns regarding *de jure* (by law) segregation and racism entrenched in U.S. law just as the McCarran-Walter Act had earlier reflected the Cold-War period of U.S. foreign policy concerns. The 1965 act abolished the quota system and replaced it with a seven-category preference system that was more liberal and generous with respect to immigration levels. It raised total legal immigration to 160,000, to be distributed on the basis of 20,000 persons per country for all nations outside the Western Hemisphere, and placed an overall limit of 120,000 on Western Hemisphere nations, but without individual national limits. The first several of the seven preferences opened up immigration for family reunification, and the act had a couple of other high preference categories for certain desired occupational skills.[36]

Democratic president Lyndon Johnson pushed Congress to enact the law in honor of the slain president. In order to secure its passage, the open-door policy for Western Hemisphere nations was ended. A 1964 law ended the Bracero program that had been passed in 1942 to enable agricultural and railroad workers to temporarily come to and work in the United States. That action soon resulted in increasing backlogs for applicants from Latin America, and especially from Mexico. It essentially fueled undocumented (illegal) immigration. Congress amended it in 1978, to increase slightly a worldwide limit of 290,000, but kept the basic seven-category preference system. As we have seen, special "parole" programs were established to handle refugee waves from Cuba, Vietnam, and Soviet country refugees. Finally, on March 17, 1980, Congress passed the Refugee Act, aimed at correcting deficiencies in existing policy by providing an ongoing mechanism for admission and aid of refugees. It changed the legal definition of refugee to remove previous geographic and ideological restriction (that is, refugees from Communist countries) and set a new ceiling for refugees (entering over and above the numbers allowed through the preference system) of 50,000 annually through 1982. It was quickly outmoded by worldwide events that increased the pool of refugees desiring to enter into the millions and for which the 50,000 limit was soon totally outmoded. These events set up political pressures resulting in the next phase: the Revolving Door era.

THE REVOLVING DOOR ERA

Beginning in 1980 with the Refugee Act, and continuing especially through to 2000, immigration policy can be described as a revolving door era in which ever-increasingly large numbers of unauthorized immigrants, mostly although not exclusively undocumented immigrants crossing the southwestern border, came and went to the United States, adding to the influx of legal immigrants, which also increased as a result of the Immigration and Nationality Act of 1965. Indeed, the most significant unintended consequence of the 1965 act was the resulting exponential growth of undocumented immigrants, a major portion of whom had been Bracero program workers or compatriots influenced by them and following chain-migration patterns forged during the years of the Bracero program. When the Bracero program ended, many of the Bracero workers continued to come as illegal immigrants. During the final few years of the Bracero program, upwards of 350,000 guest-workers a year came to the United States to work. Although every bit as motivated by racism as it was by anti-Catholicism, the movement opposing the change was certainly fueled by the fact that Hispanics from Mexico and Central America were overwhelmingly Roman Catholic. When Mexico received a quota of 20,000 legal immigrants, that quota simply could not satisfy the demand, and so the chain migration continued unabated but illegally, as undocumented immigrants. Until 1986, moreover, many came illegally, worked for a season or two, then returned to Mexico for a while, before re-crossing again. When Congress enacted the Immigration Reform and Control Act of 1986 (IRCA; 104 Stat. 4981), which significantly imposed a new tool designed to stop the illegal flow by imposing employer sanctions on those who knowingly hired undocumented immigrants, it resulted in a temporary decline in illegal border crossings and also resulted in those already residing in the United States in unauthorized status (whether undocumented or visa-overstayers) to remain rather than returning to their nations of origin expecting to easily recross some time later. More than three million undocumented immigrants who satisfied the requirements of IRCA's amnesty program had their status changed to legal resident aliens. Those members could now acquire a legal work permit card (commonly called a green card, although it was by then actually a white card). Many nuclear families were separated by this process—husbands from wives, fathers or both parents from their children. To be reunited legally, family members in Mexico or Central America who wished to join their family members residing in the United States faced ever-increasingly long backlogs, typically stretching to seven years or longer before a legal visa would be available. Rather than face years apart, they too crossed illegally as undocumented entrants, to reunite with their family members. The estimated number of unauthorized immigrants climbed each year after 1986, numbering 7.9 million by 2000.[37]

Seeing that the employer sanctions provision of IRCA was failing to halt the exponential rise of undocumented immigrants, Congress tried other legislative actions.

The vast majority of undocumented immigrants came seeking work and participated in the labor force at a percentage rate exceeding that of U.S. citizens. Nonetheless, Congress subscribed to the notion that welfare services were drawing them to the United States, and as a result, Congress passed two laws in 1996 designed to "demagnetize" the draw of welfare benefits. The first law was the Personal Responsibility and Work Opportunity Act of August 22, 1996 (H.R. 3734—Pub. L. 104-193). It enacted as national law and policy many of the provisions of California's Proposition 187. Officially the "Save Our State" initiative, Proposition 187 was passed to deny a host of benefits to illegal immigrants and even some legal immigrants designed to send a message to Congress to crack down on undocumented immigration. It had been overturned by a federal district court as unconstitutional in *LUCLAC et al. v. Wilson et al.* (November 20, 1995 (908 F. Supp. 755, C.D. Cal. 1995) because it denied welfare services to immigrants, both legal and illegal. Congress also folded several provisions into the omnibus fiscal 1997 spending bill (The Illegal Immigration Reform and Immigrant Responsibility Act of September 30, 1996, H.R. 3619—Pub. L. 104-209).

As economic conditions improved and the anti-immigrant fervor eased, several adjustments to the restrictions of the 1996 laws were passed in December 2000, aimed at restoring some benefits to legal immigrants. For example, the Legal Immigration and Family Equity Act (LIFE) of 2000 reinstated Section 245(i) of the Immigration Act of 1952 that allowed undocumented immigrants to apply for visas without first leaving the United States while they waited for adjustment to lawful permanent resident status. Illegal aliens who were in the United States for at least six months could be barred from reentry for up to 10 years. About 640,000 undocumented immigrants were covered by this law, but applicants had to pay a $1,000 penalty fee and other filing fees.[38]

With the terrorist attacks of September 11, 2001, the Revolving Door era came to a fiery end ushering in the current phase of immigration policymaking, the Storm Door era.

THE STORM DOOR ERA

Several legislative enactments demarcate the beginning of immigration policymaking that may be viewed as the Storm Door era, an attempt to establish by law "Fortress America." Various laws were passed between 2000 and 2006 that were designed to "harden" and to "take control" of U.S. borders, particularly the southwestern border, by asserting a border management approach to immigration policymaking.

The first such action was the USA Patriot Act of 2001 (H.R. 3162, signed into law by President George W. Bush on October 26, 2001). Its name is an acronym for United and Strengthening America by Providing Appropriate Tools Required to Intercept and Obstruct Terrorism Act. It grants to the Justice Department broad powers to refuse admission, to monitor foreign students and resident aliens, and to detain and expedite the removal of noncitizens suspected of links to terrorist organizations merely upon certification of the Attorney General as to their being threats to national security on whatever grounds. The law received much criticism for being too sweeping and too dangerous to constitutional checks and balances.

A year later, on November 19, 2002, Congress enacted the Homeland Security Act (H.R. 5005; Pub. L. 107-296, 116 Stat. 2135). It is a law of hundreds of pages in the U.S. Code, merging 22 federal agencies and reorganizing 170,000 federal employees (the Department of Homeland Security, DHS). It is the most sweeping reorganization of the federal bureaucracy since the creation of the Department of Defense in 1947. With respect to immigration policymaking, it establishes within the new DHS two bureaus, each headed by an undersecretary: the Bureau of Border

Transportation Security, and the Bureau of Citizenship and Immigration Services.[39]

Congress passed the Intelligence Reform and Terrorism Prevention Act of 2004 (Pub. L. 108-458, signed into law by President Bush on December 17, 2004). Among its various sections, it established a Director of National Intelligence (DNI) to oversee the work of 15 intelligence agencies and a National Counterterrorism Center, and authorized annually the addition of 2,000 agents to the Border Patrol (Immigration and Customs Enforcement, or ICE), for five years. It also set new standards for information that must be contained in driver's licenses and made it easier to track suspected terrorists referred to as lone wolves.

In May 2005, Congress passed the Real ID Act (Pub. L. 109-12; 119 Stat. 302). It modified national law by elaborating on the ways to authenticate and on issuance procedures used by state and local governments for state's driver's licenses and state-issued photographic identification cards (for persons not able to have a driver's license). It also waived several environmental restrictions that could potentially interfere with construction of a border fence.

In 2006, Congress enacted and President Bush signed into law the Secure Fence Act (Pub. L. 109-367). It approved $1.2 billion to construct a steel fence along the 2,000-mile southern border with Mexico. To date, just over 600 miles have been constructed, and in 2010–2014 bills have been introduced to authorize an additional 350 miles. The most significant impact of the border fence has been to induce immigrants to cross elsewhere—through Arizona, Texas, and New Mexico—where the fence has not been built. There, the terrain has proven to be more dangerous and has resulted in hundreds of deaths of undocumented immigrants attempting the crossing, some while attempting to walk across the desert, others while being smuggled in vans that were inadequately ventilated or controlled for excessive heat.

In March 2006, Congress passed a renewed USA Patriot Act (referred to in the media as Patriot Act II). This law made it easier for the DHS to remove aliens (called expedited removal), and the numbers of those deported soared, as did the number of those who voluntarily departed. Finally, in January 2017, Republican president Donald Trump signed his "Travel Ban" executive order barring entry of persons from seven predominantly Muslim countries, and advocated the building of a wall along the southern border with Mexico for which he said Mexico would have to pay. By another executive order, he ordered the immediate cessation of two of President Barack Obama's executive actions: Deferred Action for Childhood Arrivals (DACA) and Deferred Action for Parental Accountability (DAPA), designed to protect Dreamer children and their parents from deportation as unauthorized immigrants. President Trump increased staffing of the Border Patrol, and other policies designed to "harden border control." These policy shifts or attempted shifts will be discussed more fully in the next chapter.

CONCLUSION

This brief overview of immigration policymaking demonstrates the complexity of immigration policy, the frequency of unanticipated consequences, and the impact of push factors beyond the scope of influence of the U.S. policy to effectively control the immigration process. Attempts to decrease immigration by passing legislation designed to lessen or control pull factors have generally proven to be far less impactful on the immigration flow than have push factors. A great many stakeholder groups, and politicians, have rather consistently worked for or against immigration over the history of the United States. Subsequent sections will provide biographical essays for some of those stakeholders.

NOTES

1. Michael LeMay, *From Open Door to Dutch Door* (New York: Praeger, 1987), 122.

2. Michael LeMay, *The Perennial Struggle*, 3rd ed. (Upper Saddle River, NJ: Prentice-Hall, 2009), 13, 123.

3. Decennial censuses for 1900 to 2000, American Community Survey for 2014, Census Bureau population projections released March 2015.

4. Michael C. LeMay, ed., *Transforming America: Perspectives on Immigration*, vol. 1 (Santa Barbara, CA: ABC-CLIO, 2013), 4–10.

5. Michael C. LeMay, *U.S. Immigration Policy, Ethnicity, and Religion in American History* (Santa Barbara, CA: Praeger, 2018), 13–18.

6. Ibid., 18–20.

7. Michael LeMay, *Religious Freedom in America: A Reference Handbook* (Santa Barbara, CA: ABC-CLIO, 2018), 35–40.

8. LeMay, *U.S. Immigration Policy, Ethnicity, and Religion*, 129–65.

9. Michael LeMay, *From Open Door to Dutch Door* (New York: Praeger, 1987), 54–55.

10. Emma Lazarus, "The New Colossus," *Catalogue of the Pedestal Fund Art Loan Exhibition at the National Academy of Design* (New York: The Academy, 1883), 9.

11. LeMay, *From Open Door to Dutch Door*, 57.

12. Maldyn Jones, *American Immigration* (Chicago: University of Chicago Press, 1960), 263.

13. Ibid., 263.

14. William S. Bernard, ed., *Immigration Policy: A Reappraisal* (New York: Harper and Row, 1950), 16.

15. Thomas Sowell, ed., *Essays and Data on American Ethnic Groups* (Washington, DC: Urban Institute Press, 1978), 77–78.

16. Thomas Pitkin, *Keepers of the Gates* (New York: New York University Press, 1975), 45–46.

17. Benjamin Ringer, *"We the People" and Others* (New York: Tavistock, 1983), 670.

18. Ibid., 687–88.

19. LeMay. *From Open Door to Dutch Door*, 67.

20. Ringer, *"We the People" and Others*, 705.

21. Robert Divine. *American Immigration Policy, 1924–1952* (New Haven, CT: Yale University Press, 1957), 4.

22. Bernard, *Immigration Policy*, 13. The law is excerpted in Michael C. LeMay and Elliott Robert Barkan, eds., *U.S. Immigration and Naturalization Laws and Issues: A Documentary History* (Westport, CT: Greenwood Press, 1999), 103–6.

23. As cited in Harry Kitano, *Japanese Americans: The Evolution of a Subculture* (Englewood Cliffs, NJ: Prentice-Hall, 1969), 17. See also Jonathan Lee, Matsuoka Fumitake, Edmond Yee, and Ronald Nakasone, eds., *Asian American Religious Cultures*, 2nd ed. (Santa Barbara, CA: ABC-CLIO, 2003), and https://oag.ca.gov/history/19webb (accessed 7/14/2018).

24. LeMay, *U.S. Immigration Policy*, 20–22.

25. Cited in John Higham. *Strangers in the Land: Patterns of American Nativism, 1866–1925* (New Brunswick, NJ: Rutgers University Press, 1955), 302.

26. LeMay, *From Open Door to Dutch Door*, 82. For excerpts of the law, see LeMay and Barkan, eds., *U.S. Immigration and Naturalization Laws and Issues*, 133–35.

27. Cited in Higham, *Strangers in the Land*, 318.

28. Vinson as quoted in Marion Bennett, *American Immigration Policies: A History* (Washington, DC: Public Affairs Press, 1963), 48.

29. Divine, *American Immigration Policy*, 53.

30. Bennett, *American Immigration Policies*, 68–69. See also excerpts in LeMay and Barkan, eds., *U.S. Immigration and Naturalization Laws*, 163–65.

31. LeMay, *From Open Door to Dutch Door*, 96–101.

32. Barry Chiswick, ed., *The Gateway: U.S. Immigration Issues and Policies* (Washington, DC: American Enterprise Institute, 1982), 28.

33. U.S. Congress, Senate, Committee on the Judiciary, *The Immigration and Naturalization System of the United States*, 81st Congress, 1515: 455.

34. Chiswick, *The Gateway*, 32. See also Jones. *American Immigration*, 286.

35. Chiswick, *The Gateway*, 32.

36. Grant McClellan, ed., *Immigrants, Refugees, and U.S. Policy* (New York: H.W. Wilson, 1981), 45.

37. Details of the 1965 act are excerpted in LeMay and Barkan, eds., *U.S. Immigration and Naturalization Laws*, 257–61.

38. Jeffrey S. Passel and D'Vera Cohn, "Unauthorized Immigrant Totals Rise in 7 States, Fall in 14," Pew Research Center, November 18, 2014, https://www.pewhispanic.org/2014/11/18/unauthorized-immigrant-totals-rise-in-7-states-fall-in-14/.

39. Michael LeMay, *U.S. Immigration: A Reference Handbook* (Santa Barbara, CA: ABC-CLIO, 2004), 174–75.

CHAPTER 2

ENACTING THE IMMIGRATION AND NATIONALITY ACT OF 1965

INTRODUCTION: IMMIGRATION LAW AND THE NATURE OF AMERICAN SOCIETY

Throughout American history, immigration law has helped shape what sort of nation America is, in fact, and what sort of a nation it will become in the future. In President John F. Kennedy's words, the United States is a "nation of immigrants." In myriad ways, immigration and immigration law shape what happens to and in the United States, in work, culture, politics, and other ways.

The immigration process is shaped by immigration law. Since 1970, in part as a reaction to the surge in Asian and Hispanic immigration, several American states have passed "English-only" laws (a.k.a. English as the official language). That reaction echoes the Americanization movement of the 1920s and 1930s discussed in Chapter 1. Proponents of laws to make English an official language react in no small measure out of a xenophobic fear that the exponential rate of immigration by so many Spanish-speaking persons could result in developing within the United States extremist factions akin to the separatist movement in French-speaking Quebec that had troubled Canadian politics for several decades. Such fear also girds those who oppose the immigration of so many adherents of Islam and argue that, as a result, the national government or state governments must enact laws to prohibit "sharia law" or to ban outright the immigration of Muslims. Will some future star players of the Super Bowl or the World Series be

Samoan, or Haitian, or Mexican, or from some other ethnic heritage of groups flooding into the United States since 1970? Will soccer replace baseball as the national pastime? Will future Miss Americas increasingly be brown, not white? The very nature of American society—its culture, economics, and politics—is profoundly affected by the immigration process.

To better understand the passage of immigration reform laws, it helps to grasp the nature of the perceived problems with which such laws are intended to cope. And to fully grasp the nature of what currently is the primary immigration problems—namely, a seeming loss of control of the borders due to undocumented immigration, racial bias in the administration of immigration policy, and inflexibility in the law with respect to demand for visas—one needs to go back to the foundational law, the Immigration and Nationality Act of 1965 (Pub. L. 89-236, 79 Stat. 911), also often referred to as the Kennedy immigration law. It amends the 1952 law of that name. As discussed in Chapter 1, prior to its enactment, the immigration flow was controlled by the national origins acts and their amendment by the McCarran-Walter Act of 1952. Many migration patterns, especially of the unauthorized immigration flow, were established during the 1940s. In particular, the Bracero Program, which was established during World War II to bring in much-needed but temporary agricultural laborers, allowed annually the legal entrance of hundreds of thousands of "guest workers" from Mexico and Central America outside the confines of the quota system. The chain migration patterns established by the Bracero Program persist to this day.

Although the McCarran-Walter Act largely reaffirmed the quota system, two provisions were included in order to assure its passage, which did open new doors to immigration. The act established a token quota for previously excluded groups from the "Asia-Pacific Triangle." This opened up a spigot, so to speak, allowing a trickle of immigration from the Asia Pacific and Oceania regions. They came in still small numbers for the first time since the 1880s, when the exclusion of Asians was established. Asian exclusion was later enshrined in the quota system acts of the 1920s. Even more importantly, the McCarran-Walter Act passed only after inclusion of the "Texas Proviso," which exempted employers of illegal aliens from the harboring provisions of the law, thereby legalizing the hiring of illegal aliens. The Texas Proviso, which was included to secure support for the bill from southwestern growers, stated that "no employer could be found to have violated federal law for hiring illegal aliens."[1]

THE EARLY CIVIL RIGHTS MOVEMENT—SETTING THE STAGE FOR IMMIGRATION REFORM

The black civil rights movement was propelled forward into American politics by the 1954 Supreme Court decision *Brown v. Board of Education of Topeka, Kansas* (347 U.S. 483, 497, decided May 17, 1954). The case was brought to the Supreme Court by the National Association for the Advancement of Colored People (NAACP) and was its greatest legal victory in its battle against *de jure* (by law) segregation. In *Brown*, the Court finally overturned the separate-but-equal doctrine of the *Plessy v. Ferguson* (1896) decision. The *Plessy* decision, like many of the immigration laws and decisions discussed in Chapter 1, established a constitutional principle that served to justify Jim Crowism and the pervasive use of de jure segregation. In sharp contrast, *Brown* gave a constitutional blessing to the effort and policy of racial desegregation. *Brown* failed to be immediately enforced, and in the short run, little practical change resulted from the decision. It would take more than a decision by the nine justices of the Court to seriously alter the norms, values, and institutional racism of the nation; it would take a truly national mass movement. That came with the direct-action approach begun with the Montgomery, Alabama, bus boycott of 1955–1956. The boycott was precipitated in early December 1955, when Rosa Parks refused a bus driver's demand that she give up her seat to a white man, as required by a 1945 Alabama state law requiring the Alabama Public Service Commission to enforce racially segregated seating on all bus companies under its jurisdiction. The NAACP, a group of black ministers, and professors from Alabama State College formed the Montgomery Improvement Association (MIA) to direct and coordinate what became a 382-day-long boycott of the City Lines bus company.[2]

In 1956, a federal district court ruled that the Montgomery city ordinance violated the U.S. Constitution. The district court decision was challenged but upheld by the U.S. Supreme Court in *Browder v. Gayle* (352 U.S. 903, 1956). In 1957 the Rev. Martin Luther King Jr. and other black clergymen established the Southern Christian Leadership Conference (SCLC). The SCLC developed the strategy of nonviolent protest throughout the South to oppose racial segregation in all its forms. King's philosophy of nonviolent protest rested on six principles: (1) active resistance to evil, (2) attempts to win over one's adversaries through understanding,

(3) attacking the forces of evil rather than the people perpetrating it, (4) a willingness to accept suffering without retaliation, (5) refusing to hate one's opponent, and (6) the conviction that the universe is on the side of justice. He articulated that philosophy in his famous *Letter from a Birmingham Jail* (April 16, 1963) and his even more famous *I Have a Dream* speech (August 28, 1963).

During the 1960 presidential campaign, when King was arrested and given a four-month prison sentence for an alleged driving offense in Georgia, the Democratic candidate for president, Senator John F. Kennedy (D-MA), intervened and won his early release. In gratitude, Martin Luther King Sr. quietly backed the senator and urged blacks to support his candidacy. Kennedy narrowly won the election, and the 68 percent of the black vote he received arguably provided a critical margin in his victory.[3]

The direct-protest, civil-disobedience campaigns of the civil rights movement pushed the Johnson administration, and the Judiciary Committees of Congress headed by Representative Emanuel Celler (D-NY) and Senator Philip Hart (D-MI), to back two landmark laws signed into law by President Johnson. The first, the Civil Rights Act of 1964 (Pub. L. 88-352, 78 Stat. 241, July 2, 1964), passed by wide margins in both chambers of Congress (71–27 in the Senate, by 69 percent; and 289–126 in the House, by 70 percent). The second, the Civil Rights Act of 1965 (Pub. L. 89-110, 79 Stat. 437, August 6, 1965), also passed by comfortable margins. In the Senate, the vote was 77–18 on May 26, 1965; and in the House, on July 9, 1965, by 333–85. These two laws resulted in a dramatic closing of the gap between black and white voter turnout and solidified black support for Democratic presidential candidates ranging from 82 to 94 percent from the 1964 election to the 2000s. That electoral support was instrumental in moving the federal government, manifested by the Johnson administration, Congress, and the Supreme Court, to move to end the racially explicit bias in U.S. immigration law as well.[4]

THE 1960 ELECTION OF JOHN F. KENNEDY

On November 8, 1960, Democratic senator John Fitzgerald Kennedy (JFK) narrowly defeated Republican vice president Richard M. Nixon, by which Kennedy became the youngest man ever to be elected president of the United States and the first Catholic to become president. The popular vote was 49.7 percent for Kennedy to 49.5 percent for Nixon. Kennedy won the Electoral College Vote (ECV) by a bit more comfortable margin—303 to 219 votes. Kennedy's election eased the way for what became a frontal assault on the quota system as the United States' approach to immigration law.[5]

The first years of President Kennedy's term in office were marked by racial tension and calls to end the racially biased and highly restrictive immigration policy of the quota system. As Chapter 1 describes, by 1960 the quota system had become clearly and increasingly viewed as inadequate to cope with the immigration process. There was fairly widespread consensus that the immigration system "was broken" and in need of a major overhaul. President Kennedy's election placed in the White House a chief executive who strongly desired a major revision in the approach to immigration policy and who was able to put that desire on the agenda of the U.S. Congress.

During Kennedy's first two years in office, however, the Cuban Missile Crisis and foreign policy issues so dominated the nation's and the administration's political agenda that little was done to attend to his desire to amend immigration policy. After the missile crisis ended, however, a dramatic rise in agitation over civil rights took place, which effectively turned inward the focus of the Kennedy administration and, indeed, of the nation. The civil rights movement marked a change in the national attitude toward racism that served to undercut the highly restrictive and openly racially biased quota system. The sort of bigotry prevailing throughout the 1940s and 1950s that had contributed to the lopsided majorities in favor of the quota system became increasingly less acceptable by the mid-1960s.

Ironically, black migration from the South to the Northeast and Midwest was linked to reduced European immigration. Only after the flow of Europeans to northern and midwestern cities was reduced so drastically by the quota acts, the Great Depression, World War II, and the Korean War did a large number of job opportunities for blacks open up. Blacks first began moving north in great numbers during World War I, and that migration north increased following the restriction mandated by the immigration laws of 1921, 1924, and 1929. Those laws effectively curtailed European immigration from a comparative flood to a trickle, to even negative net immigration during World War II. Women and blacks not serving in the military (which was still largely segregated during most of the war years) began meeting much of the labor demand for the industrial and service sectors of the economy in northern cities of the United States. The very groups urging enactment of laws to restrict immigration during the Pet Door era that were so often and so blatantly based on racial and ethnic grounds thereby accelerated, albeit unintentionally, the migration of blacks northward. Soon these new migrants were resented even more than were the SCE Europeans who had preceded them.

Also, by the mid-1960s, the remaining labor supply in rural areas in the South dwindled or migrated to fill the growing job opportunities in expanding industrial centers in the South, such as Atlanta, Georgia. This reduced pressure on blacks to move northward, and black migration from the South virtually ended during the 1960s. Indeed, during the early 1970s more blacks moved into the South than left the region, somewhat reversing a nearly century-long trend.

The success of the Kennedy administration's economic policy and a post–Korean War economic recovery ended the recession that had plagued six of the eight years of the President Eisenhower period. The U.S. economy of the early to mid-1960s was healthy. Unemployment rates dropped to 4 percent, essentially deemed full employment. There was also a steady growth of the Gross Domestic Product (GDP). These two trends reduced opposition to immigration reform. Even organized labor espoused a more liberal immigration policy.

In July 1963, President Kennedy sent his immigration reform proposal to Congress. It ended the quota system and established a preference system, with a cap of 20,000 visas per country on a first-come, first-served basis. Senator Philip Hart (D-MI) and Representative Emanuel Celler (D-NY), serving on the Senate and the House immigration subcommittees of each chamber's Judiciary Committee, introduced companion bills. Opposition to the bills by some key congressional leaders, like Senator James Eastland (D-MS), and then the assassination of President Kennedy in November 1963, delayed passage of the bill.

President Kennedy was assassinated in Dallas, Texas, on November 22, 1963. His vice president, Lyndon B. Johnson (D-TX, and a former Senate majority leader), assumed the office. Johnson ran for election in 1964, selecting Senator Hubert H. Humphry (DFL-MN) as his running mate.

By landslide proportions, the Democratic ticket won the 1964 presidential election. The Johnson-Humphrey ticket won 486 ECV and 61.1 percent of the popular vote to the Republican ticket of Senator Barry Goldwater (R-AZ) and little-known New York representative William Miller's 52 ECV and 38.5 percent of the popular vote. The landslide was so great that the Goldwater-Miller ticket won only six states: Alabama, Arizona (Goldwater's home state), Georgia, Louisiana, Mississippi, and South Carolina. Immigration reform was not a high-profile issue in the 1964 election, as both Johnson and Goldwater stressed foreign policy issues.[6]

ENACTMENT OF THE IMMIGRATION AND NATIONALITY ACT OF 1965

By the mid-1960s, moreover, the traditional supporters of the national origins quota system were disorganized and largely inactive. Senator Edward Kennedy (D-MA), the youngest brother of the slain president, led the Senate forces advocating for a change in immigration law. He met with past opposition leaders of immigration reform, such as the American Coalition, the American Legion, the Daughters of the American Revolution, and the National Association of Evangelicals. They registered no significant opposition to eliminating the quota system. Senator Kennedy argued persuasively for the bill that President Kennedy's administration had submitted to Congress in 1963 but had failed to pass. President Johnson reintroduced the legislation on January 13, 1965. Once again, it was introduced in the House by Rep. Emanuel Celler, by then chair of the House Judiciary Committee, and in the Senate, again sponsored by Sen. Philip Hart. Having served as Senate majority leader (1961–1965), President Johnson was one of the best nose counters in Washington, D.C., and his landslide victory in 1964 swept into the 89th Congress "on his coattails" an unusually large number of more liberal Democratic noses for him to count. Senator Hart's bill had 32 official cosponsors, including both Senator Robert Kennedy (D-NY) and Senator Edward Kennedy (D-MA).

As the bills worked their way through the two chambers and the assorted congressional committees, Senators Sam Ervin (D-NC) and Everett Dirksen (R-IL) fought a rearguard battle to preserve the quota system. They won some eventual but minor revisions to the administration's proposal dealing with the process of determining the preference-based visas, but not preserving the more rigid quota system. Representative Michael Feighan (D-OH), chair of the House Subcommittee on Immigration, also had been effective in the use of delaying tactics in 1963–1964. In July 1963, Feighan was appointed chair of the Joint Committee on Immigration and Nationality Policy.

The Celler-Hart bill (H.R. 2580) sought to balance five goals: (1) to preserve the family unit and to reunite separated families; (2) to meet the need for highly skilled workers; (3) to help ease population problems created by emergencies caused by such events as Communist aggression or natural disasters that resulted in large numbers of refugees; (4) to better the understanding of people cross-nationally through exchange programs; and (5) to bar from the United States those aliens who were likely to represent adjustment problems because of their physical or mental health, criminal history, dependency, or for national security reasons.

In the U.S. Senate, a key compromise provision was crafted by Senators Dirksen and Ervin. That compromise provision, crucial to the final passage of the bill, set an overall ceiling of 120,000 for the Western Hemisphere. This compromise figure replaced the prior status of unlimited immigration from the Western Hemisphere. The Dirksen-Ervin compromise number was based on the actual flow of immigration during the few years immediately preceding the act. Their compromise in the Senate enabled the measure to pass comfortably and with significant bipartisan support in both chambers of Congress.

The measure passed in the House on August 25, 1965, 318–95, or by 74 percent. The successful passage of the measure in the U.S. House of Representatives was significantly bipartisan. Yea votes on the measure were cast by 209 Democrats and 109 Republicans. The 95 votes in opposition were from 71 Democrats (mostly by ideologically conservative Democrats who mostly represented districts in southern states) and 24 Republicans. There were 19 not voting (4 percent): 13 Democrats and 6 Republicans.[7] The measure passed in the U.S. Senate on September 22, 1965 by an even wider margin—76 percent; 52 Democrats and 24 Republicans. There were 18 nay votes (18 percent); 14 Democrats, 3 Republicans, and 1 independent, with 6 (6 percent) not casting votes on the measure's roll call vote.

A member's party affiliation was the strongest indicator of how a member of Congress was likely to vote on the 1965 act. Both major parties in Congress met in their respective caucus—the Democratic Party Caucus and the Republican Conference. A congressional caucus is a group of members of the U.S. Congress who meet on occasion to pursue common legislative objectives. Caucuses are formed as congressional member organizations through the U.S. House of Representatives. Even if Senate members join, they are governed under the rules of the House chamber. They are not always called caucuses and are sometimes titled coalitions, conferences, task forces, or working groups. In 1965, other caucuses beyond the party caucuses that might have influenced a legislator's position on the bill had not yet formed. Several would become influential by 1986, but in 1965 only the party caucuses met. The Black Congressional Caucus formed in 1969. The Hispanic Congressional Caucus formed in 1976. The Border Security Caucus formed in 2014.[8]

Another concept useful in understanding why the 1965 bill passed is that of the "gateway" states that led the way in pursuing more open immigration politics. Gateway states are those with high percentages of the foreign-born within their populations. Traditionally considered as gateway states are California, Texas, Florida, Illinois, New Jersey, New York, and New Mexico. But by the 1960s, immigrants (both authorized and unauthorized) particularly from Mexico, were beginning to expand out to more states seeking new destinations for settlement and greater opportunities to incorporate into American society. As they spread across the country, they began to change the very concept and culture of nationalism. As James Kellas notes: "Nations . . . are inclusive and are culturally or politically defined."[9] He goes on to state:

> In many countries—including particularly the United States—ethnic groups have an important influence on foreign policy. A multiethnic state based on immigrants is likely to have more involvement in nationalism abroad than a nonimmigrant multinational state. A political system with a nondisciplined party system and dependent more on passive funding, such as that of the United States, gives greater scope to ethnic political influence than those such as Britain, or France, with greater party discipline and less private funding. But in nearly all states, ethnic groups have a significant, if often hidden, influence in the making of foreign policy.[10]

We might add that influence applies as much if not more to immigration policymaking.

New policy approaches to immigration control caused dramatic shifts in the flow of immigration—some intended, others unintended consequences of laws. Post-1965, they resulted in a marked increase in overall immigration, a drastic shift in the flow of unauthorized immigration, and a radical change in the composition of the authorized immigration flow that led to dramatic demands to change the direction of U.S. immigration policymaking. Senators from states that had a higher percentage of immigrants as their share of the population (that is, the expanding number of gateway

Table 2.1   The Top States, Ranked by Immigrants' Share of Their Population, and Whether Their Senators Cast a Yea or Nay Vote on the Immigration and Nationality Act of 1965

State	Share/Population	Yea Vote	Nay Vote	No Vote Cast
California	27.8	2	0	–
New York	20.5	2	0	–
New Jersey	18.7	2	0	–
Florida	18.3	1	1	–
Hawaii	17.2	2	0	–
Nevada	17.1	2	0	–
Texas	15.1	1	–	1
Arizona	14.8	1	1	–
Massachusetts	13.8	2'0	–	
Rhode Island	11.9	2	0	–
Illinois	11.3	2	0	–
Washington	10.6	2	0	–
Connecticut	10.4	2	0	–
Colorado	9.8	2	0	–
Virginia	9.7	0	1	1
New Mexico	9.3	1	0	1

Source: Table by author. Data from Michael LeMay, *U.S. Immigration* (Santa Barbara, CA: ABC-CLIO, 2004), 170–71.

Table 2.2 Southern State Senators Yea or Nay Vote on the 1965 Act

State	Nay Votes	Yea Votes	No Vote Cast
Alabama	2	0	–
Arkansas	1	1	–
Georgia	2	0	–
Louisiana	1	1	–
Mississippi	2	0	–
Missouri	0	2	–
North Carolina	1	1	–
South Carolina	2	0	–
Texas	0	1	1
Virginia	1	0	1
West Virginia	1	1	–

Source: Table by author. Roll Call Vote Data at: https://www.govtrack.us/congress/votes/89-1965/s232 (accessed 7/17/2018).

states, which are categorized here as having 9 percent or more of their population who are foreign-born) were more likely to have voted yea on the bill. Senators from southern states, which in 1960 meant more rural states with lower foreign-born percentages of their populations, were more likely to have voted nay on the measure. These facts are detailed in Tables 2.1 and 2.2. Table 2.1 presents the top states ranked by the share of immigrants in the state population and whether their senators cast a yea or nay vote on the 1965 act. Table 2.2 lists how senators from southern states cast a yea or nay vote on the 1965 bill.

President Lyndon B. Johnson (LBJ) signed the immigration bill into law on October 3, 1965, in front of the Statue of Liberty in New York harbor. In his remarks upon signing the bill, LBJ stated:

> This bill that we sign today is not a revolutionary bill. It does not affect the lives of millions. It will not reshape the structure of our daily lives, or really add importantly to either our wealth or our power. Yet it is still one of the most important acts of this Congress and this administration. For it does repair a very deep and painful flaw in the fabric of American justice. It corrects a cruel and enduring wrong in the conduct of the American Nation.[11]

LBJ was right about the law correcting a cruel and enduring wrong, but he could hardly have been less prescient about the law's affecting the lives of millions, nor about its not reshaping the structure of the daily lives of those millions of Americans, nor of its not impacting the wealth and power of the United States. The Immigration and Nationality Act of 1965 reshaped America. However, President Johnson was optimistic about the change in immigration policy and law that would result from the end of the quota system. In his remarks on signing the law, he goes on to state:

> Today, with my signature, this system is abolished. We can now believe that it will never again shadow the gate to the American nation with the twin barriers of prejudice and privilege. Our beautiful America was built by a nation of strangers. From a hundred different places or more, they have poured forth into an empty land—joining and blending in one mighty and irresistible tide. The land flourished because it was fed from so many sources—because it was nourished by so many cultures and traditions and peoples ... Now under the monument which has welcomed so many to our shores, the American nation returns to the finest of its traditions today. The days of unlimited immigration are past. But those who do come will come because of what they are, and not because of the land from which they spring ... Over my shoulder here you can see Ellis Island, whose vacant corridors echo today with the joyous sounds of long-ago voices. And today we can all believe that the lamp of this grand old lady is brighter today—and the golden door that she guards gleams more brilliantly in the light of an increased liberty for the peoples from all the countries of the globe.[12]

The following summarizes the major provisions of the Immigration and Nationality Act of 1965:

1. It abolished the national origins quota system after a transition period to June 30, 1968.
   After that date, immigrants admissible under the act were subject to numerical limitations specified in accordance with percentage limitations and in order of the priority specified in section 203 of the act. It specified that any immigrant born in a colony or other dependent area of a foreign state unless a special immigrant as specified in the Act or an immediate relative of a U.S. citizen, shall be chargeable to the foreign state.

It abolished the Asian Pacific Triangle provision of the 1952 McCarran-Walter Act.

2. It allowed the use of quota numbers unused in the previous year as a pool of additional numbers for each year of the transitional period, for preference applicants chargeable to overcharged quotas. Those visas were to be made available in the chronological order in which they qualified (essentially, on a first-come, first-served basis).

3. It revised previous preference categories into a new system of preferences, strongly favoring (at 74 percent of total annual immigration) relatives of citizens and permanent resident aliens. The preference category was applied to any alien seeking permanent immigration status who was seeking entrance to the United States from any Eastern Hemisphere nation-state. Any immigrant was presumed to be a nonpreference immigrant until that person established to the consular officer and immigration officer issuing a visa that he or she was entitled to a preference status, or that he or she is an immediate relative of a U.S. citizen. The consular officer was not authorized to grant a visa until provisions listed in section 204 of the act were established.

4. It required that an alien coming to work in the United States and not entitled to a preference obtain certification from the secretary of labor that he or she would not displace nor adversely affect the wages and working conditions of workers in that same field in the United States.

5. It included refugees as one of the preference categories.

6. It set an annual ceiling of 170,000 on immigration of aliens in the preference and nonpreference classification with a 20,000 limit for any single foreign state.

7. It established as "immediate relative" (previously called "nonquota") status for parents of adult U.S. citizens.

8. It increased the dependent area immigration (previously "subquota") to 1 percent of the 20,000 maximum allowable numbers available to that governing country, that is, from 100 to 200 annually.

9. It set the filing date of the petition to determine the chronological order of preference categories.

10. It required that applicants be considered in the order of their preference class.
11. It created a Select Commission on Western Hemisphere immigration to study the economic, political, and demographic factors affecting immigration. It required the attorney general to report to Congress on each approved petition for immigrant status, stating the basis for his approval and such facts establishing the beneficiary's qualifications for the preferential status.
12. It set a ceiling of 120,000 on immigration from the Western Hemisphere nations after July 1968. It defined the term "special immigrant" to mean an immigrant who was born in any independent foreign country of the Western Hemisphere or in the Canal
13. Zone, and the spouse and children of any such immigrant.
14. It included all independent countries of the Western Hemisphere in "special immigration" status (previously called "nonquota" systems).
15. It defined the term "profession" to include but not be limited to architects, engineers, lawyers, physicians, surgeons, and teachers in elementary or secondary schools, colleges, universities, academies, or seminaries.
16. It specified that the study commission should study the following matters:
    (1) Prevailing and projected demographic, technological, and economic trends, especially as they pertain to Western Hemisphere nations;
    (2) Present and projected unemployment in the United States by occupations, industries, geographic areas, and other factors, in relation to immigration from the Western Hemisphere;
    (3) The interrelationships between immigration, present and future, and existing and contemplated national and international programs and projects of Western Hemisphere nations, including programs and projects for economic and social development;
    (4) The operation of U.S. immigration laws as they pertain to Western Hemisphere nations, including the adjustment of status for Cuban refugees, with emphasis on the adequacy of such

laws from the standpoint of fairness and from the standpoint of the impact of such laws on employment and working conditions in the United States;

(5) The implications of the foregoing with respect to the security and international relations of Western Hemisphere nations; and

(6) Any other matters which the Commission believes to be germane to the purposes for which it was established.

The study commission was to report on or before July 1, 1967, and on or before January 15, 1968.[13]

Briefly, the seven preferences used to allocate immigration visas within each foreign state are as follows:

1. First preference: spouses and unmarried sons and daughters of U.S. citizens.
2. Second preference: spouses and unmarried sons and daughters of permanent resident aliens.
3. Third preference: members of the professions and scientists and artists of exceptional ability (sometimes referred to as the Einstein preference).
4. Fourth preference: married sons and daughters of U.S. citizens.
5. Fifth preference: brothers and sisters of U.S. citizens.
6. Sixth preference: skilled and unskilled workers in short supply.
7. Seventh preference: refugees.[14]

As intended, the law resulted in some significant changes to the immigration flow in the decade following its enactment. For example, total authorized immigration increased by 60 percent. The number of immigrants from some countries increased markedly: Greek immigration rose by 162 percent; Portuguese immigration increased by 382 percent; overall Asian immigration rose by 663 percent. Asian nations exemplified some of the most remarkable changes: from India, immigration rose by more than 3,000 percent; from Korea, by 1,328 percent; from Pakistan, by 1,600 percent; from the Philippines, by nearly 1,200 percent; from Thailand, by more than 1,700 percent; and from Vietnam, by more than 1,900 percent. As expected, European countries that previously had quotas larger than

Table 2.3   Legal Immigration to the United States, 1964–2016

Year	Number Arriving	Year	Number Arriving
1964	292,248	1991	1,827,367
1965	296,697	1982	973,977
1966	323,040	1993	904,191
1967	361,972	1994	804,415
1968	454,448	1995	720,462
1969	358,579	1996	915,900
1970	373,326	1997	798,378
1971	370,478	1998	654,568
1972	384,685	1999	646,451
1973	400,063	2000	849,807
1974	394,861	2001	1,064,318
1975	386,194	2002	1,059,902
1976	502,289	2003	730,542
1977	426,315	2004	957,883
1978	601,442	2005	1,122,373
1979	460,348	2006	1,266,129
1980	530,639	2007	1,052,415
1981	596,600	2008	1,107,126
1982	594,131	2009	1,120,818
1983	559,763	2010	1,042,625
1984	543,903	2011	1,062,040
1985	570,009	2012	1,031,631
1986	601,506	2013	990,553
1987	601,708	2014	1,016,518
1988	643,025	2015	1,051,031
1989	1,090,924	2016	1,183,505
1990	1,563,483		

Source: Table by author. Data from Migration Policy Institute, "Legal Immigration to the United States, 1820–Present," https://www.migrationpolicy.org/programs/data-hub/charts/Annual-Number-of-US-Legal-Permanent-Residents (accessed 12/1/2019).

the new 20,000 per state provision of the 1965 law declined overall by 38 percent. European countries with some of the more dramatic declines include: Austria by more than 76 percent; Ireland by more than 77 percent; Norway by 85 percent; and the United Kingdom by nearly 120 percent.[15]

Table 2.3 presents a detailed overview of the legal immigration numbers admitted into the United States from 1964, the year before enactment of the 1965 law, to 2016. The data in Table 2.3 show a very steady increase in the number of legal immigrants entering the United States as a result of the 1965 act and its amendments.

The act's third preference category, the provision for professionals, was especially important for opening up immigration from Asia (and producing a high positive "brain drain" flow). Korean and Philippine health professionals entered in exceptionally large numbers. They, in turn, could then use the family preference categories to bring in their family members. By 1980, more than 70,000 Filipino physicians entered the United States under the third preference, such that their numbers exceeded those of native-born black doctors. Nurses and other medical technicians from Asia and Ireland also used this preference category to enter in large numbers. The Trump administration has been highly critical of the family preference category, which it refers to as "chain migration" and has proposed a drastic reduction in this category.

The refugee preference category, the seventh, was almost immediately outmoded. The act set the seventh preference at 10,200, which seemed generous in 1965. Events in Cuba, Vietnam, and Haiti, however, soon outstripped that limit's ability to cope with the demand for entrance by refugees, as it does to this day. That unforeseen surge in refugees, and the impact of other unanticipated consequences of the Immigration and Nationality Act, led to a number of amendments.

A combination of world economic developments, major political upheavals, and the unanticipated consequences of the 1965 immigration law all interacted with significant impact on the flow of immigration into the United States during the 1970s—what has been called "The Fourth Wave." Fourth-wave immigration began in the late 1960s, comprised of three primary groups: legal immigrants admitted as permanent residents, refugees, and the undocumented. Under the quota system, as we have seen, immigrants entering the United States came overwhelmingly from Europe. By the mid-1980s, they came from Third World nations—largely

Asian and Latin American. Of the 544,000 legal immigrants who entered in 1984, to cite but one exemplary year, more than 10 percent (57,000) were from Mexico, followed by the Philippines (42,000), and Vietnam (37,000). In sharp contrast, legal immigrants from Great Britain numbered only 14,000, ranking ninth overall as an immigrant-sending nation-state that year.[16]

The end of black migration from the South resulted in an increased demand for a new source of low-wage labor in America's cities—which by the 1970s was no longer concentrated in northern industrial cities. In fact, the industrial Northeast and even the Midwest began, by the mid-1970s, an extended period of relative economic stagnation. Demand for labor was strongest in the South and West, the "Sun Belt" states, led by Texas and California.

The number of refugees seeking entrance skyrocketed. Large numbers fled here from Asia. So too, were those arriving from El Salvador and Haiti.

AMENDING ACTS TO THE 1965 LAW

The 1965 act, as discussed previously, was itself an amendment of the 1952 act. It has been amended several times since its passage, each amendment attempting to remedy apparent defects in the earlier versions of the law. This section discusses those various amendments to the Immigration and Nationality Act in chronological order of their enactment.

In 1966, Congress first amended the 1965 Act when it enacted a law adjusting the status of refugees from Cuba. It was known as the Cuban Adjustment Act of 1966 (Pub. L. 89-732, 80 Stat. 1161, November 2, 1966). In brief, the act empowers the attorney general of the United States to adjust the status of any alien who is a native of Cuba who was inspected and admitted or paroled into the United States subsequent to January 1, 1959, and had been physically present in the United States for at least two years. Furthermore, the change in legal status was applicable to the spouse and child of any such alien. Their status was adjusted to legal permanent resident, and they were given a green card and could begin the process for naturalization.

In 1972, in what was the largest landslide presidential election in modern history, the Republican ticket of President Richard Nixon and

Vice President Spiro Agnew won a whopping 520 ECV (96.7 percent of the ECV), 60.7 percent of the popular vote, and 49 states (losing only Massachusetts and the District of Columbia). The Democratic candidate, Senator George McGovern, and his vice presidential nominee, Sargent Shriver, won only 17 ECV and 37.5 percent of the popular vote.[17] Despite the massive margin of their electoral victory, the Nixon-Agnew administration did not survive their second term in office.

In the 1976 presidential election, Jimmy Carter became the first president elected from the deep South since Zachary Taylor in 1848. The refugee crisis continued during the Carter administration. As previously discussed, the 1965 act defined as refugees those fleeing communism or trying to leave the Middle East. It did not consider as refugees those fleeing right-wing dictatorships in the Western Hemisphere, such as the infamous Francois "Papa Doc" Duvalier in Haiti. The collapse of the South Vietnamese government in 1975 led to another large pool of refugees fleeing communism. Between 1975 and 1979, more than 200,000 Vietnamese came to the United States. Given his strong religious and humanitarian values, it is not surprising that, as president, Jimmy Carter would address the refugee problem as an important reform of immigration policy. At first, President Carter, acting through his attorney general Griffin Bell, responded to this sudden refugee flow by using executive parole power to permit Cubans, Vietnamese, and other refugees to enter in numbers far exceeding the refugee preference category numbers. In doing so, President Carter was following precedents set by Presidents Dwight Eisenhower and Lyndon Johnson. As discussed in Chapter 1, President Eisenhower used his executive authority to establish "parole" and "mortgages" against the quota system during his presidency. Likewise, President Johnson issued a proclamation, in 1968, reaffirming the adherence of the United States to the UN Protocol on the Status of Refugees. Congress finally responded to the "refugee problem" after the fall of the South Vietnamese government, followed by Cambodia and Laos, to Communist forces. Those events sent hundreds of thousands of refugees to seek to come to the United States. In 1975 Congress passed the Indochina Migration and Refugee Assistance Act (89 Stat. 87, May 23, 1975). It established the Indochina Refugee Resettlement Programs. These assistance programs made available more than $1 billion of assistance to help resettle

Indochina refugees, many of whom were referred to as "boat people," who fled from Thailand, Malaysia, Indonesia, Singapore, the Philippines, and Hong Kong.

In 1976, Congress once again amended the Immigration and Nationality Act of 1965 (Pub. L. 94-571, 90 Stat. 2703). The 1976 amendments primarily cover the lack of preference categories for aliens from the Western Hemisphere. They apply to Western Hemisphere immigration the seven preference categories established for the Eastern Hemisphere under the 1965 act.

The 1976 amendments included a provision requiring all professionals qualifying for third preference status to have received an offer of employment prior to entry. Third preference category aliens, from either hemisphere, must comply with two independent (i.e., administered by two separate agencies/departments) requirements: (1) establishing their professional credentials, administered by the Immigration and Naturalization Service (INS); and (2), a job offer with labor certification (by the secretary of labor). The INS formulated various criteria for determining third preference eligibility.

The refugee crisis and the growing anxiety over an estimated one million undocumented immigrants entering the United States annually spurred Congress to establish a Select Commission on Immigration and Refugee Policy (SCIRP) in 1978. Opened in May 1979, the Select Commission was comprised of members of Congress, the executive branch, and the public. Congress was represented by the following: from the U.S. Senate, Charles Mathias (D-MD), Alan Simpson (R-WY), Edward Kennedy (D-MA), and Dennis DeConcini (D-AZ); and from the House, Peter Rodino (D-NJ), Elizabeth Holtzman (D-NY), Robert McClory (R-IL), and Hamilton Fish (R-NY). The executive branch was represented by Secretary of State Cyrus Vance, Attorney General Benjamin Civiletti, Secretary of Labor Ray Marshall, and Secretary of Health, Education and Welfare Patricia Harris. From the public commission, members included Joaquin Otero of the Brotherhood of Railway and Airline Clerks, Judge Cruz Reynoso of the California Court of Appeals, Rose Ochi of the office of the Mayor of Los Angeles, and Reubin Askew, the former governor of Florida, who was designated as its chairman. By the time the Commission was underway in October 1979, however, President Carter appointed Askew to another position, and Carter named the Reverend Theodore

Hesburgh, then president of Notre Dame University and former chairman of the Civil Rights Commission, as the new SCIRP chairman. Dr. Lawrence Fuchs, a distinguished professor at Brandeis University and an acknowledged ethnic and immigration scholar, was appointed as the staff director of the Commission.[18]

When the "boat people" from Indochina began to arrive in massive numbers in 1979, President Carter used his executive authority to respond to the crisis and promised to work diligently to move Congress to enact legislative reforms by amending the refugee preference category of the 1965 immigration law. In a 1967 Protocol, the United Nations defined a refugee as follows:

> Any person who, owing to a well-founded fear of being persecuted for reasons of race, religion, nationality, membership in a particular social group or political opinion, is outside of the country of his nationality and unable or, owing to such fear, is unwilling to avail himself to the protection of that country, or who, not having a nationality and being outside the country of his former habitual residence, is unable, or owing to such fear, unwilling to return to it.[19]

Cuba and Vietnam alone made permanent exiles of more than 2.5 million persons. Between 1975 and 1979, some 300,000 refugees from Vietnam and Cambodia entered the United States through presidential action. Congress reacted by passing the Refugee Act of 1980.

THE REFUGEE ACT OF 1980

On March 17, 1980, Congress passed the Refugee Act of 1980 (Pub. L. 96-212, 94 Stat. 102). It amends the Immigration and Nationality Act of 1952 (66 Stat. 163), and the Migration and Refugee Assistance Act of 1960 (74 Stat. 504). It raised the annual ceiling for refugees from 17,400 to 50,000, created a process for reviewing and adjusting the refugee ceiling to meet emergencies, and required annual consultation between Congress and the president. It created within the Office of Refugee Resettlement the Office of U.S. Coordinator for Refugee Affairs. The Coordinator was to monitor, coordinate, and implement overall refugee policy, which was administered in one respect or another by the Immigration and Naturalization Service in the Department of Justice, the Office of Refugee

Resettlement in the Department of Health and Human Services, and the Bureau of Refugee Programs at the Department of State.

The 1980 Refugee Act changed the definition of refugee to that of the UN Protocol. That change in definition increased at one time the number of persons potentially eligible to enter the United States from 3 million to nearly 15 million. Although the issue of refugee status is a complex one that involves political, social, economic, and legal ramifications, the trends in political turmoil among Third World nations led to what has been called "the global refugee crisis."[20] Indeed, the *1981 World Refugee Survey* put the number of refugees in the world at 12.5 million. Subsequent refugee crises raised that number to more than 15 million, and international movements of people were, by 1985, higher than in any other period of recorded human history.[21]

During the 1980s, the industrialized nations became almost inured to the Third World waves of refugees. But 1989 witnessed a refugee movement unseen since the end of World War II. Hundreds of thousands of Europeans migrated from East to West: 100,000 Soviets, 250,000 East Germans, 300,000 Bulgarian Turks, 230,000 Poles, and 20,000 Romanians. This outpouring of eastern Europeans fleeing to the West partially explains why reduction in East/West tensions has not been significantly relieved by the crisis nature of the world's refugee problem. The trends discussed here changed the very image of the refugee, from the emaciated Ethiopian child seeking relief from famine in a dusty desert camp to today's refugee as one seeking better economic opportunity or political stability and liberty rather than simply those fleeing war or natural disaster. Despite those changes, most of the world's refugees are still fleeing their nations of origin simply to stay alive.

In its various provisions, the Refugee Act of 1980 allowed as many as 70,000 persons annually to enter because of their having a well-founded fear of persecution based on race, religion, nationality, or membership in a social group, or because of political opinions. In 1984, for example, 61,750 refugees were admitted into the United States. From 1960 to 1985, as mentioned, 800,000 refugees came from Cuba, 340,000 from Vietnam, 110,000 from Laos, 70,000 from the then USSR, nearly that many from Kampuchea (formerly Cambodia), 30,000 from Yugoslavia, 25,000 each from China and Taiwan, about 20,000 from Romania and Poland, and about 10,000 each from Czechoslovakia, Spain, and Hungary.

Religious persecution was still a compelling factor in refugee movements. About two-thirds of Soviet Jews fleeing the Soviet Union came to the United States (the other third went to Israel). The United States received about three times as many refugees as any other receiving nation and almost as many as all the other receiving nations in the world combined.

The plight and problems caused by the flow from Haiti, deemed "economic refugees," who were also predominantly black, raised perplexing issues for U.S. policymakers. The Vietnamese and other Indochinese refugees were largely political allies whom the members of Congress felt some moral obligation to assist and to whom the American public was generally inclined to help. Poor black Haitians were another matter. Vietnamese refugees (other than the Hmong) were mostly well-educated, middle-class persons, about two-thirds of whom had held white-collar occupations in Vietnam, and nearly a quarter of whom were from professional, technical, and managerial occupations. Less than 5 percent were farmers and fisherman. Given their backgrounds, the Vietnamese tended to acculturate more rapidly than any previous groups of Asian immigrants. Haitians, by marked contrast, were treated as illegal immigrants fleeing dire economic conditions, not political repression, and were not allowed to enter under refugee status. Arriving in ever-increasing numbers starting in 1972, their legal status was clouded for years by the Department of State while the government decided what to do with them. As economic refugees, they were accorded neither public support nor aid, as had been given to Cubans, Vietnamese, Hungarians, or Soviet Jews. The Haitians were held in detention camps for years, and even upon their release, they received no help in finding jobs, housing, or, indeed, anything else to acculturate to life in the United States, as were the political refugees.

Haitian refugees were for the most part illiterate, had few job skills suited to the American economy, and, as French-Creole speakers, had language problems that made them easily exploitable. As a result, they often lived in conditions of near slavery as migrant workers. Public opinion saw them as a special threat to the labor market. Their migration focused attention on the increasing problem of "illegal aliens" who entered the United States as undocumented, and who were estimated at between three million and six million during the 1970s and 1980s. The issue of illegal immigration has dominated the debate over immigration policy ever since 1980.

PUSHING FOR THE IMMIGRATION REFORM AND CONTROL ACT (IRCA) OF 1986

In the 1980 presidential election, the former Republican governor of California, Ronald Reagan and his running mate, George H. W. Bush, were elected in another landslide-type win. Reagan/Bush won 489 ECV (90.9 percent) and 50.7 percent of the popular vote to the Democratic ticket of Jimmy Carter and Walter Mondale, which garnered only 49 ECV (9.1 percent) and 41 percent of the popular vote. The third-party ticket of John Anderson and Patrick Lucey won no Electoral College votes but did win 6.6 percent of the popular vote. The Democratic ticket carried only the District of Columbia and the states of Georgia, Hawaii, Maryland, Minnesota, Rhode Island, and West Virginia. The Reagan election signaled a dramatic change in American politics. A center-left administration was replaced by a center-right one, and a period of Republican Party ascendency began. It rang the death knell of the old New Deal coalition. In the 1984 presidential election, Reagan's win was even greater. Reagan-Bush won 525 ECV (97.6 percent), and 58.8 percent of the popular vote over the Democratic ticket of Walter Mondale and Geraldine Ferraro, who won only the District of Columbia and Mondale's home state of Minnesota and received 40.6 percent of the popular vote.[22] The huge winning margins are important to note because they gave President Reagan an undisputed "mandate," which he used to shift American politics dramatically to the right across numerous public policy areas. In terms of immigration policy and law, the focus on the "immigration problem" shifted from the refugee problem to the "illegal alien" problem.

Various methods have been used to estimate the number of unauthorized immigrants entering the United States, but the Reagan administration used a metric based on apprehensions of undocumented immigrants attempting to enter at the southern border.

In 1984, the INS apprehended 1.3 million undocumented immigrants and estimated that two to three times as many had slipped through. In 1978, SCIRP estimated the total illegal immigration population at between 3.5 million and 6 million. A National Academy of Sciences study released in 1985 placed the total between 2 million and 4 million. But by anyone's measures, Hispanics comprised about two-thirds of the illegal flow, led by Mexicans driven by poverty and unemployment across the highly porous 2,000-mile Mexican-U.S. border.

The exponential increase in unauthorized immigration contributed to the enormous political pressure to "control the border," and to "close the back door" by "demagnetizing" the draw of the U.S. economy. The fact that the richest nation with the largest economy in the world shared a 2,000-mile border with a country suffering with a failed economy meant the push and pull factors compelled an inexorable migration flow. The illegal influx reflected an unanticipated consequence of the prior policy shift to end the Bracero Program in 1964. With the end of the Bracero Program and enactment of the Immigration and Nationality Act of 1965, legal immigration from Mexico plummeted from 350,000 guest workers annually to 20,000 legal immigrants annually by 1970. Undocumented entrants simply replaced the Bracero flow; they were essentially the same workers.

The volume of overall legal immigration also rose dramatically, although not exponentially, during the 1970s, to about 4.5 million. This was the highest level since the 1910–1920 decade and the fourth highest level for any decade in the nation's history. The 1980 census enumerated 5.6 million foreign-born persons who had entered during the 1970s, representing the total for legal immigration and the estimated number who entered illegally. Muller and Espanshade put net immigration at 6.6 million for the 1970s. It is likely that the flow into the United States during the decades of the 1970s and 1980s was at the highest level for any period in the twentieth century. This new "Fourth Wave" was overwhelmingly Asian and Hispanic: 34 percent were from Asia, 34 percent from Central and South America, and 10 percent from the Caribbean. Only 16 percent came from Europe. The remaining 6 percent were from Canada or from "unspecified nations." In contrast, prior to 1960, 69 percent came from Europe.[23]

Moreover, the trend in increased Hispanic population growth in the United States has continued and even increased since 1980. According to the 2010 census, of the total U.S. population of 308.7 million who live in the United States, 50.5 million (16 percent) were Hispanic or Latino, an increase of 15.2 million since the 2000 census. That number (50.5 million) exceeds what had been projected by the Population Reference Bureau, who had estimated they would be at 47 million by the 2020 census count. Hispanic growth rate has been at 39 percent since 1980, about half attributable to immigration and half to births. Central and South American groups have grown the fastest since 1980, increasing by two-thirds, while Mexicans increased by one-third. In 1980 the Hispanic population was about

20.1 million, or 6.5 percent of the U.S. total population. On average, Fourth Wave immigrants were better educated than those who had come before 1980. A higher percentage of them had college degrees, and they were more highly urbanized—with nearly 90 percent settling in 10 metropolitan areas within the United States. They were concentrated in six gateway states: California, Florida, Texas, Illinois, New York, and Arizona.

Mexican immigrants, who by 1990 made up nearly 63 percent of Hispanic immigrants, especially undocumented immigrants, tended to come from rural and small towns in Mexico, and they were fleeing dire poverty. Prior to 1986 and passage of IRCA, Mexican migrants exhibited a "sojourner" attitude. Since they often resided in the United States along the border region close to their native areas, they periodically returned to their place of origin, thereby keeping strong family, social, and cultural ties. Mexicans—especially the undocumented—considered the border more of a nuisance than a barrier. Moving back and forth across the border, they exhibited a slower rate of naturalization and political incorporation than did non-Hispanic groups.

Although both push and pull factors are and always have been involved in immigration, push factors seem to have become more important since 1980. Worldwide population growth has contributed to the flow as a dominant push factor. As noted in the final report of the Select Commission on Immigration and Refugee Policy (SCIRP):

> One of the greatest pressures for international migration is and will be world population growth. Projections of this growth show more than a 50 percent increase in 1975 to the year 2000, from 4 billion to 6.35 billion ... 92 percent of this growth will take place in countries whose resources are least able to accommodate the needs of new population ... World economic and political instability would be threatened by the sudden, large-scale population moves which could result from widespread political or economic chaos in developing nations.[24]

Enactment of the Refugee Act of 1980 clearly showed that Congress was ready, willing, and able to reexamine immigration policy. Failures by the INS to enforce policy and control the border, coupled with the rising number of legal and unauthorized immigrants, led to broad support for new policy and a bipartisan effort to enact an amendment to the 1965 law. As discussed previously, SCIRP had been established to study immigration policy. Its recommendations became the foundation for the immigration reform acts of 1986 and 1990. Its recommendations became the basis for imposing the "employer-sanctions" approach central to IRCA.

THE CRISIS OF BORDER CONTROL

What resulted from the surge of immigration from South and Central America, Asia, Africa, and the Caribbean was a growing sense of crisis: a widespread dissatisfaction in the media, general public opinion polls, and within the government at both the national level and among states especially impacted by the unauthorized immigration flow. A general sense emerged that immigration was out of control, that the nation had lost control of its borders.

Seemingly millions of illegal immigrants resided in the United States and more were being added at historic and exponential rates. Even for those who entered legally, the INS seemed unable to keep track of them to assure they obeyed the terms of their visas. The inefficiency of the INS and its inept recordkeeping was brought to light during the Iranian hostage crisis. The nation was shocked to learn that the INS knew neither how many Iranian students were living in the country nor how many were doing so illegally (having broken the conditions of their visas). Problems of corruption flowed naturally from the tremendous pressures for immigration coupled with the restrictions on legal immigration and the inefficiency and corruption of the INS.

By far the most controversial problem, the one that stirred the greatest debate, was the economic impact. One study concluded that the undocumented contributed more revenue to the state than it spent on them. Another concluded that the undocumented contributed less than the estimated $3,000 cost per year to educate a public school student.[25] The sense that immigration was a crisis compelled Congress to undertake "reform" of immigration law and to consider a new method of "employer sanctions" as a means to demagnetize the pull of the U.S. economy.

SCIRP issued its final report in January 1981, which ran more than 450 pages, and its staff report in excess of 900 pages. It recommended "closing the back door" to unauthorized, undocumented immigrants, and a modest increase in legal immigration (from 279,000 to 350,000) to reunify families. Its recommendations set the agenda for all subsequent discussions of and proposals to reform immigration law. An important contribution was the shared information it provided to all the disputants—information pertinent to alternative solutions and about the other parties' positions.

The Reagan administration responded to the SCIRP findings by establishing a Task Force on Immigration and Refugee Policy on March 6, 1981. The Task Force was chaired by Attorney General William French Smith, and it presented its recommendations to President Reagan at three meetings in July 1981. Its major proposals were the following:

1. *Amnesty.* Aliens living in the United States illegally since January 1, 1980, would be permitted to remain, being made eligible for resident-alien status after being in country for 10 years, and would then be free to seek naturalization. The Task Force estimated their number at 5 million persons.
2. *Guest Workers.* A program to allow 50,000 Mexicans to annually enter to work temporarily, gradually increasing in numbers over several years until up to 100,000 annually.
3. *Employer Sanctions.* Employers with more than four employees who "knowingly hire" illegal aliens would be subject to fines up to $1,000 per violation.
4. *Boat People.* Boats carrying Haitians would be intercepted. Detention camps would be established to hold as many as 6,000 people pending hearings on their deportation.
5. *Enforcement.* Increase the budget of the INS by 50 percent and add 1,500 officers to the Border Patrol to enhance enforcement of immigration and labor laws.
6. *Immigration Limits.* Allow 610,000 new immigrants to enter the United States annually, with a special preference to persons from Canada and Mexico.[26]

The Task Force's boldest proposals were politically controversial: (1) to allow the Coast Guard to intercept boats carrying Haitians so they could be returned to Haiti; and (2) to create a counterfeit-resistant Social Security card (dubbed in the media a "national ID card"). The latter proposal, however, was dropped from the Task Force's final report.

By fall 1981, both the House and Senate Judiciary subcommittees on immigration had completed their hearings. Their chairmen, Senator Alan

Simpson (R-WY) and Representative Romano Mazzoli (D-KY), essentially crafted the SCIRP recommendations into legislative proposals and with what they considered provisions necessary to achieve cooperation of the various competing groups. By March 1982, identical Simpson-Mazzoli bills were introduced into their respective chambers (S. 2222 and H.R. 5872), and incorporating some aspects of the Reagan Task Force proposals. Their bills also set up a new procedure for asylum adjudication. It specified a U.S. Immigration Board to hear appeals. Its members were to be appointed by the president and to be independent of the attorney general.

The Simpson-Mazzoli bill did not fare so well in the House. A version of the bill passed the Senate. It would have reduced the role of the Department of Labor in the certification process, allowing for the possibility that the INS, an agency less sensitive to domestic labor conditions, would ignore or overrule the DOL.

Senator Edward Kennedy (D-MA) offered several amendments, among other things doing away with the H-2 temporary worker expansion provisions. Groups like the Mexican American Defense League (MALDEF), the Spanish International Network (SIN), the national Spanish-language network, and the National Council of La Raza lobbied against the Simpson-Mazzoli bill, calling it "the most blatantly anti-Hispanic bill ever." The Hispanic Caucus strongly opposed the bills, offering 100 amendments to the employer-sanctions provision alone. The Hispanic Caucus, led by Edward Roybal (D-CA), lobbied Speaker Tip O'Neill (D-MA) to kill the bills. The Simpson-Mazzoli measure received only tepid support from the House Democratic leadership. The Speaker scheduled floor action only out of courtesy to the Reagan White House and the Republican House leadership. After three days of emotional, even bitter late evening debates, the bill died as the 97th Congress adjourned.

In the 98th Congress in 1983, Simpson and Mazzoli renewed their efforts at immigration reform, again introducing identical versions of their bills. Representative Edward Roybal (D-CA) introduced an alternative bill focusing on tougher labor laws and minimum wage laws rather than the employer-sanctions approach. Senator Jesse Helms (R-NC) unsuccessfully tried to delete the amnesty provision. The Senate passed its version by late April, by 63–33. But in the House, the Mazzoli bill once again moved sequentially through referrals to several committees: Education and Labor, Agriculture, Ways and Means, and Energy and Commerce.

Speaker O'Neill pulled the bill from floor consideration. After various amendments were considered, some adopted, most defeated, the bill finally passed in 1984, by a sharply divided House (Democrats by 138–125, and Republicans by 91–73).

Since the House and Senate passed different versions of the bill, the measures were sent to a House-Senate Conference Committee. The conference committee deliberated during the 1984 presidential election (between September 13 and October 4, 1984). The conference committee was unable to achieve compromises to pass a unified bill to send to the president. The 98th Congress adjourned with the conference committee dissolved, and the reform measure once again died.

The failure to pass the bill out of the conference committee nonetheless laid an important base for the future. A proposed change by Representative Barney Frank (D-MA) for a strong antidiscrimination provision would have created a special counsel in the Department of Justice to handle charges of employment discrimination. It became part of the base of the bills going forward in 1985. Representative Charles Schumer (D-NY) emerged as a key player to try to bridge a gap between farm labor advocates and growers over a guest worker provision, working closely with Simpson, Mazzoli, and Frank during six days of intense shuttle diplomacy. Schumer tried, but failed, to secure a compromise on the hotly debated cap on federal support for state and local governments for costs incurred through the legalization program.

In May 1985, Senator Simpson introduced a new version of his bill, without the cosponsorship of Representative Mazzoli. His version contained a compromise on the amnesty program that would take place only after a presidential commission had certified that the new law resulted in a substantial reduction in illegal immigration. His bill also placed a $1.8 billion limit on federal reimbursement to states for costs to process undocumented aliens through the program. Senator Edward Kennedy introduced an amendment that granted amnesty at the same time as employer sanctions would take effect. That proposed amendment failed by a vote of 26–65, as did a temporary guest worker proposal from Senator Pete Wilson (R-CA) to give growers of perishable crops a large, mobile, temporary work force of foreign workers to pick fruits and vegetables. Wilson's proposal went down 48–50. He then offered a new proposal, for 350,000 guest workers to be allowed in annually. It passed by a narrow margin, signaling that any House bill to survive would have to include a guest-worker program. The Senate bill passed in September 1985, 69–30.

In the House, Representative Peter Rodino (D-NJ) introduced a bill cosponsored by Representative Mazzoli that was very similar to the bill that died in the final days of the 1984 conference committee. As in previous years, the various Hispanic groups and the American Civil Liberties Union opposed both the House and the Senate versions. Working through the Hispanic Caucus and the Black Congressional Caucus, they opposed the employer-sanctions approach, arguing it would inevitably increase discrimination against all Hispanics. They opposed the bill's guest-worker program, arguing that historically such workers had been highly exploited. Growers insisted on a guest-worker program and that the provisions for such in both the House and Senate bills were too small.

The Reagan White House strongly backed the Senate version. The Senate Judiciary Committee rejected attempts to make the Senate version more like the House version. After the 1985 conference committee seemed unable to agree on a compromise version of the bill, it once again seemed the bill was "a corpse going to the morgue."[27]

ENACTMENT OF IRCA

A small group of legislators long committed to passage of immigration reform, however, refused to let it die. They crafted the final key compromises that enabled passage in October 1986. The September 1986 deadlock over the farm workers provision was broken by a compromise crafted by Representative Schumer, working with Representative Rodino and Representatives Hamilton Fish Jr. (R-NY), Howard L. Berman (D-CA), Leon Panetta (D-PA), and Dan Lungren (R-CA). They secured the support of Senator Simpson and Representative Mazzoli.

After a decade or more of dealing with proposals to reform immigration law, Congress was finally in a better mood and position to act than it had been in any previous year. The Mexican economy deteriorated in 1985 and the peso plunged in value. That spurred more "push" unauthorized migration. The INS reported a record high of 1.8 million apprehensions at the border. The growing conservative mood of the country, clearly indicated by President Reagan's landslide victory in 1984, convinced liberal opponents of the bill that continued resistance was likely to result in even more restrictive legislation in 1987.

The bill's tangled history made compromises possible in 1986. Nearly everyone involved desperately wanted some sort of bill to pass. Previous fights meant there was less need for continued political posturing. There was no longer a looming presidential election to complicate such compromise moves by legislators representing the various interests of the competing factions. In the words of Representative Mazzoli, who urged its passage: "It's not a perfect bill, but it's the least imperfect bill we will ever have before us."[28]

The key shift came when the Hispanic Caucus split on the compromise bill 5–6. With their affiliates, the Hispanic Caucus vote was 20 for to 17 against the bill. Their split enabled the Black Congressional Caucus to split as well, 10 for to 8 against. With their affiliates, the 29 members of the Black Caucus voted 15 for the measure to 14 against. The total vote in the House was 301 in favor to 197 against, with the Democrats splitting their votes 196 (65 percent) for the bill to 88 (45 percent) against, with 17 not voting. Republicans in the House split their 231 votes at 105 (35 percent) in favor to 108 (55 percent) against the measure, with 17 not voting.

The House passed the compromise conference committee measure by 238–173 on October 15, 1986. The Senate approved it 63–24 on October 17, 1986. President Reagan signed it into law on November 6, 1986, as the Immigration Reform and Control Act of 1986 (Pub. L. 99-603, 100 Stat. 3445).

The 1988 presidential election continued the Republican Party ascendency. Their ticket of George H. W. Bush and Dan Quayle won 426 ECV (79.2 percent) and 53.4 percent of the popular vote, carrying 42 states. The Democratic ticket of Michael Dukakis (former governor of Massachusetts) and Senator Lloyd Bentsen (D-TX) carried only 8 states, winning but 111 ECV (20.6 percent) and 45.6 percent of the popular vote.[29] Their landslide-proportion victory gave them a mandate that they used to push for legal immigration reform.

THE IMMIGRATION ACT OF 1990 (IMMACT)

As discussed previously, the legislative push to enact IRCA had heavily emphasized the issue of illegal immigration. IRCA was passed only after protracted struggle and only by incorporating several key compromises. Those very compromises necessary to achieve a majority to pass the bill, however, resulted in unanticipated consequences when the law was implemented. As a result, Congress took up once more the issue to reform immigration with provisions not addressed by IRCA, or that were intended to refine its approach when problems in IRCA's implementation became obvious. Between 1988 and 1990, Congress undertook several measures to reform legal immigration, and they culminated the effort of reform begun by SCIRP in 1979. In 1990, Congress passed the Immigration Act of 1990, known as IMMACT (104 Stat. 4981). IMMACT contained elements of virtually all the ideas and bills since the SCIRP final report.

The Senate passed another Edward Kennedy–Alan Simpson bill on March 15, 1988, by a vote of 88–4. It addressed numerous aspects of legal immigration not dealt with by IRCA and contained a few provisions designed to address problems seen as failures of IRCA implementation. It identified separate tracks for family and nonfamily immigration and increased total legal immigration. It tipped the ratio of independent to family-related immigration, and it separated refugees from family-related immigrants. It called for establishing an eligibility for entrepreneurs who created at least 10 new jobs, investing at least $1 million in new jobs, and created separate avenues of entrance for immigrants with needed job skills and more than doubled such visas from 54,000 to 150,000 aimed at drawing more skilled and better-educated workers.

The Kennedy-Simpson bill was a slightly modified version of one passed in the Senate in 1988 but not voted on in the House that was sponsored by Senator Paul Simon (D-IL). Simon's bill contained an amendment to end direct federal benefits to undocumented immigrants and a provision to grant stays of deportation to immediate relatives of persons in the process of legalizing under IRCA. In a response to the repression of the pro-democracy movement in mainland China, the Simon bill allowed for an increase in the annual immigration level from Hong Kong, from 2 percent to 3.5 percent of the worldwide total, and permitted Chinese students already in the United States to remain for four years and qualify for legal residency.

Senator Dennis DeConcini (D-AZ) sponsored a bill to halt deportation of Salvadorans and Nicaraguans as a companion bill to one in the House sponsored by Representative Joseph Moakley (D-MA). The manner in which IRCA was implemented aggravated problems that Salvadorans and Nicaraguans were facing, prompting Senator DeConcini to sponsor the new measure set at 7 percent of the total, and a bill by Representative Howard L. Berman that set it at 22,000. Still another measure was introduced by Representatives Peter Rodino and Romano Mazzoli. It differed from the Kennedy-Simpson-Simon bill in that it neither imposed a ceiling on annual admissions of immediate relatives of U.S. citizens nor offset such admissions against other family-sponsored immigration.

In 1987–1989 Congress passed several laws that modified on the fringes the 1965 Immigration and Nationality Act. In 1987, it passed the American Homecoming Act (a.k.a. the Amerasian Homecoming Act). It was written in 1987, passed in 1988, and implemented in 1989 (H.R. 3171, Pub. L. 97-359, 96 Stat. 1716). It was an appropriations bill providing for the admission of children born in Vietnam between certain specified dates to Vietnamese mothers and American fathers, together with their immediate relatives. Although they were admitted as nonquota immigrants, they received refugee-program benefits.

In 1988, Congress passed the U.S.–Canada Free Trade Agreement Implementation Act (Pub. L. 100-449, September 28, 1988. 102 Stat. 1851, 19 U.S.C. 2112). In it, Congress facilitated the temporary entry of Canadians on a reciprocal basis, with Canada accepting U.S. emigrants. In a 1989 appropriations bill, the Foreign Operations Act of 1989 (Statutes at Large, 1989b: 3908), Congress adjusted to permanent resident status certain Soviet and Indochinese nationals who were paroled into the United States between certain dates after denial of refugee status by the INS. And in December 1989, Congress again amended the 1965 act by passing the Immigration Nursing Relief Act of 1989 (Pub. L. 101-238, passed 12/18/89; and Senate bill, 11/20/1989). It adjusted to permanent resident status without numerical limitations certain nonimmigrants employed as registered nurses for three years, in response to a severe nursing shortage.

These "tinkering" reforms, largely amending the 1965 Immigration and Nationality Act at its fringes, culminated in legal immigration reform that plugged IRCA-related loopholes, known as the Immigration Act of 1990, or IMMACT (104 Stat. 4981). One of the act's authors, Senator Edward Kennedy, described it as follows:

> This bill, like all major legislation, represents many years of work, and many
> efforts at compromise. The measure is the culmination of a decade-long effort

which began in 1979 with the Select Commission on Immigration and Refugee Policy. This commission's work laid the basis for the most comprehensive reforms of the nation's immigration laws in our history. This effort has been a two-step process. In 1986 we enacted a far-reaching measure to deal with illegal immigration. In this bill, an equally far-reaching measure of legal immigration will be achieved . . . Our goal has been to reform the current immigration system—which has not changed in 25 years—so that it will more faithfully serve the national interest, and be more flexible and open to immigrants from nations which were so short-changed by current law . . . This compromise creates two separate preference systems for immigrant visas—one for close family members, another for independent immigration. This two-track system was first recommended by the Select Commission.[30]

Senator Alan Simpson, the bill's cosponsor, stressed yet another aspect of the measure:

But the bill provides, for the very first time, a mechanism through which the national level of immigration in the United States will be reviewed by the President and the Congress every three years. So never again will we go 25 to 30 years without carefully reviewing immigration levels, how they should be adjusted to bring our immigration policy more into line with our national interests.[31]

IMMACT passed in the House by a vote of 264 in favor to 118 against, with 50 not voting. It split voting blocs much like IRCA did, but with greater unanimity among some of the caucus blocs. In the total Congress roll call vote (combining House and Senate votes), by party affiliation, the Democrats voted in favor by 218 votes (62 percent) to 58 (46 percent) with 35 (13 percent) not voting. Among Republicans, 131 (38 percent) voted in favor of the bill, 68 (54 percent) against, with 18 (34 percent) not voting.

The major provisions of IMMACT are as follows:

- It increased total immigration under the overall flexible cap of 675,000 immigrants beginning in fiscal year 1995, preceded by a 700,000 level during the fiscal years 1992 through 1994. The 675,000 level consisted of three tracks: 480,000 family-sponsored immigrants (71 percent), 140,000 employment-based immigrants (21 percent), and 55,000 "diversity immigrants" (8 percent). It revised all grounds for exclusion and deportation, significantly rewriting the political and ideological grounds. For example, it repealed the bar against admission of communists as nonimmigrants (for example, coming as tourists or students), and limited the exclusion of aliens on foreign policy grounds.

- It authorized the attorney general to grant temporary protected status to undocumented alien nationals of designated countries subject to armed conflict or natural disasters (for example, El Salvador, Guatemala, and Honduras).
- It revised and established new nonimmigrant admission categories by:

  1. Redefining the H-1(b) temporary worker category and limited admissions to 65,000 annually; and

  2. Creating new temporary worker admissions categories, some with annual caps on the number of admissions.

- It revised and extended through fiscal year 1994 the Visa Waiver Pilot Program.
- It revised naturalization authority and requirements by:

  1. Transferring the exclusive jurisdiction to naturalize aliens form the federal and state courts to the attorney general; and

  2. Amending the substantive requirements for naturalization: revised and reduced to three months state residency requirements, added another ground for waiving the English-language requirement; lifted the permanent bar to naturalization for aliens who applied to be relieved from U.S. military service on the grounds of alienage who previously served in the service of the country of the alien's nationality.

- It revised enforcement activities in several ways:

  1. Broadened the definition of "aggravated felony" and imposed new legal disabilities on aliens convicted of such crimes.

  2. Revised employer-sanctions provisions of the Immigration Reform and Control Act of 1986.

  3. Authorized funds for the increase by 1,000 of the personnel level of the Border Patrol.

  4. Revised criminal and deportation provisions.

  5. Recodified 32 grounds for exclusion into nine categories, including revising and repealing some of the grounds (especially health grounds).[32]

IMMACT was passed with the support of, or over the opposition of, many of the same groups and congressional voting coalitions as were involved in the enactment of IRCA. Its major authors in the U.S. Senate were Edward Kennedy, Alan Simpson, and Paul Simon. In the House, its chief author was Representative Bruce Morrison (D-CT). It passed on the last day of the session, and then only after a last-minute flap that nearly killed the bill as patched together in the conference committee. The last-gasp flap was engineered by the Hispanic Caucus members. They held up consideration of the conference committee report on October 26 over opposition to a small pilot program included in the conference committee's bill to establish a forgery-proof driver's license that could be used by employers to screen out unauthorized workers. They argued that the program was the first step down the slippery slope towards a national identification card. California Democratic Representatives Edward Roybal and Esteban Torres rallied other Hispanic Caucus members, who worked the House floor to persuade their liberal colleagues to vote against the provision on civil rights grounds, arguing that the program was a clear threat to privacy and individual liberties. Hispanic caucus members won over Black Congressional Caucus members, many of whom had significant Hispanic populations in their districts, and who were frustrated by President Bush's veto of a renewal of the 1964 Civil Rights Act. They also won over some liberal Democrats who opposed it on civil rights grounds. They even persuaded some Republicans who were against the overall bill to vote against the conference committee report. The roll call vote on the conference committee report was 186–235.

Proponents then came up with the idea of a concurrent resolution to strip out the license provision from the conference committee report. By a voice vote, both chambers agreed to strip out the license provision, allowing the House to vote to adopt the conference committee report 264–118.[33]

Surprisingly, Senator Simpson, who earlier had held up the bill in conference until he got a deal that included the driver's license pilot program, dropped it without a floor fight. Also surprisingly, Representative John Moakley had won from the House-Senate conference a stay of deportation for Salvadorans living in the United States without authorization. Moakley had worked for the deportation stay for seven years and had not expected Senate proponents of the bill serving on the conference committee to include it in the conference committee report.

Even with dropping the pilot program for a tamper-proof license, the conference committee report bill faced some opposition in both chambers. Representative John Bryant (D-TX) opposed it because "the simple fact that today in the United States of America, we admit 530,000 legal immigrants to this country every year, more than all other countries of the world combined admit to their countries, at a time in which we are unable to meet the basic needs of our own citizens, and unable to pay the bills of our country."[34]

Representative Tom Campbell (R-CA) objected to the provision allowing investors to immigrate (often referred to as the "millionaires" provision). He argued the provision was inserted into the conference committee report version of the bill by three senators who lacked the power to get the provision included during deliberations in the two-year session, but were able to get it included by reason of the desperately late hour in the Congress, putting the three senators in a position to insist on their way. As he put it in the House debate on the conference report: "Standing alone, a provision in the immigration law that favors those with wealth would fail because the overwhelming majority of the people's representatives would oppose such a stark departure from what we think of America. We must not let the shortness of time stampede us into a fundamental breach of faith."[35]

Representative Thomas Lewis (R-FL) objected to the bill on the grounds it had no compensation for the increased costs to state and local governments in states that received the bulk of immigration entering the country—which included Florida. Other strong opposition to the conference report was voiced by several senators. For example, Senator Nancy Kassebaum (R-KS) objected to the provision that expanded the secretary of state's authority to exclude any alien if the admission would compromise a compelling U.S. foreign policy. As she stated it:

> I am concerned about the procedure used to adopt this proposal. It was not debated or discussed by either body or by the committees of jurisdiction. Yet we are presented with a fait accompli—as part of a back-room deal we are making significant changes in U.S. immigration policy . . . This is an issue of great concern to me, and next session I intend to promptly revisit this issue.[36]

Her objection to the bill was echoed by Senators Daniel Patrick Moynihan (D-NY), Bob Kerrey (D-NE), Alan Cranston (D-CA), Terry Sanford (D-NC), and Paul Sarbanes (D-MD).

Proponents of the bill stressed different provisions that solidified their support. Representative Bruce Morrison, the chief author and chair of the conference committee, stressed the bill's increased support for the

INS and its strident measures against alien smuggling and its authorization of an additional 1,000 Border Patrol personnel. Representatives Lamar Smith (R-TX) and William McCollum (R-FL) favored its provision to increase job-skills related immigration. Representatives Howard Berman and John Moakley emphasized its provisions regarding refugees from El Salvador. Representative John Porter (R-IL) stressed the bill's provision for the investment category of new immigrants. Senator John Chafee (R-RI) advocated for the bill noting its provision to rectify problems of IRCA.

CONCLUSION

The Immigration and Nationality Act of 1965 revised the fundamental law governing legal immigration to the United States. With its various amendments, the 1965 law governs immigration to this day. It amended the Immigration and Nationality Act of 1952 and in doing so replaced the quota system, with its racial and ethnic biases, established by the National Origins Quota Acts of 1921, 1924, and 1929, with a seven-category preference system. The preference system was applicable to all persons seeking entrance into the United States as permanent resident immigrants on a first-come, first-served basis with an annual limit of 20,000 immigrants from each country of the Eastern Hemisphere. It set a seventh preference category for refugees that at just more than 10,000 was considered to be generous at the time.

The refugee category proved to be inadequate nearly immediately, and the law was amended several times thereafter in 1966, 1976, 1980, 1986, and 1990. Each subsequent amendment addressed a perceived problem, flaw in, or unanticipated consequence of the 1965 Act.

The coalitions of outside lobbying groups and organizations that were primary stakeholders in favor of or opposing the 1965 act proved to be remarkably stable and have been involved in the battles over immigration reform ever since the 1965 act. The coalition of legislators in both chambers of Congress has also been essentially stable. The political party caucuses in both chambers have been the most significant factor influencing how members voted on immigration reform bills and proposals. For the 1965 act, the Black and Hispanic caucuses had not yet formed. The Black Congressional Caucus was founded in 1971. The Hispanic Political Caucus formed in 1976. After they were established, they have proven to be important players in the immigration reform struggles in Congress ever since.

The short- and long-term effects of the Immigration and Nationality Act of 1965 have been profound, and they have quite literally reshaped American government, politics, and society. Those short- and long-term effects are discussed in more detail in the next chapter.

NOTES

1. Nathan Glazer, ed., *Clamor at the Gates: The New American Immigration* (San Francisco: Institute for Contemporary Studies, 1985), 52–55.

2. Michael LeMay, *The Perennial Struggle*, 3rd ed. (Upper Saddle River, NJ: Prentice-Hall, 2009), 284–96.

3. Bill Clinton, "Remarks to the Convocation of the Church of God in Christ at Memphis, Tennessee," November 13, 1993. The American Presidency Project, www.presidency.usb.edu/showelection.php?Year=1960.

4. "Civil Rights Act of 1964," History.com, January 4, 2010. Available at: https://www.history.com/topics/black-history/civil-rights-act; and "The Voting Rights Act of 1965—Overview," FindLaw.com. Available at: https://civilrights.findlaw.com/other-constitutional-rights/the-voting-rights-act-of-1965-overview (accessed 7/23/2018).

5. "John F. Kennedy Elected President," This Day in History: November 8, 1960, History.com, July 17, 2019. Available at: https://www.history.com/this-day-in-history/john-f-kennedy-elected-president (accessed 7/19/2018).

6. The American Presidency Project, www.presidency.usb.edu/showelection.php?Year=1964.

7. "TO PASS H.R. 2580, IMMIGRATION AND NATIONALITY ACT AMENDMENTS," GovTrack, Civic Impulse, LLC. Available at: https://www.govtrack.us/congress/votes/89-1965/s232 (accessed 7/17/2018).

8. United States Senate, "Glossary Terms: Caucus," https://www.senate.gov/reference/glossary_term/caucus.htm (accessed 7/20/2018).

9. James Kellas, *The Politics of Nationalism and Ethnicity* (New York: St. Martin's Press, 1991), 4.

10. Ibid., 158.

11. President Lyndon B. Johnson's Remarks at the Signing of the Immigration Bill, Liberty Island, New York, October 3, 1965. Available at: http://www.lbjlibrary.org/lyndon-baines-johnson/timeline/lbj-on-immigration (accessed 7/20/2018).

12. Ibid.

13. Michael LeMay, *Anatomy of a Public Policy: The Reform of Contemporary Immigration Law* (Westport, CT: Praeger, 1994), 12–13. Author's summary of Pub. L. 89-236; 79 Stat. 911, October 3, 1965.

14. Michael LeMay, *U.S. Immigration: A Reference Handbook* (Santa Barbara, CA: ABC-CLIO, 2004), 4–5; Author's summary of Pub. L. 89-236; 79 Stat. 911, October 3, 1965.

15. LeMay, *U.S. Immigration*, 5.

16. Thomas Muller and Thomas Espanshade, *The Fourth Wave* (Washington, DC: The Urban Institute, 1985), 12.

17. American Presidency Project, www.presidency.usb.edu/showelection.php ?Year=1972.

18. Box 68, folder 10/20/76, H.R. 13535, "Immigration and Nationality Act Amendment of 1976" of the White House Records Office, legislative files at the Gerald R. Ford Presidential Library. Available at www.fordlibrarymuseum.gov/library/document/0055/1669712.pdf (accessed 7/21/2018).

19. Elizabeth Ferris, ed., *Refugees and World Politics* (New York: Praeger, 1985), 2–3.

20. Mary M. Kritz, *U.S. Immigration and Refugee Policy: Global and Domestic Issues* (Lexington, MA: Lexington Books, 1983), 157.

21. Ferris, *Refugees and World Politics*, 105.

22. Michael C. LeMay, *The American Political Party System* (Santa Barbara, CA: ABC-CLIO, 2017), 41.

23. Muller and Espanshade, *The Fourth Wave*, 15.

24. Select Commission on Immigration and Refugee Policy, *Final Report* (Washington, DC: U.S. Government Printing Office, 1981), 19–20, and as cited in LeMay, *U.S. Immigration*, 11.

25. Kritz, *U.S. Immigration and Refugee Policy*, 191–285; and Muller and Espanshade, *The Fourth Wave*, chapters 4–6.

26. LeMay, *Anatomy of a Public Policy*, 37.

27. Ibid., 48.

28. "House Passes Compromise Immigration Bill," *Washington Post*, October 16, 1986, A-5; as cited in LeMay, *Anatomy of a Public Policy*, 55.

29. Dave Leip, US Election Atlas. Available at: https://uselectionatlas.org/RESULTS/data.php?year=1988&datatype=national&def=1&f=0&off=0&elect=0 (accessed 7/26/2018).

30. *Congressional Record—Senate*, October 26, 1990, S-17109.

31. *Congressional Record—Senate*, October 26, 1990, S-17109.

32. *Congressional Record—House*, October 26, 1990, H-13203-13240; summarized in Michael C. LeMay, *Guarding the Gates: Immigration and National Security* (Westport, CT and London: Praeger Security International, 2006), 143–44.

33. *Congressional Quarterly Weekly Report*, November 3, 1990: 3753.

34. *Congressional Record—House*, October 27, 1990, H-12359.

35. *Congressional Record—House*, October 27, 1990, H-12359.

36. *Congressional Record—Senate*, October 26, 1990, S-17114.

CHAPTER 3

THE SIGNIFICANCE OF THE 1965 ACT

INTRODUCTION: IMMIGRATION AND REMAKING AMERICA

Since the first immigration law was passed in 1819, the flow of immigration and the immigration law addressing the issue have always had a profound impact upon the United States, especially when a particular law concerned comprehensive reform. The Immigration and Nationality Act of 1965 is no exception and, in important ways, it remade America.

The 1965 law clearly enacted a comprehensive reform of U.S. immigration policy. The 1965 law accounted for substantial increases in population growth after 1970. As a direct result of the law's comprehensive reforms, it allowed for a dramatic increase in the size of the immigration wave that followed its enactment—soon reaching and then exceeding the size of the immigration wave to one greater than that of any other period in U.S. history. An equally dramatic and intended effect was how the law changed the composition of the immigrant wave—the so-called "preference immigrants," as to their region and countries of origin, their religious affiliations, the "human capital" they brought with them, and their far more diverse backgrounds of ethnicity and race than that of prior eras.

This chapter will show how preference immigrants shaped where Americans lived by contributing significantly to the urban and metropolitan areas of the United States. The birth rate among immigrants is significantly greater than that of the native stock, thereby resulting in immigrants contributing a major portion of the population growth of the United States. Immigrants had a significant impact on how, when, and where Americans worshiped. They had an enormous economic impact on national, state, and local governments. Immigrants came to the United States to work, and they participated in the labor force at a higher percentage rate than did the native-born.

The 1965 law had some equally profound unanticipated consequences associated with the exponential increase in undocumented immigration. Authorized and unauthorized immigrants have had dramatic demographic effects; they quite literally contributed to the "browning" of America. This chapter details the short-term effects and long-term impact of the 1965 act and discusses those likely effects for the future.

SHORT-TERM EFFECTS OF THE IMMIGRATION AND NATIONALITY ACT OF 1965

As previously noted, the Immigration and Nationality Act of 1965 had a provision for a three-year transition from the quota system to the preference system. The preference categories were not to take effect until after 1968. As shown in Table 2.3, in 1965, 1966, and 1967, the numbers of legal immigrants arriving and who were allowed to enter the United States, as intended by the quota system, ranged in numbers from 290,000 to 360,000. Those annual totals only enumerate the legal immigrants entering the United States. They do not include undocumented immigrants who, by 1976, were estimated to be at about 3 million, and by the enactment of IRCA in 1986, were estimated to be at 6 million to 6.5 million. Another reason why changes in the immigration flow was gradual between 1965 and 1970 was the depressing effect that the Vietnam War had on international migration. Furthermore, sending nations of origin needed a few years to adjust to the requirements of the new law. The low point in the foreign-born population among the total U.S. population was in 1970 when the 9.6 million foreign-born then residing in the United States equaled 4.7 percent of the total population. It was not until the mid-1980s, when the effects of the amendments of 1976 and 1980 are felt, particularly with respect to refugee admissions, that annual legal immigration to the United States began to exceed 500,000.

An important short-term effect of the 1965 law was changes in the region of birth of the persons naturalized between 1961 and 1970. In that decade, Europeans still predominated at slightly more than 62 percent, Asians to just less than 13 percent, and North Americans (which includes Canadians and Mexicans) to just shy of 21 percent. Eventually, between 1965 and 2016, nearly 40 million legal immigrants arrived, averaging about 783,000 per year for the 50-year period (see Table 2.3). A dramatic impact of the 1965 reform law is evident as to the region of origin of legal immigrants. Europeans dropped from more than 62 percent of all legal immigrants naturalizing in 1970 to less than 12 percent by 2000. During that same time, the naturalization rate among Asian immigrants rose from 13 percent to 38 percent, and the rate of naturalization among North Americans rose from 21 percent to 40 percent. The number of foreign-born residents in the United States as a percentage of the total U.S. population rose from 4.7 percent in 1970, to 6.2 percent in 1980, to 7.9 percent by 1990, to 11.1 percent in 2000, to 13.3 percent in 2014, and it is projected by the U.S. Census Bureau to reach 14.3 percent by 2020 and 18.8 percent by 2060, when the number of foreign-born residents in the United States is projected to exceed 78 million.

During the Senate debate over the 1965 bill, Edward Kennedy, one of the measure's chief sponsors in the U.S. Senate, addressed his colleagues shortly before the bill's passage. In his remarks, Senator Kennedy stressed the "short-term" impact of the bill:

> Mr. President, the bill we are considering today accomplishes major reforms in our immigration policy. This bill is not concerned with increasing immigration to this country, nor will it lower any of the high standards we apply in the selection of immigrants. The basic change it makes is the elimination of the national origins quota system in line with the recommendations of the last four Presidents of the United States and Members of Congress from both parties ... [For] forty-one years the immigration policy of our country has been crippled by this system. Because of it we have never been able to achieve the annual quotas authorized by the law. We have discriminated in favor of some people over others, contrary to our basic principles as a nation, simply on the basis of birth. We have separated families needlessly. We have been forced to forego the talents of many professionals whose skills were needed to cure, to teach, and to enhance the lives of Americans ... There will be some increase in total immigration to the United States—about 50,000 to 60,000 per year. This [increase] results from changing the law from an individual country quota system to a worldwide system ... We are talking about 60,000 people, in a population nearing 200 million that is growing, without immigration, at a rate of 3 million per year ... This legislation opens no "floodgate." Rather, it admits about the same number of immigrants that current law would allow, but for the national origin restrictions.[1]

Indeed, in echoing the spirit of the Civil Rights Act of 1964, the Immigration and Nationality Act of 1965 was a reassertion of and return to the nation's liberal tradition in immigration law. Senator Kennedy called the approach of the quota system "un-American" and argued that the 1965 law restored a sense of "fair play" in coping with immigration decisions as to who should be allowed to enter and who should be restricted.[2]

Yet another short-term effect concerned a perceived flaw in one provision of the 1965 act. The seventh preference category of the 1965 act, its refugee provision, which in 1965 was considered to be generous, allowed only 10,000 refugees to enter the United States annually. The refugee provision was immediately viewed as woefully inadequate in the face of a refugee crisis first involving Cuban boat people. Within a year, in November 1966, Congress reacted to that obvious flaw in the 1965 act to address the plight of the Cuban refugees. Consistent with the foreign policy goals of the Kennedy and then of the Johnson administrations, and in part reacting to the Cuban missile crisis in 1962, Congress passed a special act to adjust their status to permanent residence (Act of November 2, 1966: 80 Stat. 1161). President Lyndon Johnson had earlier used his executive authority to grant asylum for Cuban refugees by directing the Department of State, Department of Justice, and the then Department of Health, Education, and Welfare (today the Department of Health and Human Services) to immediately make all necessary arrangements to permit those fleeing Cuba to seek freedom by an orderly entry into the United States. Congress confirmed President Johnson's asylum policy into law by the 1966 act adjusting their status.

POST-1970: LONG-TERM IMPLICATIONS OF THE IMMIGRATION AND NATIONALITY ACT OF 1965—THE BROWNING OF THE AMERICAN POPULATION

All the changes in the U.S. population over the years since 1970 are not, obviously, solely the result of immigration. Nonetheless, the immigration of "non-whites" was sufficiently significant to cause a political backlash among some of the native stock who felt the United States was changing too quickly and from their perspective, too negatively so. Many among the white native stock, especially, were aware of the changes leading to the "browning" of America. Census Bureau data show that in 1970, whites comprised 87.6 percent of the total population (178,119,000 out of

203,210,000). Blacks made up 11.2 percent of the population (77,082,000 of 203,210,000). By 2010, the total U.S. population had increased to 307,007,000. The 2010 census found the whites' percentage of the total population had fallen to 79.5 percent (244,298,000) and blacks' had risen to 39,641,000 (12.9 percent). By 2015, the total U.S. population was 325,540,000, with whites at 256,306,000 (declining further, to 78.7 percent); and blacks at 42,137,000 (remaining at 12.9 percent). In 2010, Asians were at 14,410,000 (4.5 percent) and Hispanics at 44,447,000 (14.5 percent). By 2015, Asians reached 16,527,000 (5 percent), and Hispanics 57,711,000 (17.7 percent).[3]

THE ECONOMIC IMPACT OF THE 1965 ACT—FINANCIAL COST/BENEFITS OF IMMIGRATION

Arguably, the most controversial impact of the 1965 act is its relative cost versus benefits to the U.S. economy and to state and local economies. The body of discourse on the economic effects of immigration is considerable and quite varied. The reported results of those studies varies depending on the assumptions of the scholars doing the analysis of the overall benefits versus costs—finding either a drain on or gain of resources. Immigration costs are measured in public education, health, prisons and jails, the criminal justice system, state and local court systems, and assorted welfare services. These costs are assessed as a net drain on state and local governments. Critics of unauthorized immigration maintain that illegal aliens take jobs from native-born workers, especially blacks and other Hispanics. State governments, especially those in states with high percentages of foreign-born, argue—sometimes in federal courts—that federal immigration laws impose a huge financial burden upon them. Several states sued, unsuccessfully, in federal courts to require the federal government to refund the state government for the billions of dollars that, those states maintained, were saddled on the states due to the failure of the federal government to adequately control the nation's borders.

However, other scholars and studies dispute the burden argument, methods, and the way in which the cost-benefit ratio is measured. Advocates in favor of immigration contend that in the long run the United States benefits economically, culturally, and socially from immigration. Legal and unauthorized immigration brings workers who create wealth. They point out that the United States benefits from the "brain drain" effect wherein highly talented individuals with strong entrepreneurial spirits migrate from the developing nations to the United States, bringing with them their talents and hard-work ethic (i.e. human capital). They add to the labor force and, with their high birth rates, continue to add to the employee base upon which an increasingly aging native-born population depends for the solvency of the Social Security and Medicare systems.

The cost debate was thrust to center-stage national attention in 1993 when economist Donald Huddle completed a groundbreaking report for the Carrying Capacity Network, an environmental group concerned over rapid population growth. His study, the Net National Cost of Immigration, was the first attempt to systematically measure the cost-benefit ratio of immigration.[4] Huddle calculated that for every 100 unskilled immigrants who were working, 25 unskilled native-born workers were displaced. In his 1993 report, Huddle placed the net costs at $42.5 billion, and in 1997, he estimated that those costs had risen to $68 billion.

A 1994 Urban Institute study by Jeffrey Passel and Rebecca Clark, however, disputed Huddle's findings. They maintained that Huddle failed to account for the positive impact of immigrant businesses and consumer spending. They argued that Huddle had overstated costs and displacement effects, calculating that immigrants paid more than $70 billion in taxes, a whopping $50 billion above Huddle's estimates.[5]

Because different approaches to measuring the cost-benefit ratio use different assumptions in their calculations, it is difficult to assess which is more accurate. Their estimates of economic gains and losses differ substantially. The Government Accountability Office (GAO) issued a report in 1995 that examined three national studies of costs and benefits associated with undocumented immigrants (unauthorized immigrants such as visa overstayers were not included in any of the three studies examined by the GAO). The GAO concluded undocumented immigrants cost more than they generated in revenues to federal, state, and local governments. The GAO report found net costs ranged from $2 billion (Urban Institute) to about $19 billion (Huddle). The GAO found that the primary fiscal benefits are the positive impact on Medicare and Social Security systems and the Social Security Trust Fund.[6]

A 1998 study by Stephen Moore noted that undocumented immigrants using fraudulent Social Security numbers pay into the system through payroll withholding taxes collected, but since they are unauthorized, they cannot draw on those accounts when they reach age 65. This creates a one-generation windfall to the Social Security and Medicare systems that helps ease the financial hardship to the system by the baby-boom generation of about 40 million people who started collecting benefits in 2011. A 1998 Social Security Trust Fund Report estimated that immigrants, over the next 25, 50, and 75 years, would contribute on average $19.3 billion, $22.3 billion, and $25.8 billion, respectively, to the Social Security Trust Fund. Moore estimated that, in 1997, total immigrant income was $390 billion, generating $133 billion in taxes.[7]

In sharp contrast, George Borjas, a Cuban immigrant and professor of public policy at the John F. Kennedy School of Government at Harvard University, argues that immigration has a detrimental effect, claiming that the lower educational levels of immigrants mean that they will remain at an economic disadvantage that in the long run will result in a greater use of welfare. However, the National Research Council concluded that on balance, immigration (they measured legal immigration) had little negative effect on wages and job opportunities of most native-born Americans, and concluded that estimates of the costs to state and local taxpayers had been badly inflated. Another study, by Walter Ewing, concluded that immigrants, on average, paid $1,800 in taxes to state and local governments above what they cost in welfare services and benefits received. Ewing noted, however, that costs to state and local government are higher than costs to the federal level, as the states provide more of the social services and that state and local governments depend for a greater percentage of their revenues on property and sales taxes, whereas the federal government receives a greater percentage of its revenues from income taxes collected to a greater extent though payroll withholding.[8]

Those economic impact studies do not cover less tangible but positive impacts. For example, they do not measure the impact on the economy of immigrants who come as entrepreneurs. Immigrants founded 223 of the Fortune 500 companies. Those companies generated $6.1 trillion in revenue in 2019, and they employed 12.5 million people. An estimated 3.2 million immigrants are running their own companies—many small businesses that add to the diversity and therefore to the stability of local economies that are thereby less dependent on one or two big employers.

The federal Commission on Immigration Reform (CIR) was established in 1990 to study U.S. immigration policies. It was chaired by Representative Barbara Jordan (D-TX) and is often referred to as the Jordan Commission. It submitted a series of reports between 1994 and 1997, and the Commission made many recommendations to improve border control and to better cope with unauthorized immigration.

A related impact of the 1965 act in that regard was that the law spurred the establishment of several "think tank" organizations to study public policy, and immigration policy in particular. A think tank is an institute, corporation, or group organized to study a particular subject, such as a policy issue or a scientific problem, and to provide information, ideas, and advice to deal with it. Many such think tank organizations are nonprofits and nonpartisan organizations. Examples of such think tank organizations that study immigration policy include the following: the Border Policy Research Institute, founded in 2005; the Center for Immigration Studies, founded in 1985; the Center for Migration Studies, established in 1964; the Immigration History Research Center at the University of Minnesota, created in 1965; the Pew Hispanic Center, founded in 2001; and the Southern Poverty Law Center (SPLC), founded in 1971. The SPLC is an advocacy organization as well as one that studies and analyzes civil rights policy (including immigrant rights). Two of the oldest such think tanks that have produced groundbreaking studies of immigration are the Rand Corporation (founded in 1946), and the aforementioned Urban Institute (founded in 1912).

In part, the 1965 law and the changes it influenced on American society, led to the development of numerous immigration-related advocacy organizations. Table 3.1 lists 30 such organizations established after the 1965 law, and specifies the year in which they were founded.

Table 3.1 Immigration-Related Advocacy Organizations Established Post-1960

Name of Organization	Year
American Conservative Union	1973
American Immigration Control Foundation	1983
American Immigration Law Foundation	1987
Americans for Prosperity	2004
American Refugee Committee	1978
Americans for Legal Immigration PAC	2004
Association of Patriotic Arab-Americans in the Military	2001
Border Action Network	1999
Business Roundtable	1972
Catholic Legal Immigration Network, Inc.	1988
Center for American Progress	2003
Central American Refugee Center	1983
Federation for American Immigration Reform	1979
Freedom Works	1984
Heritage Foundation	1973
Humane Borders	2000
Human Rights First	1978
Mexican American Legal Defense and Education Fund	1968
Mothers Against Illegal Aliens	2006
MoveOn.org	1998
MRS, U.S. Conference of Catholic Bishops	1970
National Immigration Forum	1982
National Immigration Law Center	1979
National Network for Immigrant and Refugee Rights	1986
No More Deaths	2004
Numbers USA	1996
Southern Poverty Law Center	1971
United Farm Workers	1965
United We Dream	2013
V-DARE	1999

Source: Table by author. Data from National Immigration Law Center, https://www.nilc.org/ get-involved/links/aro/natres/ (accessed 12/1/2019).

THE IMPACT ON URBAN AND METROPOLITAN AREAS OF THE UNITED STATES

The 1965 act continued immigration's impact on the urbanization of the United States begun just after the U.S. Civil War. In 1860, there were only 392 cities in the United States, of which only 58 were in the 10,000–25,000 population size range—small cities by today's standards. The total U.S. population in 1860 numbered just more than 31 million, of whom about 6 million—9 percent—were city dwellers. Among places categorized as cities in 1860, 6 were in the 100,000–250,000 range, 7 ranged between 50,000 and 100,000, and 19 were between 25,000 and 50,000 in population. In the 1860 census, New York was the first city, and at that time, the only city, to exceed one million in population. In the 1860 census, 13.2 percent of the population was foreign born.

A century later, in 1960, the foreign-born population numbered slightly more than 14 million and comprised 6.2 percent of the total U.S. population. The foreign-born were decidedly urban in residency. In the 1960 census there were more than 6,000 cities, and they contained 64 percent of the total U.S. population. Of those cities, five exceeded one million and had 9.6 percent of the total urban population. Sixteen cites were between 500,000 and 1,000,000 and comprised 6.2 percent of urbanites. There were 30 cities that ranged between 250,000 and 500,000, in which 6 percent of the urban population resided. There were 81 cities whose populations ranged between 100,000 and 250,000, comprising 6.5 percent of the urban population. In the 1960 census year, 201 cities ranged between 50,000 and 100,000, making up 7.7 percent of the urban population; 432 cities were between 25,000 and 50,000, and they contained 8.3 percent of the total urban population of just more than 125 million. There were 1,134 small cities ranging between 10,000 and 25,000 in population, in which 9.8 percent of the urban population resided. Cities between 5,000 and 10,000 in population numbered 1,394 and comprised 5.5 percent of the total urban population. Finally, 2,152 urban places achieved the size necessary to be defined as a city by the Census Bureau (that is, populated by more than 2,500); they comprised 4.2 percent of the urban population.[9]

By the 1970 census, the total urban population in the United States exceeded 149 million of the nation's total population of just more than 203 million. In 1970, 18,769 places qualified as urban—in which 73.5 percent of the nation's total population resided. There were eight cities in excess of one million in population, comprising 9.2 percent of the urban population. Cities ranging between 500,000 and one million in population numbered 20, and comprised 6.4 percent of the urbanites. There were 30 cities in the 250,000–500,000 size range, making up 5.1 percent of the total urban population. A total of 100 cities ranged in size from 100,000 to 250,000, and made up 7.0 percent of the total urban population. There were 240 cities between 50,000 and 100,000 in size, and made up 8.2 percent of the urban population. There were 520 cities that were 25,000 to 50,000 in size, making up 8.8 percent of the urbanites. There were 1,385 cities of 10,000 to 25,000, making up 10.5 percent of the urban population. Places of 2,500 to 5,000 numbered 1,839 in the 1970 census, comprising 6.4 percent of the urban population. Finally, places ranging in size between 2,500 and 5,000, officially city-sized, numbered 2,295 and 4.0 percent of the urban population.[10]

Net immigration between 1965 and 1980 grew by the following annual averages for the years as follows: 1965 to 1969, 419,000; 1970 to 1974, 359,000; and 1975 to 1979, 416,000. In the 1980 census, the foreign-born population numbered 14,079,900 and comprised 6.2 percent of the total U.S. population. Among those foreign born, 4,743,300 were born in Europe; 2,539,800 were from Asia; 842,900 were from Canada; 2,553,100 were from Central America, which includes 2,199,200 from Mexico; 1,258,000 from the Caribbean (including, for example, Cuba, Dominican Republic, Haiti, Jamaica, and Trinidad and Tobago); and 561,000 from South America (e.g. Argentina, Colombia, and Ecuador).[11]

In the decade 1991–2000, nearly 11 million legal immigrants arrived— more than in any previous decade. Senator Ted Kennedy had been correct about the short-term effects of the 1965 law, but woefully wrong as to its long-term impact. In 2001–2010, another 10 million legal immigrants settled in the United States, increasing the U.S. population by about 1 percent every year. As of the 2010 census, a quarter of the under-18 residents are immigrants or their children. According to a 2009 Pew

Hispanic Center study, 8 percent of all babies born in the United States were children whose parents included at least one who was of illegal immigrant status.

In the 2000 census, the top 10 gateway states had about eight million Mexican immigrants who comprised just over 86 percent of Mexican immigrants residing in the United States. In the 1990–1999 decade, new immigrants—both legal and unauthorized—disproportionately settled in urban America, profoundly shaping the diversity of cities and their cultural, social, and political life.

According to the 2010 American Community Survey (ACS) of the Census Bureau, the number of foreign-born in the United States was estimated to be nearly 40 million, or 13 percent of the total population. Immigrants from Latin America, the largest region of birth, comprised 53 percent of all foreign-born. Immigrants from Asia made up 28 percent of the foreign-born; versus 12 percent from Europe, 4 percent from Africa, 2 percent from North America, and less than 1 percent from Oceania. Among the 21.2 million foreign-born from Latin America, 11.7 million (or 55 percent) were born in Mexico. Of the total foreign-born population, 29 percent were born in Mexico.

Since 1970, Mexican and Central American immigrants, whether legal or unauthorized, have impacted the nation's metropolitan areas in particular. Hispanics continue to be one of the nation's fastest growing minorities. A mid-census report (in 2005) showed that Hispanics accounted for half of all the population growth in the United States from 2000 to 2005. Their political power is likewise growing, although it still lags far behind their potential power based on population numbers, which are concentrated. In 2004, nine states (Arizona, California, Florida, Colorado, New York, Texas, New Mexico, Illinois, and New Jersey) elected 96 percent of all Latino elected officials. As of that 2005 mid-census, those nine states had 82 percent of the total Latino population.[12] In their search for jobs, those migrants flocked to and are concentrated within metropolitan areas, contributing significantly to the growth of metropolitan America. This is illustrated in Table 3.2, which presents data on the top 25 metropolitan areas of the United States ranked by their percentage growth rate from 2000 to 2009. Note that most of these fast-growing (10 percent or greater)

Table 3.2   Top 25 Metropolitan Areas Ranked by Percentage Growth, 2000–2009

Rank	Metropolitan Area	Percent Growth
1	Raleigh-Cary, NC	41.2
2	Las Vegas, NV	38.3
3	Austin-Round Rock, TX	36.4
4	Phoenix-Mesa-Scottsdale, AZ	34.2
5	Charlotte-Gastonia-Concord, NC	31.2
6	Atlanta-Sandy Springs-Marietta, GA	28.9
7	Riverside-San Bernardino, CA	27.3
8	Orlando-Kissimmee, FL	26.6
9	Dallas-Fort Worth-Arlington, TX	24.9
10	Houston-Sugar Land-Baytown, TX	24.4
11	San Antonio, TX	21.1
12	Nashville-Davidson-Murfreesboro, TN	20.6
13	Sacramento-Arden Arcade-Roseville, CA	18.6
14	Jacksonville, FL	18.3
15	Denver-Aurora-Broomfield, CO	17.1
16	Portland-Vancouver-Beaverton, OR-WA	16.3
17	Tampa-St. Petersburg-Clearwater, FL	14.7
18	Washington-Arlington-Alexandria, DC-VA	14.2
19	Richmond, VA	12.9
20	Kansas City, KS-MO	12.6
21	Oklahoma City, OK	12.0
22	Seattle-Tacoma-Bellevue, WA	12.0
23	Columbus, OH	11.7
24	Miami-Fort Lauderdale-Pompano Beach, FL	10.8
25	Minneapolis-St. Paul, MN	10.1

Source: Table by author. Data from: https://www2.census.gov/library/publications/2011/compendia/statab/131ed/2012-statab.pdf, Table 21 (accessed 8/14/2018).

metropolitan areas are located in the "Sun Belt" states of the American South and Southwest, all with high concentrations of Hispanic populations.

Table 3.3 shows the top 25 states arrayed by percentage growth in their populations from 2000 to 2010. A few of these states will perhaps surprise the reader as to their rank by percentage growth during that decade, but remember, percentage change is on the prior census population for that state, and some of the smaller states had a much smaller base from which to measure the percentage change (e.g. Utah, Idaho, Wyoming, Arkansas, and South Dakota).

Finally, Table 3.4 presents the foreign-born in the 15 largest metropolitan areas, detailing their percentage of the total population of each specified metropolitan area, and the percentage of the foreign-born in those metropolitan areas who were born in Latin America, Asia, Africa, Europe, or elsewhere.

Of the nation's Hispanic population, 45 percent live in just 10 metropolitan areas, according to tabulations of the 2010 American Community Survey (ACS) by the Pew Hispanic Center. Among the top 60 metropolitan areas by Hispanic population, Hispanics are a majority in 13 metropolitan areas. Mexicans are by far the largest Hispanic-origin group in the United States, now comprising 65 percent of the total Hispanic population, and are the largest Hispanic-origin group in 50 of the 60 metropolitan areas, making up more than half of the Hispanic population in 46 of them; and in 33 of them, Mexicans are bigger than any other racial or ethnic group. Mexican immigrants have spread out from the gateway states since the 1960 census, but as Table 3.5 shows, they are still are heavily concentrated in gateway states. Table 3.5 shows the distribution of Mexican immigrants by state of residency, for selected states, for each decennial year from 1960 to 2000.

ELECTORAL IMPACT OF THE 1965 ACT

Ironically, the very concentration of the Hispanic population within U.S. urban and metropolitan areas has contributed to their less effective electoral power. Several scholars have documented that Hispanic voting power lags far behind their potential power, that is, as based

Table 3.3 Top 25 States Ranked by Percentage Change in Population, 2000–2010

State	Percentage Change, 2000–2010
Nevada	35.1
Arizona	24.6
Utah	23.8
Idaho	21.1
Texas	20.6
North Carolina	18.5
Georgia	18.3
Florida	17.6
Colorado	16.9
South Carolina	15.3
Delaware	14.6
Washington	14.1
Wyoming	14.1
Alaska	13.3
New Mexico	13.2
Virginia	13.0
Hawaii	12.3
Oregon	12.0
Tennessee	11.5
California	10.0
Montana	9.7
National Average	**9.7**
Arkansas	9.1
Maryland	9.0
Oklahoma	8.7
South Dakota	7.9

Source: Table by author, adapted from data online at: https://www.census.gov/library/publications/2011, Table 14 (accessed 8/14/2018).

Table 3.4 The Foreign-Born in the 15 Largest Metropolitan Areas in the United States, 2010, Percent of Total: Latin America, Asia, Africa, Europe, Other

Metropolitan Area	Percent of Total	Latin America	Asia	Africa	Europe	Other
Miami	38.8	86.8	5.0	0.9	5.7	1.6
Los Angeles	34.3	56.4	35.6	1.6	5.1	1.4
San Francisco	30.0	31.6	53.7	1.8	9.8	3.1
New York	28.8	51.0	27.4	3.8	16.7	1.1
Houston	22.3	66.6	23.9	3.9	4.5	1.2
Washington, D.C.	21.8	40.0	35.4	13.9	9.2	1.2
Chicago	17.6	48.6	25.5	2.3	23.6	1.0
Dallas	17.5	64.4	24.1	5.7	4.6	1.2
Boston	16.8	38.4	31.1	8.0	19.4	3.1
Seattle	16.8	20.9	49.8	6.4	16.6	6.3
Phoenix	14.4	64.2	19.3	3.3	9.1	4.2
Atlanta	13.5	51.7	27.6	9.5	9.2	2.0
Philadelphia	9.5	30.1	40.3	7.8	19.9	2.0
Minneapolis	9.5	25.6	39.0	21.4	10.8	3.3
Detroit	8.6	14.5	50.4	3.1	25.2	6.8

Source: U.S. Census Bureau, 2010 Community Survey.

on their numbers within the population. Reported Hispanic voting typically is about half the rate of white reported voting, rising or declining depending on whether the election takes place in presidential or midterm congressional years. Table 3.6 illustrates that pattern. It presents reported voting data for elections from 1972 to 2004, comparing the Hispanic vote with the white vote in each presidential or congressional election year.

Since 1964, the U.S. Census Bureau has fielded the Voting and Registration Supplement to the Current Population Survey every two years. In 2016, 61.4 percent of the citizen voting-age population reported voting, as

Table 3.5   Distribution of Mexican Immigrants by State of Residency, 1960–2000

Gateway State	1960	1970	1980	1990	2000
Arizona	6.3	4.5	3.3	3.7	2.6
California	41.9	52.7	57.0	62.9	35.4
Illinois	4.8	6.2	7.7	4.9	6.1
New Mexico	1.8	0.8	0.8	0.9	0.8
Texas	35.9	26.5	22.6	14.9	16.4
All Other States	9.4	9.4	8.5	12.8	35.3

Source: Table by author. Data from Table 6.1 in Michael C. LeMay, *Illegal Immigration* (Santa Barbara, CA: ABC-CLIO, 2007), 170.

did 61.8 percent in 2012. In 2016, for only the second time since the Census Bureau has reported on the matter, non-Hispanic black votes decreased from 12.9 percent in 2012 to 11.9 percent in 2016. Hispanic voting continued to be approximately half of the white reported voting in 2016.

Table 3.7 presents the results of the 2016 presidential election. It details the percentage of the vote won by the two major party candidates from various population demographic groups as measured by *New York Times* exit polls. It demonstrates that Democrat Hillary Clinton won the "minority" vote—blacks, Latinos, Asians, Jewish voters—by super majorities, ranging from 65 percent to 88 percent. As those demographic groups become an ever-larger percentage of the population, and as immigrant groups such as Hispanics and Asians increasingly naturalize, register, and turn out to vote, they may well portend a dramatic shift in the relative power positions between the two major political parties in the United States. In the past, such ethnic group loyalty and partisan affiliation has been shown to last for a generation (two decades or more).

By 2040, the United States may well go the way of California in terms of political party affiliation. In 1994, California was a two-party competitive state with the Republicans dominating the statewide offices and Governor Pete Wilson leading the campaign to pass the "Save Our State" initiative, Proposition 187. He won his reelection, and the initiative won handily. It proved to be a Pyrrhic victory, however, as his and the Republican Party's stand on the issue of immigration and

Table 3.6   Hispanic versus White Electoral Percentages, 1972–2004

Year	Hispanic Reported Voting	White Reported Voting
1972	37.4%	64.5%
1974	22.9%	46.3%
1976	31.8%	60.9%
1978	23.5%	47.3%
1980	29.9%	60.9%
1982	25.3%	47.3%
1984	32.6%	61.4%
1986	24.2%	47.0%
1988	28.8%	59.1%
1990	21.0%	46.7%
1992	28.9%	63.6%
1994	20.2%	47.3%
1996	26.7%	56.0%
1998	20.0%	43.3%
2000	45.1%	60.5%
2002	18.9%	44.1%
2004	28.0%	60.3%

Source: Table by author, adapted from Table 4.1, LeMay, *The Perennial Struggle*, 3ed, 2009: 150. Data from Louise Honor, ed., *Hispanic Americans: A Statistical Sourcebook* (Palo Alto, CA: Information Publications, 2002) 94–103; and updated to 2004 from the *Statistical Abstract of the United States, 2006*, Table 405: 263.

especially Hispanic immigration into the state alienated an entire generation of voters who considered Wilson and his party "anti-immigrant, anti-Hispanic." It cost them dearly in the long run. Their stand was clearly on the wrong side of history. Hispanic and Asian voters grew increasingly numerous, activated, registered—and they voted for the Democrats. The Republican Party's campaign to pass Proposition 187 turned the state into the bluest of blue states. By the 2010 census, California's total population was 40 million. The native-born comprised 73 percent of the population, and the foreign-born

Table 3.7   Election Results, Clinton versus Trump, by Assorted Groups

Group	Clinton	Trump
White	37%	58%
Black	88%	8%
Hispanic/Latino	65%	29%
Asian	65%	29%
Other	56%	37%
Protestant	39%	58%
Catholic	45%	52%
Jewish	71%	24%
White Evangelicals	16%	81%

Source: https://www.nytimes.com/interactive/2016/11/08/us/politics/election-exit-polls.html (accessed 8/18/2018).

27 percent. Whites split their votes, but the foreign-born went overwhelmingly Democratic. In the 2016 presidential election, for example, Democrat Hillary Clinton won 61.5 percent of the vote and took all 55 of the state's Electoral College votes, to Trump's 31.5 percent of the vote. Democrats took the U.S. Senate seat (Kamala Harris) and 39 U.S. House seats to the Republicans' 14. In the California Senate, Democrats held 16 seats to the Republicans' 4; and in the State Assembly, there were 55 Democrats to the Republicans' 25. Things only got worse for the Republicans in the 2018 midterm elections. All the major statewide executive offices were won by Democrats. In the California State Senate, there were 29 Democrats to 11 Republicans; and in the State Assembly, 61 Democrats to 18 Republicans (with one vacant seat).[13]

Perhaps President Donald Trump's immigration policies (for example, to build the wall, to expel historic numbers of immigrants using expedited removal, to separate children from their parents who entered at the border seeking asylum and were met with "zero tolerance," and to attacks on sanctuary cities) will turn an entire generation of today's immigrants and their children against the Republican Party, as did Governor Pete Wilson in California as a result of Proposition 187.

As the numbers of the foreign-born in the population reach the pro-jected 18.8 percent of the population level by 2050, they well may reject the Republican Party so solidly as to relegate it to minority party status. If that comes to pass, then President Trump's 2016 win will be as Pyrrhic a victory as was Governor Wilson's in California in 1994.

THE EXPONENTIAL RISE IN UNAUTHORIZED AND UNDOCUMENTED IMMIGRANTS—THE APPARENT INABILITY TO CONTROL THE U.S. BORDERS

The number of persons crossing the U.S. borders without authorization began to swell after 1970, from about an estimated quarter million in 1970 to nearly 1 million in 1980, to nearly 2 million in 1986. The SCIRP report placed the number of illegal immigrants then resident in the United States at between 3.5 million and 6 million. Hispanics, especially those from Mexico and Central America, made up the bulk of those without papers. SCIRP estimated that about two-thirds of the undocumented immigrants were from Mexico, driven north by grinding poverty and enor-mous unemployment. Many who came had been temporary workers during the Bracero Program years, or were relatives or compatriots of those who had come at that time. Mexicans comprised about 60 percent of Hispanic immigrants and tended to come from rural and small town areas in Mexico. They typically exhibited a sojourner attitude, residing close to their native areas and often returning to their places of origin, thereby keeping strong family, social, and cultural ties. They came from near feudal societies. Those who often moved back and forth saw the border as more of a nuisance than a barrier.

Estimates of their numbers vary considerably and are best viewed as "guesstimates," since persons here illegally do not identify themselves for fear of deportation. Their numbers are most often estimated on the basis of apprehensions at the border. Illegal aliens rose from about 3.2 million in 1986 to 9.3 million in 2002. Nearly two-thirds of them resided in six states: California (27 percent), Texas (13 percent), New York (8 percent), Florida (7 percent), Illinois (6 percent), and New Jersey (4 percent). In 2005, the Pew Center for Hispanic Studies esti-mated that the total numbers of unauthorized immigrants was between 10.5 million and 11 million.

Table 3.8 Estimated Total Legal Immigrants versus Apprehensions at the U.S. Border versus Mexican Undocumented Immigrant Apprehensions at the Border, 2000–2013

Year	Total Legal Immigrants	Total Apprehensions	Mexican Apprehensions
2000	849,807	1,678,438	1,636,883
2001	1,064,318	1,266,214	1,224,047
2002	1,059,902	955,310	917,993
2003	703,542	931,557	882,012
2004	957,883	1,106, 395	1,086,006
2005	1,122,373	1,189,075	1,023,905
2006	1,266,129	1,089,092	981,066
2007	1,052,415	876,704	808,688
2008	1,107,126	723,825	661,766
2009	1,120,818	556,041	503,386
2010	1,042,625	439,382	404,385
2011	1,062,040	340,252	286,154
2012	1,031,631	364,765	265,755
2013	990,553	420,789	267,734

Source: Table by author, adapted from Michael C. LeMay, *Illegal Immigration,* 2nd ed. (Santa Barbara, CA: ABC-CLIO, 2015), 220. Data from DHS, 2011, Yearbook of Immigration Statistics, Washington, DC: Department of Homeland Security and 2011–2014 annual reports, online at: http://www.dhs.gov/sites/default/files/publications/ois.

Table 3.8 details a picture of the legal immigrants compared to the total illegal immigrant apprehensions at the southern border and Mexican undocumented immigrants among the total apprehensions at the border. Many estimates of the undocumented assess that for every person apprehended at the border, two to three more enter, that is, are not apprehended.

As the undocumented immigrant numbers rose steadily over the years since 2000, political pressure increased to crack down at the borders and, in order to do so, to increase the number of border patrol agents in the DHS. As Table 3.9 shows, however, there is close to an inverse

Table 3.9 Total Illegal Apprehensions by Fiscal Year, 2000–2017, Compared to the Total Number of Border Patrol Agents

Year	Total Apprehensions	Total Number of Agents
2000	1,643,679	9,212
2001	1,235,718	9,821
2002	929,809	10,045
2003	905,065	10,717
2004	1,139,282	10,819
2005	1,171,396	11,264
2006	1,071,396	12,439
2007	858,638	14,923
2008	705,005	17,499
2009	540,085	20,119
2010	447,731	20,058
2011	327,577	21,444
2012	356,873	21,394
2013	414,397	21,391
2014	479,371	20,863
2015	331,333	20,273
2016	408,870	19,828
2017	303,916	19,437

Source: USBP Southwest Border-Apps: FY 1960–FY 2017, and BP Staffing FY 1992–2017, Border Patrol Agents by Fiscal Year, https://www.cpb.gov/newsroom/media-resources/stats? title=border (accessed 7/6/2018).

relationship between apprehensions at the borders and the number of Border Patrol agents between 2000 and 2017. As can be seen in Table 3.8, in 2000 there were 1,633,679 apprehensions when the Border Patrol had 9,212 agents. By 2017, the number of apprehensions actually fell, to 303,916, an eightfold decrease, even as the number of Border Patrol agents increased to 19,437, or an increase of more than 300 percent.

The exponential rise in border apprehensions of undocumented immigrants since 1970 led to a pervasive sense in the public and among members of Congress that the nation had lost control of its borders. As shown in Table 3.8, Mexicans dominated the undocumented immigrant flow, but it is interesting to note that in 2014, non-Mexicans (mostly Central Americans) exceeded Mexican border crossers apprehended that year. The need to fix the illegal immigrant problem dominated immigration policymaking from 1980 to 1984 and influenced the 1984 presidential election and President Reagan's landslide victory of 525 Electoral College votes and 58.8 percent of the popular vote. Illegal immigration and the need to "regain control of the borders" played an important role in the 1984 election. The sense that control of the border was lost was perhaps the strongest factor leading to adoption of the employer sanctions approach in the Immigration Reform and Control Act (IRCA) of 1986, which, as discussed, marked the beginning of the Revolving Door era of immigration policy, 1986 to 2001.

However, the failure of the employer sanctions device to effectively control the illegal immigration flow, where apprehensions at the border dipped only slightly after IRCA and by 1990 were back up to pre-IRCA levels, led to the sense among Republican members of Congress that the amnesty program of IRCA simply drew more undocumented immigrants. Since 1990, Republicans in Congress and the Republican Party more generally have been adamant in their opposition to any legalization program, which they label as amnesty (the Democrats refer to it as "earned legalization.") That opposition was only strengthened after the terrorist attacks of September 11, 2001. The failure of the INS to control the borders was viewed as a major factor in the attacks, and the agency was blamed for

Table 3.10 Unaccompanied Children Apprehended by the U.S. Border Patrol at the Southwest Border, FY 2014

Country	Number of UAC	Percentage of Total UAC
El Salvador	16,404	24.36
Guatemala	17,057	25.3
Honduras	18,244	27.09
Mexico	15,634	23.21
Total	67,339	100

Source: https://www.cbp.gov/newsroom/stats/southwest-border-unaccompanied-children/fy-2014, published November 24, 2015 (accessed 3/30/2018).

Table 3.11   Pew Research Center Immigration-Related Public Opinion Polling Data, 2018

Granting Permanent Legal Status to DACA Children—Dreamers

	Percent Opposed	Percent in Favor
Total	21	74
Republican/Lean Republican	40	50
Democrat/Lean Democrat	6	92
Men	47	47
Women	33	54
18- to 49-Year-Olds	34	57
50+-Year-Olds	45	45
College Graduates	36	58
Non-College Graduates	42	48
Conservatives	44	46
Moderates/Liberals	35	58

Building a Wall on the Southwest U.S.-Mexico Border

Total	60	37
Republican/Lean Republican	24	67
Democrat/Lean Democrat	85	13
Men	20	77
Women	29	67
18- to 49-Year-Olds	36	60
50+-Year-Olds	14	83
College Graduates	24	74
Non-College Graduates	24	72
Conservative	17	81
Moderates/Liberals	40	55

Source: https://www.pewresearch.org/fact-tank/2018/01/19/public-backs-legal-status-for-immigrants-brought-to-u-s-illegally-as-children-but-not-a-bigger-border-wall/ (accessed 4/6/2018).

letting the hijackers into the country. The INS was among the agencies merged into the Department of Homeland Security (DHS) by the Homeland Security Act of 2002. Title IV, Section 402 of the act transferred responsibilities from the INS within the Department of Justice (DOJ) to the newly created DHS.

Another notable development in recent years has been the vexing problem of children who come across the U.S. southern border unaccompanied by an adult (UAC). Although this problem is commonly perceived as a Mexican migration problem, in point of fact, UAC from Mexico are actually the lowest in numbers and as a percent of total UAC. More such children are from the Central American nations of El Salvador, Guatemala, and Honduras. Those coming from Central America cross the border illegally into Mexico and then proceed from its southern border to the north, to reach the U.S. border with Mexico. They do so in two ways: walking in caravans of hundreds to even thousands of persons; and some traveling on "the Beast," the nickname for a freight train that travels from south to north across Mexico, and on top of which many unauthorized immigrants ride in a perilous journey. They reach the border in the hope to cross, again illegally as undocumented migrants, into the United States. A snapshot of the issue, and the relative UAC numbers coming from Mexico versus children from Central America, is detailed in Table 3.10, which presents the numbers of UAC from those countries, and their percentage of the total UAC.

Not surprisingly, public opinion polling on immigration reform varies among voters depending on a number of characteristics of voters and on the polling source. Table 3.11 presents data from a 2018 poll by the Pew Research Center on two immigration reform issues: support for a Dreamer Act, and support for or opposition to the building of a border wall.

THE INCREASING RELIGIOUS DIVERSITY OF THE UNITED STATES

Another effect of the 1965 act and the tens of millions of immigrants who have entered the United States since its enactment has been a dramatic increase in the religious diversity of the nation. The United States is arguably the most religiously diverse nation-state in the world. As we have seen, the 1965 act shifted the source of immigrants from Western Europe

Table 3.12   Religious Diversity in America as Seen in the 2010 Census Data

Religious Group	Number/2010 Census	Percentage in 2010 Census
Total U.S. Population	308,745,538	100.0%
Evangelical Protestant	50,013,107	16.2
Mainline Protestant	22,568,258	7.3
Black Protestant	4,877,067	1.6
Catholic	20,800,000	23.0
Mormon	10,600,000	2.9
Jehovah's Witnesses	800,000	0.02
Eastern Orthodox	500,000	0.016
Other Christian	400,000	0.012
Jewish	6,141,325	2.0
Muslim	2,600,000	0.08
Buddhist	2,000,000	0.07
Hindu	400,000	0.01

Source: Table by author. Data from 2010 census, https://www.census.gov/2010census.

to Latin America, the Caribbean, Africa, and Asia. The post-1970 immigrants brought a new array of denominational and religious affiliations. Some of those affiliations have been considered "cults" or "sects" by the majority native stock (the so-called White Anglo Saxon Protestants, or WASPs). A quick overview of American religious diversity can be seen in Tables 3.12 and 3.13, which array data on religious group affiliation as self-identified by respondents in the 2010 census or the Pew Research Center's Religious Landscape Study in 2010.

Many people among the majority Protestant denominations considered the new immigrants affiliating with nontraditional Protestant or non-Christian belief communities to belong to "cults." Those minority religious groups experienced various forms and degrees of discrimination, compounding anti-ethnic or antiracial prejudices with anti-immigrant sentiment. Sabbatarian groups (such as Seventh Day Baptists, Seventh Day Adventists, the Church of God, and Judaism) hold that the Sabbath (Shabbat in Judaism) must be observed on Saturday as their holy day.

Table 3.13   Religious Landscape Study, U.S. Religious Diversity, 2010

Religious Denomination/Group	Percentage of U.S. Population, 2010
Christians	70.6
Evangelical Protestant	25.4
Mainline Protestant	14.7
Historically Black Protestant	6.5
Catholic	20.8
Mormon	1.6
Orthodox Christian	0.5
Jehovah's Witnesses	0.8
Other Christians	0.4
Non-Christian Faiths	6.9
Jewish	1.9
Muslim	0.9
Buddhist	0.7
Hindu	0.7
Other World Religions	1.5
Unaffiliated (Religious "Nones")	22.8
Atheist	3.1
Agnostic	4.1
Nothing in Particular	15.8

Source: Table by author. Data from the 2010 census and the Pew Research Center, Religious Landscape Study. Retrieved from: www.pewforum.org/religious-landscape-study.

Mainline Protestants, Catholics, and Orthodox Christians observe Sunday as the holy day. When prejudice is compounded, it is not only stronger, it is more resistant to change. One can argue that President Trump's compounding anti-Muslim with anti-immigrant rhetoric exacerbates prejudices against both.

Discrimination based on religion is not as prevalent in the United States as it was in Europe, and many groups fled to the United States to escape persecution, such as the Hasidic Jews fleeing pogroms in

Russia and Eastern Europe in the late nineteenth and early twentieth centuries. A number of Supreme Court cases concerned challenges to local ordinances or state laws, known as the "blue laws," over the constitutionality of such laws. Protections afforded by the free exercise and establishment clauses of the First Amendment were invoked in those suits by such religious groups as the Amish, Mennonites, Jehovah's Witnesses, Baha'i, Muslims, Seventh Day Adventists, Hare Krishna, Black Muslims, Hasidic Jews, and Rastafarians.[14]

A good example of such a case is the 8–1 Supreme Court decision in *Lemon v. Kurtzman* (403 U.S. 602, 1971). In it the court provided what came to be known as the *Lemon* test as to when a state or local law passed the constitutional line against establishment. *Lemon* concerned a local government, a school district, and whether it could use public money from the Pennsylvania Nonpublic Elementary and Secondary Education Act (1968) to fund educational programs that taught religion-based lessons, activities, and studies. The case is considered a landmark one because it set the precedent for many subsequent decisions. *Lemon* stipulated a three-point test that has since 1971 been applied to virtually all such cases in which public policy action by state or local government is constitutionally challenged on the basis of the establishment clause. The *Lemon* test asks: (1) Did the law have a secular purpose? (2) Was the law neutral on religion, neither advancing nor inhibiting religion? And (3) did the law not favor an excessive government entanglement in religion? In *Lemon*, the court decided that the Pennsylvania law was an unconstitutional violation of the establishment clause.[15] It reached a similar conclusion in 1973 in the *Nyquist* case (413 U.S. 756). These free exercise of religion and establishment clause cases set precedent that protected discrimination against immigrant groups espousing these minority religious beliefs and practices.

Occasionally, state laws—and more often local ordinances—have set aside Sunday as a day of rest prohibiting certain stores to be open to sell their wares, thereby requiring employees to work on the Sabbath or discriminating against those members of a religious faith who celebrate Saturday as their Sabbath day. A number of cases have challenged these laws, brought to the courts by members of the Jewish faith, by Seventh Day Adventists, and by Jehovah's Witnesses. In *Thornton v. Caldor* (472 U.S. 703, 1985), the Court decided 8–1 that private companies are free to fire

Table 3.14   Charges of Religious-Based Discrimination, 2000–2016

Year	Complaints Received
2000	1,939
2001	2,127
2002	2,572
2003	2,532
2004	2,466
2005	2,340
2006	2,541
2007	2,880
2008	3,273
2009	3,386
2010	3,790
2011	4,151
2012	3,811
2013	3,721
2014	3,549
2015	3,502
2016	3,825

Source: Table by author. Data from Religious-based charges, FY 1979–FY 2018, U.S. Equal Employment Opportunity Commission, https://www.eeoc.gov/eeoc/statistics/enforcement/religion.cfm (accessed 12/1/2019).

people who refuse to work on any day they claim to be their Sabbath because the First Amendment applies only to government, not to private employers.

The Court had to decide two cases in which the conflict was between two sacred First Amendment rights: free exercise of religion versus free speech. In R.A.V. v. City of St. Paul (505 U.S. 377, 1992) the Supreme Court held that "hate speech" was protected free speech when the court unanimously struck down a St. Paul, Minnesota, ordinance that proscribed cross burning as a hate crime. Writing the majority opinion for the Court, Justice Antonin Scalia found the ordinance "an unconstitutional content-based regulation of speech."[16]

Table 3.15   Religious-Related Hate Crime Statistics, 2015

Religion	Incidents	Offenses
Anti-Jewish	664	695
Anti-Catholic	53	59
Anti-Protestant	37	47
Anti-Islamic	257	301
Anti-Other Religion	96	104
Anti-Multiple Religions	51	57
Anti-Mormon	8	8
Anti-Jehovah's Witnesses	1	1
Anti-Orthodox	46	50
Anti-Other Christian	15	18
Anti-Buddhist	1	1
Anti-Hindu	5	5
Anti-Sikh	6	6
Anti-Atheist	2	2

Source: Table by author. Data from FBI Statistics, 2015, retrieved from: https://ucr.fbi.gov/
hate-crime/2015/tables-and-data-declarations/1tabledatadecpdf.

Finally, there is the problem of a conflict between religious belief and practice that involved the ritual sacrifice of animals (in this case, chickens). In the case of *Church of Lukumi Babalu Aye, Inc. v. City of Hialeah* (508 U.S. 520, 1993), Justice Anthony Kennedy delivered the unanimous opinion of the court. The Yoruba people were brought as slaves to Cuba, and they brought with them practices of the Santeria religion. Descendants of these enslaved people were among refugees and immigrants who came to the United States, and they continued to practice Santeria there. The Church of Lukumi Babalu Aye was a small Santeria sect in Hialeah, Florida. The court ruled that the city may not enact laws that suppress religious belief or practices, enacted by city officials who did not understand, failed to perceive, or chose to ignore that fact that their official actions violated the nation's essential commitment to religious freedom.[17]

Minority religions, which so often have been brought to the United States by immigrants and refugees, particularly refugees from religious persecution in their nations of origin, have also been the target of religious-based discrimination in the United States. Table 3.14, for example, lists the number of complaints about religious-based discrimination investigated by the Equal Employment Opportunity Commission (EEOC). The table details that from 2000 to 2016, the EEOC received annually 2,000 to nearly 4,000 such complaints that it investigated.

Similarly, Table 3.15 presents FBI data on reported religious-based hate crime incidents and offenses that occurred in 2015.

FEAR OF NATURAL PANDEMIC DISEASES ENTERING THE UNITED STATES WITH IMMIGRANTS

Microscopic agents of disease—germs and viruses—are silent fellow travelers that accompany humans as they migrate. We cannot prevent their migration as humans travel from place to place. Medical science has shown that when natural agents of disease—pathogens—migrate to new areas and essentially confront a new and "virgin" population (one with little or no immunity), they can cause epidemics with severe morbidity and mortality rates. They can become killers on a grand scale (the Flu Pandemic of 1918–1919 took an estimated 50 million lives worldwide).[18] The speed and ease with which humans travel today means that human carriers of disease can quickly spread infection across wide expanses. Oceans are no barriers in the day of jetliner traffic. At best, medical science can only react to their spread to lessen the duration and intensity of epidemic outbreaks to hopefully prevent them from becoming pandemics. Immigration policymakers and implementers can reduce the morbidity and mortality rates of epidemic outbreaks, but they cannot prevent them from occurring. The AIDS and Ebola pandemics proved that point.

Many of the newly emerging pathogens with the potential to cause pandemics likely have jumped from animals, primates for instance, to humans. An estimated 20 percent of all major infectious diseases began in primates. Viruses can leap between species when bodily fluids are shared, as when one animal hunts, kills, and eats another. Then the virus mutates and can make the leap from animals to humans. Hunters of wild animals (known as bush meat hunters) are essentially sentinel populations regarding primate retroviruses that make the jump from primates to humans. HIV began in monkeys in Africa, and the first humans contracted HIV by butchering infected chimps. Similarly, SARS began in China, among bats, infected cats sold in markets, and jumped from civet cats to humans, and soon was spread by air travel to more than 25 countries, including to the United States. As humans increasingly clear forests and expand ever deeper into what was once unexplored wilderness, they expose themselves to new animals and their microbes. Once a virus, especially the newly emerging viruses for which we have no immunities or effective vaccines, reaches and begins to spread in cities, especially highly populated ones, it is difficult to ring it off and stop its spread. The 2014–2015 Ebola pandemic began in West Africa once it spread to major cities, from which it spread to neighboring countries; and a couple of cases were brought to the United States by immigrants or by U.S. medical personnel who were combating the Ebola pandemic. Likewise, Middle East respiratory syndrome (MERS) began in Saudi Arabia in 2012, likely jumping from camels to humans. It is now found in 23 countries, most recently to South Korea, and in 2015 it spread to Thailand, likely brought there by an air traveler. Such diseases can easily travel from abroad to the United States among immigrants who are infected but not yet symptomatic. The incubation periods of many virus-based diseases are longer than the international travel times of migrants. Their spread is therefore difficult to control. Epidemic outbreaks become increasingly difficult to contain from spreading and more difficult to cure once a person has been infected.

Viruses mutate at an even greater rate than do germs, and epidemiologists warn a pandemic on the scale of the great influenza pandemic of 1918–1919 may well be inevitable. Of particular concern with respect to the high rate of unauthorized (and therefore of persons neither screened nor inspected at the borders) is the potential for international terrorist organizations to intentionally spread infectious diseases as agents of bioterrorism. Smallpox is considered to be the most dangerous of the top 50 bioweapon pathogens, only 13 of which have any vaccines or treatments. Today, virtually the entire U.S. population is virgin soil.

FEAR OF THE DANGER POSED BY INTERNATIONAL TERRORISM

The "war" on terrorism declared by the George W. Bush administration after the September 11, 2001, attacks engaged the United States in global conflict. Alan Cranston described it as a war about sovereignty after the first attack on the World Trade Center in 1993:

> The bombing of the World Trade Center in New York was a direct and ominous import into our country of terrorism creating so much havoc elsewhere, carried out by militant and fanatic Islamic fundamentalists in retaliation for various perceived grievances including our intervention in the sovereignty struggles of the Middle East. Its toll was six dead, 1,000 injured. There are dark warnings of events to come as terrorists proclaim that they will wage a holy war against the United States and its citizens wherever they may be as long as we keep our "infidel" forces in Islamic lands in what they view as an irreverent violation of their sacrosanct sovereignty by the Great Satan.[19]

The attacks of September 11, 2001, on New York and Washington, D.C., clearly demonstrated that international terrorists can strike almost anytime and anywhere. The nature of the threat is clear: "Terrorism will remain a threat to Americans at home and abroad. But even as the United States engages in isolated strikes against terrorists and their sponsors, it will also fortify the homeland and reign in its overseas commitments in an attempt to cordon itself off from such threats."[20]

The continued influx of both legal and unauthorized immigrants raised fears of international terrorists entering the United States through the porous borders, and led the federal government to pressure state and local law enforcement agencies toward taking a more active role in immigration enforcement. ICE is stretched thin; for example, it had 200 agents to cover all of Colorado, Idaho, Montana, and Wyoming in 2018. And ICE agents are responsible for more than immigration control. They are responsible for child pornography, money laundering, and narcotics as well as human smuggling. With an estimated 10 million to 11 million unauthorized immigrants in the United States by 2018 estimates, ICE finds itself at loggerheads. Their failure or inability to respond promptly when local governments do call regarding apprehended unauthorized immigrants contribute to the problems local law enforcement localities have with increasing their involvement. Local law enforcement agencies often lack the funds, their officers lack the training, and their detention facilities lack the resources to hold undocumented immigrants for more than a few nights. Anything longer than that becomes onerous.

Los Angeles and Orange County, California, have reached agreements with federal agencies like ICE and CBP to get the training for their officers and are reviewing the citizenship status of inmates and those being held for criminal investigations for felony crimes. Florida and Alabama have also entered into such agreements to train members of their state patrols to identify and detain undocumented drivers. Bills proposed to force local governments to enforce civil immigration laws have been unsuccessful in part because groups such as the National League of Cities and a number of self-designated "sanctuary cities" have lobbied against those bills as being unfunded mandates and that such laws, if enacted, would divert local resources to federal obligations.

The drivers' license reform law (called the Real ID Act) and the zero-tolerance policy directives of the Trump administration, which have involved incarceration of refugees and asylum-seekers that have entered the United States without authorization, have raised constitutional issues. Some critics fear such laws and policies raise the bar for persons seeking asylum from religious and political persecution, and grant to the secretary of homeland security and the attorney general unprecedented powers to circumvent the judicial branch in matters pertaining to border security. They fear that rather than closing the door to those who would exploit our asylum laws to do harm, it will more likely close the door on real refugees fleeing political and religious persecution or excessive gang violence precisely when the United States needs allies in the fight against international terrorism.

Building the nearly 700-mile fence along the southern border—the so-called "border wall"—has induced undocumented immigrants to try crossing elsewhere—through Arizona, Texas, and New Mexico, for example, where the climate and terrain are more dangerous, and led to several hundred deaths in 2018 and 2019. The zero-tolerance policy is directly linked to five deaths of children seeking asylum in 2019 alone. The increased enforcement to control undocumented immigration via the Patriot Acts I and II have raised concerns among civil libertarians that the laws' targeting of some amount to racial profiling, and that some minorities become "suspects" merely because of their looks or names. ICE has been using expedited removal to deport unauthorized immigrants on new historic levels. The increased efforts to "control the borders" have led to detaining increasing numbers in makeshift detention camps and exacerbated the effort to cope with the problems of the "Dreamer" and of children unaccompanied by an adult (UAC), immigrants who arrive without authorization, largely from Mexico and Central America.

CONCLUSION: PROJECTIONS OF THE 1965 ACT INTO THE FUTURE

The Immigration and Nationality Act of 1965 had significant short-term and long-term impacts on American society—on its culture, on its ethnic and racial demographic composition, on its economy, on its urban and metropolitan residency patterns, on electoral politics, on the exponential rise in unauthorized immigration, on its religious diversity, on the dangers of natural pandemic disease outbreaks, and on the threat of international terrorism.

Moreover, immigration law and policy are unlikely to change the basic trends in the numbers and percentage of immigrants in the United States projected out to 2060. As the history of U.S. immigration shows, trends in immigration are more powerfully influenced by "push" factors propelling international migration than they are by laws and policies aimed at "pull" factors. The United States is already the nation-state that has received the largest number of immigrants than any other nation-state in the world, and nearly as many as the other major receiving nation-states combined. In addition to the absolute numbers, projections by the U.S. Census Bureau indicate that the immigrant percentage of the total U.S. population will continue to rise, from the current 14.3 percent to a projected 18 percent by 2050, and 18.8 percent by 2060. The "browning" of America will continue, and the nation will be a minority-majority country by about 2050. Past history, however, shows that American society can readily absorb and incorporate such large numbers of immigrants, perhaps not without problems and concerns, but clearly with remarkable ability to do so. In that process, the United States will continue to be an immigrant nation and a nation of immigrants, as it has proved itself since its inception, or will choose to be a different people with a different promise.

NOTES

1. *Congressional Record*, 89th Congress, 1st Session, 1965, Vol. III, pt. 18: 24225–29.

2. Kennedy, cited in Michael C. LeMay and Elliott Robert Barkan, eds., *U.S. Immigration and Naturalization Laws and Issues: A Documentary History* (Westport, CT: Greenwood Press, 1999), 253.

3. Bureau of the Census, *Statistical Abstract of the United States, 1980, Part 2 —Population*, online at: https://www.census.gov/library/publications/1980/compendia/statistical-abstract-of-the-United-States/101ed.html (accessed 8/13/2018).

4. Don Huddle, *The Cost of Immigration* (Washington, DC: Carrying Capacity Network, 1993).

5. Jeffrey Passel and Rebecca L. Clark, *How Much Do Immigrants Really Cost?* (Washington, DC: The Urban Institute, 1994).

6. Government Accountability Office. *Illegal Aliens: National Cost Estimates Vary Widely* (Washington, DC: U.S. Government Printing Office, 1995).

7. Stephen Moore, *A Fiscal Portrait of the Newest Americans* (Washington, DC: Immigration Forum and the CATO Institute, 1998); and Social Security Trust Fund. *Board of Trustees Report* (Washington, DC: SSTF, U.S. Government Printing Office, 1998).

8. James P. Smith and Barry Edmonston, eds., *The New Americans: Studies of the Economic, Demographic, and Fiscal Effects of Immigration* (Washington, DC: National Academy of Sciences Press, 1998); George J. Borjas, *The New Americans: Economic, Demographic and Fiscal Effects of Immigration* (Washington, DC: National Academy of Sciences Press, 1997); Walter Ewing, "The Economics of Necessity," *Immigration Policy in Focus, Report of the American Law Federation*, 4 (no. 3), May 2, 2005, 5.

9. Bureau of the Census, *Statistical Abstract of the United States, 1980, Part 2 —Population*.

10. Ibid.

11. Louise L. Honor, ed., *Hispanic Americans: A Statistical Sourcebook* (Palo Alto, CA: Information Publications, 2002), 99–103.

12. Renee Stepler and Mark Hugo Lopez, "Ranking the Latino Population in the States," Pew Research Center, September 8, 2019, https://www.pewresearch.org/hispanic/2016/09/08/4-ranking-the-latino-population-in-the-states/ (accessed 8/3/2019).

13. Roberto Suro, "California Dreaming: The New Dynamism in Immigration Federalism and Opportunities for Inclusion on a Variegated Landscape," *Journal of Migration and Human Security* 3 (2015): 1–25.

14. Michael C. LeMay, *Illegal Immigration: A Reference Handbook* (Santa Barbara, CA: ABC-CLIO, 2007), 8–9.

15. Michael C. LeMay, *Religious Freedom in America: A Reference Handbook* (Santa Barbara, CA: ABC-CLIO, 2018), 56–108.

16. Ibid., 104–5.

17. Ibid., 107–8. See also Robert S. Alley, *The Constitution and Religion: Leading Supreme Court Cases on Church and State* (Amherst, NY: Prometheus Books, 1999).

18. Michael C. LeMay, *Global Pandemic Threats* (Santa Barbara, CA: ABC-CLIO, 2016), 37.

19. Alan Cranston, *The Sovereignty Revolution* (Stanford, CA: Stanford University Press, 2004), 71–72.

20. Charles A. Kupchan, *The End of the American Era: U.S. Foreign Policy and the Geopolitics of the Twenty-First Century* (New York: Alfred A. Knopf, 2003), 160.

ANALYTICAL ESSAYS

A number of organizations are critically important to immigration law, its amend-ments, its policy implementation, and its reforms. They may be best understood as the primary "stakeholder" organizations active in advocating for or against enact-ing or implementing immigration policy. Three governmental organizations are described as to the primary role that they play in immigration policy implementa-tion and reform: the Office of the President of the United States, the Office of the Attorney General of the United States and the Department of Justice, and the Office of the Secretary of the Department of Homeland Security. Those ana-lytical essays are followed by descriptions of the organizations and roles played by several nongovernmental organizations to exemplify their advocacy role in immi-gration law and its reforms. In pursuing their advocacy, they typically sponsor or support litigation through amicus curiae (friend of the court) briefs.

U.S. GOVERNMENTAL ORGANIZATIONS

The Office of President of the United States (POTUS)

The president of the United States is both head of state and head of the federal government, i.e. the Executive Branch of the United States. By constitutional powers specified in Article II, the president directs all departments and executive agencies and is the commander-in-chief of the armed forces. The constitutional powers of the office include execu-tion of all federal law, appointment of federal executive, diplomatic, regulatory, and judicial offices, as well as concluding treaties with for-eign powers (with the advice and consent of the U.S. Senate). The president can grant pardons, reprieves, and clemency and convenes and adjourns either or both houses of Congress under extraordinary circumstances. Since the end of World War I, presidents have increasingly set the legislative agenda of the party to which the president is titular head, and directs both foreign and domestic policy. Since the federal government has primacy in all matters relating to immigration law and policy, those enumerated powers give the president an often commanding role in immigration law. For example, the first power conferred on the office by the Constitution is the power to veto legislation passed by the Congress (known as the presentment clause). Once legislation has been presented, the president may: (1) sign the bill into law; (2) veto the bill and return it to Congress, stipulating any objections, in which case the bill does not become law unless each chamber votes to override the veto by a two-thirds vote; and (3) take no action, after 10 days if the Congress is convened, the bill becomes law; or if Congress has adjourned, the bill does not become law (this is known as the pocket veto).

The president impacts immigration law in myriad ways. The president appoints some 8,000 to 14,000 federal officials ranging from ambassadors to cabinet members to other federal officers. Many of these appointees, through their actions and departmental or agency rules and regulations, affect immigration law and its implementation.

The president, when faced with a Congress that cannot or will not enact new legislation on immigration, can and often does issue executive orders, reviewable by federal courts. Executive orders can be superseded by legislation enacted by Congress. Traditionally, one of the president's significant influences on immigration matters comes through the power to nominate federal judges, including justices to the federal district courts, to the U.S. Courts of Appeal, and to the Supreme Court of the United States. Arguably, the greatest impact historically has been through the president's appointment of the chief justice of the Supreme Court, many of whom have been instrumental in landmark Supreme Court decisions on cases involving immigration law. In the biographical essays that follow, several U.S. presidents are featured.

The Department of Homeland Security (DHS)

The Department of Homeland Security was established in November 2002 under President George W. Bush and in response to the terrorist attacks of September 11, 2001. It is the third largest cabinet-level department of the

U.S. government and has supervisory authority over several agencies that implement immigration law and policy, as well as over the process of naturalization to U.S. citizenship, which further impacts immigration. The DHS workforce is 240,000 employed in 22 component units. The units most related to immigration law are: Customs and Border Protection (CBP), Immigration and Customs Enforcement (ICE), and U.S. Citizenship and Immigration Services (USCIS), each of which often involves rules, regulations, and enforcement actions that directly implement immigration law. Court challenges to DHS actions have been brought with respect to religious grounds (e.g. a "Muslim" travel ban), anti-terrorism actions challenged for being racial profiling of ethnic and religious minorities, and conflicts with cities and religious groups providing sanctuary to undocumented or unauthorized immigrants. Several such cases have resulted in federal court rulings that have put DHS actions on stays or have overturned them as unconstitutional. Especially pertinent to immigration law, the DHS is responsible for counterterrorism, cyber security, aviation security, border security, port and maritime security, and the administration and enforcement of immigration laws. In 2017, the DHS had a budget of more than $40.6 billion, and in 2019 Congress authorized an additional $5 billion to address the humanitarian crisis at immigrant detention centers at the southwestern border with Mexico. President Trump, frustrated by the refusal of the Congress to fund construction of a border wall, used his "emergency" executive authority to move $5 billion more from the Department of Defense to fund barrier construction (replacing sections of the border fence). The Supreme Court upheld his authority to do so.

When DHS was established in 2002, it was the most significant reorganization of the federal government since the National Security Act of 1947 that established the Department of Defense. The first secretary of DHS was Tom Ridge, appointed by President George W. Bush. Secretary Ridge served from 2003 to 2005. He was succeeded by Michael Chertoff (2005–2009), also appointed by President Bush. The third secretary was Janet Napolitano (2009–2013), appointed by President Barack Obama. She was succeeded by Jeh Johnson (2013–2016), who was also appointed by President Obama. President Donald Trump, in less than three years of his term of office, has fired one acting secretary of the DHS and has appointed two secretaries and two acting secretaries: John Kelly (2017),

Kirsten Nielson (2017–2018), and acting secretaries Elain Duke (2017) and Kevin McAleenan (2019).

DHS is often criticized for its excessive bureaucracy, waste, and general ineffectiveness, particularly with regard to controlling the borders and the flow of illegal immigrants and the processing of refugee and asylum seekers. It has been alleged to use racial profiling against Muslim Americans, and for its surveillance of controversial imams and Muslim mosques. It has been charged with implementing three different versions of a travel ban, resulting in stays or injunctions that two federal district judges (one in Washington and one in Hawaii) have ruled to be unconstitutional infringements on the rights of Islamic individuals. A third iteration of the travel ban was, in the main, upheld by the U.S. Supreme Court in 2018 in a 5–4 decision along partisan or ideological lines.

The Department of Justice (DOJ) and Office of the Attorney General (AG)

The U.S. Department of Justice was established in 1870 by President Ulysses S. Grant. It is home to several divisions and bureaus that have involved the DOJ in controversies over immigration policy enforcement. DOJ established a National Security Division, in 2007, which has embroiled it in controversy with Muslim Americans. DOJ houses several law enforcement agencies that have and continue to have an impact on immigration matters: the U.S. Marshals Service, the Federal Bureau of Investigation (FBI, 1908), the Federal Bureau of Prisons (1930), the Bureau of Alcohol, Tobacco, Firearms and Explosives (ATF, 1972), the Drug Enforcement Agency (DEA), the Office of Inspector General, the Executive Office of Immigration Review, the Office of Immigration Litigation, and the Office of Tribal Justice.

DOJ is led by the attorney general of the United States, several of whom have been involved in immigration-related cases: Janet Reno, the first female AG appointed by President Bill Clinton; Alberto Gonzales (2005–2007), appointed by President George W. Bush; and Sally Yates, acting AG from January 20 to January 30, 2017, who was fired by President Donald Trump for refusing to defend the constitutionality of his first Muslim travel ban against persons from six predominately Muslim countries, maintaining that the executive order was an unconstitutional infringement of the rights of Muslim immigrants.

The office of AG was established by the Judiciary Act of 1789, making the AG the chief law enforcement officer of the United States. Since then, 85 attorney generals have served. The 84th AG was Jeff Sessions, appointed by President Trump in 2017, who served through 2018. He led the DOJ's crackdown on immigration. AG Sessions was replaced by Acting AG Matthew Whitaker, and then by the current and 85th AG, William Barr. The AG represents the United States in all legal matters and gives legal advice to the president and to heads of the executive branch departments when asked to do so. The AG is appointed by the president and confirmed by the U.S. Senate and, like other cabinet-level secretaries, is subject to impeachment by the House of Representatives and trial in the Senate.

OTHER FEDERAL AGENCIES, OFFICES, COMMISSIONS, AND COMMITTEES INVOLVED IN IMMIGRATION

Bureau of Immigration and Customs Enforcement (ICE)

ICE is the bureau within the Department of Homeland Security that enforces all federal laws governing border control, customs, trade, and immigration to promote homeland security and public safety. ICE was established in 2003 with the creation of DHS and through the merger of the investigative and enforcement elements of the former Immigration and Naturalization Service (INS). In 2018, ICE had more than 20,000 employees located in more than 400 offices in the United States and in 46 foreign countries, and an annual budget of $6 billion. ICE has three operational directorates: Homeland Security Investigations, Enforcement and Removal Operations, and the Office of the Principal Legal Advisor (OPLA). The OPLA provides the legal representation in all exclusion, deportation, and removal proceedings against criminal aliens, terrorists, and human rights abusers in immigration courts across the country. OPLA provides critical legal support to ICE components focusing on customs, cyber security, worksite enforcement, ethics, employment law, tort claims, and administrative law issues. These directorates of ICE are supported by the Department of Homeland Security's directorate of Management and Administration.

United States Customs and Border Protection (CBP)

CBP is one of the world's largest law enforcement organizations, with more than 60,000 employees. Established with the creation of the DHS in 2002, it is charged with keeping terrorists and their weapons out of the United States while facilitating lawful international travel and trade. As the nation's unified border entity, CBP takes a comprehensive approach to border management and control, combining customs, immigration, border security, and agricultural protection into one coordinated and supportive activity. CBP is responsible for enforcing hundreds of U.S. laws and regulations, screening nearly a million visitors per day as well as more than 67,000 cargo containers. It arrests daily thousands of persons at the borders and seizes tons of illegal drugs. Annually, it facilitates trillions of dollars in legitimate trade, while enforcing U.S. trade laws. The CBP's mission is to safeguard the borders by protecting the public from dangerous people and materials, yet enhancing the global economic competitiveness of the United States by enabling legitimate trade and travel.

Government Accountability Office (GAO)

The GAO is an independent, nonpartisan agency that works for Congress. Often referred to as the "congressional watchdog," the GAO investigates how the federal government spends taxpayer dollars. The GAO is headed by the comptroller general of the United States, who is appointed to a 15-year term by the president from a slate of candidates proposed by Congress through a bipartisan, bicameral commission. The GAO seeks to improve the performance and accountability of the federal government by providing Congress with timely information based on objective, fact-based, nonpartisan, non-ideological, fair, and balanced studies. Its core values are accountability, integrity, and reliability.

GAO studies and analyses are done at the behest of congressional committees or subcommittees or are mandated by public laws or committee reports. The GAO supports congressional oversight by auditing agencies and operations, investigating allegations of illegal or improper activities, reporting on the effectiveness and efficiency of policies in meeting their objectives, performing policy analyses and outlining options for congressional consideration, and issuing legal decisions and opinions. The GAO advises Congress and heads of executive agencies about ways to make government more efficient, effective, ethical, equitable, and responsive. It is consistently ranked as one of the best places to work in the federal government in the annual list of the Partnership for Public Service. It has frequently produced studies on the impact of immigration laws and critical analyses of such laws as IRCA and IMMACT as well as the DHS's immigration-related policies particularly related to any discriminatory impact.

Office of Management and Budget (OMB)

The OMB is a major office within the Executive Office of the President of the United States. It serves the president in overseeing the implementation of his agenda across the entire Executive Branch. Its mission is to assist the president in meeting policy, budget, management, and regulatory objectives, and to fulfill statutory responsibilities. These include: (1) budget development and execution; (2) management, including oversight of agency performance, human capital, federal procurement, financial management, and information technology; (3) coordination of regulatory policy; (4) legislative clearance and coordination; and (5) executive orders and presidential memoranda. The director of the OMB has regularly been involved in immigration reform policy initiatives, projecting the budgetary impact of various proposed reform bills, "scoring" legislation regarding immigration reform bills, and providing oversight of the DHS's immigration agencies, such as ICE, USCBP, and USCIS. In past administrations, the OMB director has been involved in drafting immigration reform proposals for the administration.

September 11 Commission

Senators Joseph Lieberman (I-CT) and John McCain (R-AZ) sponsored legislation to establish the National Commission on Terrorist Attacks upon the United States (9/11 Commission). It was a bipartisan, independent commission created by Congress and signed into law by President George W. Bush in 2002. The 10-member commission was charged with creating a full and complete assessment of the 2001 attacks, including preparedness for it; assessing the immediate response to the attacks, and making recommendations designed to guard against future attacks. In July 2004 it released its public report, and in August 2004 it released two staff reports/monographs. This commission announced creation of the 9/11

Discourse Project. The commission formally closed on August 21, 2004. Its recommendations led to the creation of the DHS in November 2002 and the Intelligence Reform and Terrorism Prevention Act of 2004. The latter act established the director of national intelligence position. In 2006, Congress established the SAFE Port Act. In 2011, on the 10th anniversary of the attacks, the committee launched a series of hearings to review the efficacy of the law and to assess future needs.

U.S. Census Bureau

The bureau collects and does analyses of statistical data on the population, including immigrants. Its data form the basis for the most accurate official information available to project or analyze the level and distribution of legal and unauthorized immigrants throughout the United States and to track trends in the unauthorized flow (both undocumented and visa-overstayers) across time. Its numerous reports and statistical studies make possible the tracking of all immigrants. Its reports provide demographic data as to the gradual incorporation of immigrants into the major institutions of American society.

U.S. Commission on Civil Rights

The commission is an independent, bipartisan, fact-finding agency of the executive branch established under the Civil Rights Act of 1957. It investigates complaints as to discrimination and appraises federal laws and policies with respect to discrimination because of race, color, religion, sex, age, disability, or national origin. It studies and collects information regarding such discrimination and serves as a clearinghouse for such information. It regularly submits reports, findings, and recommendations to Congress and to the president, many of which concern the rights of immigrants and refugees, the problems caused by the unauthorized immigration flow, and civil rights guaranteed to all persons, including unauthorized immigrants, as basic human rights.

U.S. Commission on Immigration Reform

This bipartisan commission on immigration reform (a.k.a. the Jordan Commission after its chair, Representative Barbara Jordan [D-TX]) was authorized by the Immigration Act of 1990 (IMMACT). It was mandated to review and evaluate implementation and the impact of U.S. immigration policy and to transmit reports of its findings and recommendations to Congress. It issued its first interim report on September 30, 1994, its second report in 1995, and two final reports in 1997: "U.S. Refugee Policy: Taking Leadership," and "Becoming American: Immigration and Immigration Policy." Like the SCIRP report of 1981, the recommendations contained in these two reports formed the basis for several legislative bills aimed at better coping with the unauthorized immigration problem.

U.S. Department of Health and Human Services (DHHS)

HHS impacts immigration law through its administration of several programs, such as: the Administration for Children and Families; Health Care Financing Administration; Divisions of State Legalization Assistance; Financial Support Administration; U.S. Public Health Service Office of Refugee Health; and the Office of Planning and Evaluation. Its intergovernmental role is significant in coping with illegal immigration. It is an important actor involved with undocumented immigrants, and in 2018 it played a significant and much-criticized role in the detention and care of the children of undocumented immigrants separated from their parents at the southern border due to the zero-tolerance policy. It is likewise the primary provider and supervisor of detention camps set up for children who came across the border unaccompanied by an adult. Should an expanded guest-worker program be enacted with "earned legalization" provisions, HHS would undoubtedly have a major role in its implementation.

U.S. Department of Labor (DOL)

The Department of Labor oversees all labor-related policy and law, including matters related to temporary labor. Other agencies within the department with immigration-related policy roles are its Office of Federal Contract Compliance Program and its Wage and Hour Division. Its role related to the implementation of IRCA, to date the most directly related federal program attempting to control and to decrease illegal immigration, was significant. Strict enforcement of U.S. labor laws may be one of the most effective ways to discourage employers from using the "cheap" labor source of undocumented workers. The department also plays a role in informing Congress or in certifying the need for temporary workers. It plays an important role in H-1A, H-1B, H-2A, and H-2B guest-worker programs. Its data collection has helped to certify the extent of discrimination against workers who are or were suspected of being undocumented workers. Its Bureau of Labor Statistics is the authoritative source of data on the U.S. labor force.

U.S. Department of State (USDOS)

The State Department is primarily involved in legal immigration, of course, but its consular affairs division, which issues visas, has a role in illegal immigration mostly related to visa overstayers. It has occasionally been embroiled in scandals in which "sting operations" have led to consular officials who have been caught selling visas and work authorization cards (commonly referred to as green cards, although in fact they are now white) to illegal aliens, allowing them to enter the United States with false documents or work authorization. The State Department has been embroiled in controversy over implementation of the Trump administration's travel ban.

U.S. House Committee on the Judiciary

The Committee on the Judiciary is the standing committee of the U.S. House of Representatives that deals with all bills introduced into the Congress that concern immigration law and policy matters. Its members have become leading voices in the efforts to reform policy (or to stall or block such bills) to deal with both legal and unauthorized immigration and immigrants. It oversees border control and security issues and problems, particularly those designed to stop or block such legislative efforts. Generally speaking, any bill introduced into Congress on immigration matters, pertaining to legal or illegal immigration problems, will be sponsored by one or more members of the House Judiciary Committee and its Subcommittee on Immigration. House Judiciary Committee members favor a "piecemeal" approach to immigration reform more than they do comprehensive immigration reform. It notably favors restricting illegal immigration and a "tougher, crack-down approach," the removal of immigrants now resident in the United States in illegal status, and stronger border control management.

U.S. Senate Committee on the Judiciary

This standing committee of the U.S. Senate deals with all legislative matters concerning immigration policy and law. Like its House counterpart, its members and staff become principal actors in all immigration reform efforts. While both the House and the Senate committees are strongly supportive of efforts to beef up the Border Patrol and to increase border security at airports and seaports, the Senate Judiciary Subcommittee on Immigration has been notably more amenable to a guest-worker program than has its counterpart in the House. It has favored and has even passed (in 2013) a comprehensive immigration reform bill (S. 744), whereas the House has failed to even bring such a bill to the floor for consideration and a vote. The bipartisan bill for comprehensive immigration reform died in the House.

U.S. Social Security Administration (SSA)

The SSA's role in immigration matters is also supportive of that of other agencies. Its data bank is used to verify a person's identity and to guard against fraud, waste, abuse, and mismanagement in administration of the benefit programs based upon contributory financing of social insurance programs to ensure that protection is available as a matter of right, as contrasted with a public assistance approach whereby only those persons would be eligible for benefits, whether natural-born citizens, naturalized citizens, or legal resident immigrants who had worked in and contributed to the system. As a system, it collects benefit payments from all workers, including illegal immigrants, who pay into the system. The large numbers of illegal workers who pay into the system yet do not withdraw benefits result in net benefits estimates to be in the billions of dollars annually. Their contributions are especially important given the increasing age of the citizen workforce. Unauthorized immigrants are generally much younger and are employed at higher percentages than are citizen laborers. They therefore work longer and pay into the system for much longer periods of time, and they are significant in filling the gap or shortfall between income and payments out of the system. In no small measure, these estimated billions of dollars in contributions from unauthorized immigrants help to keep the Social Security fund system solvent. Although they are only a stopgap factor in the financial strength of the Social Security system, their impact is nonetheless important. If policy designed to cut off that unauthorized immigrant flow were to be efficient, the Social Security system would suffer a noticeable decrease of considerable size.

NONGOVERNMENTAL ADVOCACY ORGANIZATIONS INVOLVED IN IMMIGRATION LAW AND POLICY

American Civil Liberties Union (ACLU)

The ACLU was founded in 1920 by Roger N. Baldwin, a seminal figure in the human rights movement in the United States and of international human rights. He served as its executive director from 1920 to 1950, and he founded the International League for Human Rights in 1950. The ACLU arose when civil liberties were endangered and citizens were being jailed simply for holding anti-war views, and when then U.S. attorney general A. Mitchell Palmer conducted raids on aliens simply suspected of holding unorthodox opinions. During those controversial raids, noncitizen immigrants from Russia were rounded up and some 500 deported on a ship dubbed "the Soviet Ark." In the 1920s, the ACLU fought the deportation of aliens for their radical beliefs, and opposed attacks on the Industrial Workers of the World. It won release of hundreds of prisoners sentenced during World War I simply for expressing radical views. In 1942, the ACLU was one of only a few and was arguably the strongest voice protesting the treatment of Japanese American citizens in the hysteria that followed the attack on Pearl Harbor. It similarly opposed the use of loyalty oaths in the 1950s, fighting a running battle with the government's loyalty-security programs and investigations of the House Un-American Activities Committee (HUAC).

The ACLU is a nonpartisan, nonprofit, public interest law firm, the first of its kind. It works nationally and through local chapters to protect the civil rights and civil liberties of citizens as guaranteed by the U.S. Constitution. To pursue those values, ACLU relies particularly on litigation and has often become involved in immigration adjudication—either by bringing a lawsuit to a federal court, or by supporting the litigation of other organizations through amicus curiae briefs. It publishes annually many policy statements, pamphlets, studies, and reports on legal matters, frequently with regard to immigration law.

ACLU is comprised of two separate but closely affiliated nonprofits: the ACLU, a 501(c)(4) social welfare group, and the ACLU Foundation, a 501(c)(3) public charity. Both engage in litigation, advocacy, and education, but only the 501(c)(3) donations are tax deductible, and only the 501(c)(4) group can engage in unlimited political lobbying.

As of 2017, ACLU claims a national membership of 1.2 million, has an annual budget of more than $133 million, and a staff of 300 attorneys as well as several thousand volunteer attorneys. It has frequently criticized the Department of Homeland Security and its implementation of the Patriot Acts I and II. It publishes semiannually a newsletter, *Civil Liberties Alert*. It has been a leading partner in efforts to reform or amend the USA Patriot Act and to rectify what it determines are civil rights abuses in procedural matters designed to cope with homeland security issues, in particular, with the efforts of the DHS to remove unauthorized immigrants in an expedited manner. The ACLU has promoted a guest-worker program and legalization programs more generally, and advocates for enactment of the Dream Act as part of comprehensive immigration reform. It has sections for LGBT rights, civil liberties, and immigration.

Since 2008, its president is Susan Herman, who leads the ACLU in opposing the Trump administration's immigration policies, such as the executive-ordered travel ban and the "zero-tolerance" policy of the Department of Justice with respect to unauthorized immigrants entering the United States. It has funded and supported, and in July 2018 has won on constitutional grounds, a federal district court challenge against the Trump administration's executive order rescinding DACA and DAPA.

American Federation of Labor–Congress of Industrial Organizations (AFL-CIO)

Founded in 1955 when the AFL and CIO merged, the AFL-CIO claims more than 12.5 million members. It supports liberal/progressive politics and was a major stakeholder organization comprising the New Deal coalition. It has seven major constituency groups: (1) A. Philip Randolph Institute, (2) AFL-CIO Union Veterans, (3) Asian-Pacific American Labor Alliance, (4) Coalition of Black Trade Unionists, (5) Coalition of Labor Union Women, (6) Labor Council for Latin American Advancement, and (7) Pride at Work. Prior to its merger in 1955, organized labor was a leading component against immigration. That changed after the merger, and the AFL-CIO backed passage of the Immigration and Nationality Act of 1965. Labor leader Walter Reuther promoted an aggressive civil rights agenda with strong financial and other support of the AFL-CIO. During the 1970s, it backed policies toward illegal immigration control (IRCA) to reduce the unauthorized immigration flow and to enact employer sanctions. It is a leading critic of the Trump administration's immigration policies, particularly zero-tolerance, the border wall, and the travel ban.

American Immigration Law Foundation (AILF)

Founded in 1987 as a tax-exempt, nonprofit educational and service organization, AILF promotes understanding among the general public of immigration law and policy through education, policy analysis, and support of litigation. It has three core program areas: the Legal Action Center, the Public Education Program, and the Exchange Visitor Program. It has often been a critic of the USA Patriot Act and of the DHS's expedited removal program. It considers the current reaction to international terrorism influencing immigration policy to be a threat to civil liberties that is every bit as great as is international terrorism itself. AILF opposed enactment of Patriot Act II. It supported enactment of the bipartisan comprehensive immigration reform bill of 2013. It supported President Barack Obama's DACA and DAPA executive orders, and has opposed the Trump administration's efforts to rescind them.

American Refugee Committee (ARC)

ARC is an international nonprofit and nonsectarian organization that has provided multinational humanitarian assistance and training for millions of beneficiaries. It began in 1978, when a relief team deployed to the Thai–Cambodian border in the post–Vietnam War refugee crisis. ARC continues to work designing new solutions to humanitarian crises that create mass refugee situations around the globe. It does so by delivering services and providing opportunities to help refugees and displaced persons and similar persons to survive conflict and crisis, and to rebuild lives of dignity, health, security, and self-sufficiency. ARC has a staff of around 2,000 people located across the world and a 2017 budget of nearly $40 million from UN and U.S. government grants, private donations, and in-kind goods and services. It vigorously opposes the zero-tolerance policy of the Trump administration, and has blamed that policy and the separation of children from their undocumented parents or other family members as the primary cause of the humanitarian crisis on the southwestern border with Mexico. It opposes the administration's drastic cuts in the number of refugees it will allow to enter, and the changes in administrative rules for processing asylum requests, and the Trump administration's greatly expanded use of expedited removal and ICE raids to find and summarily deport unauthorized immigrants held to be guilty of any crimes committed in the United States, even nonviolent crimes. ARC opposes the administration's executive order that authorizes expanded powers of ICE and Border Patrol agents to make on-the-spot judgments about asylum claims.

Mexican American Legal Defense Fund (MALDEF)

Founded in 1968 in San Antonio, Texas, by Mario Obledo, MALDEF is a leading nonprofit advocacy Latino litigation and educational outreach institution dedicated to foster sound public policies, laws, and programs to safeguard the civil rights of the more than 40 million Latinos living in the United States. MALDEF seeks to empower Latinos to fully participate in society. In coalition with other Latino organizations, such as LULAC and LaRaza, MALDEF lobbies to promote legislation, favors a guest-worker program, and is highly critical of what it holds are the civil rights infringements of the Patriot Acts. It strongly opposed state initiatives such as California's "Save Our State" Proposition 187 as well as Arizona's 2010 anti-illegal immigrant law (SB1070), the "Support Our Law Enforcement and Safe Neighborhood Act." In 2016, Arizona reached a settlement with the National Immigration Law Center. MALDEF and other immigrants' rights groups sued after passage of the measure to end most of the law's more strident provisions. In 1996, MALDEF opposed two acts: The Personal Responsibility and Work Opportunity Act of August 22, and the Illegal Immigration Reform and Immigrant Responsibility Act of September 30. MALDEF held that both laws were racially motivated, anti-Hispanic, and anti-immigrant. It has legally opposed English-only laws and initiatives. It supported DACA and DAPA, and enactment of a Dreamers bill, and opposed rescinding of DACA and DAPA, the travel ban, and zero-tolerance policy. Its major advocacy efforts concern the civil liberties of Mexican Americans. It often files amicus curiae briefs in federal courts to pursue its legal goals. MALDEF set up an education-litigation project, and in *Plyler v. Doe* (457 U.S. 202, 1982), the Supreme Court ruled that children of undocumented persons were protected by the due process clause of the Fourteenth Amendment. In *LULAC et al. v. Richards et al.* (1987), MALDEF joined in a class-action suit that charged the state of Texas with discrimination against Mexican Americans in south Texas because the state inadequately funded colleges. It fought Arizona's SB1070 in 2010, considered to be the toughest anti-illegal immigration law in the United States and supported an amicus brief that challenged the law to the Supreme Court. MALDEF won another victory in 2010, in *Gonzalez v. State of Arizona* (624 F. 3d 1162, 9th Cir.) that struck down Arizona's Proposition 200 that restricted voter registration by requiring proof of U.S. citizenship. The court ruled it unconstitutional and a violation of federal law by forcing voters to meet onerous new identification requirements at the polls and by imposing unnecessary paperwork on those seeking to register to vote.

League of United Latin American Citizens (LULAC)

LULAC was founded in 1929, in Corpus Christi, Texas, largely by Hispanic veterans of World War I who fought to end ethnic discrimination against Latinos in the United States. It is the oldest surviving Latino civil rights organization in the United States.

LULAC is organized to promote the democratic principles of individual, political, and religious freedom, and the right to equal social and economic opportunities. LULAC works to development a U.S. society wherein the cultural resources, integrity, and dignity of every individual and group constitutes basic assets of the American way of life. Among its stated goals are to be a service organization to actively promote and establish cooperative relations with civic and congressional institutions and agencies in the field of public service, to uphold the rights guaranteed to every individual by state and national laws, to ensure justice and equal treatment under those laws, and to oppose any infringement upon the constitutional rights of an individual to vote at local, state, and national levels. It brought to the U.S. Supreme Court the case that overturned as unconstitutional many of the provisions of California's Proposition 187 (*LULAC et al. v. Wilson, et al.*, 908 F. Supp. 755, 1995). It works in coalition with other organizations to oppose the USA Patriot Acts and insists on amending some of the more egregious civil rights infringements of those acts. LULAC favors legislation for a guest-worker program such as that contained in the 2013 Senate-passed comprehensive reform bill (S. 744). It supported DACA and DAPA and opposes the Trump administration's travel ban, his rescinding of DACA and DAPA, the DOJ's zero-tolerance policy, and construction of a border wall. In 1973, LULAC established the LULAC National Educational Service Centers as a 501(c)(3) national nonprofit designed to narrow the opportunity gap for disadvantaged youth in the United States through education and leadership programs such as Upward Bound.

National Immigration Forum (NIF)

Founded in 1982, the National Immigration Forum advocates to embrace and uphold the U.S. tradition as a nation of immigrants and to build public support for public policies that welcome immigrants and refugees, and that are fair and supportive to newcomers. As such, NIF opposes President Trump's travel ban. NIF works to unite families torn apart by what it considers unreasonable and arbitrary restrictions. It advocates for fair treatment of refugees who have fled persecution, for legalization of unauthorized immigrants, and a pathway to full political incorporation and equitable access to social protections. NIF argues for fundamental constitutional rights, no matter the legal status of immigrants. It advocates for policies that strengthen the U.S. economy by working with a diverse coalition of allies—immigrant, ethnic, religious, civil rights, labor union, business groups, and state and local governments—to forge a new vision of immigration policy consistent with global realities. It fosters economic growth, attracting needed workers to the United States, and protects the rights of workers and their families. It helps newcomers to settle into their communities, and to improve their socioeconomic status, and helps localities to weave immigrants into the fabric of community life by building bonds of mutual understanding between residents and newcomers. NIF supported President Obama's executive orders of DACA and DAPA. It opposes President Trump's travel ban and the DOJ's zero-tolerance policy that separates children from their unauthorized parents.

National Network for Immigration and Refugee Rights (NNIRR)

The NNIRR is a national organization composed of local coalitions of immigrant, refugee, religious, civil rights, and labor organizations and activists. It is a forum to share information and analysis, to educate communities and the general public, and to develop and coordinate plans of actions on important immigrant and refugee issues. It promotes just immigration and refugee policy in the United States. It defends expanding the rights of all immigrants/refugees without regard to their legal status. It seeks to incorporate immigrants and refugees through organizing and advocating for their full labor, environmental, civil, and human rights. It emphasizes the change in global, political, and economic structures exacerbating regional, national, and international patterns of migration. It builds support and cooperation among its coalition to strengthen the rights, welfare, and safety of all migrants without regard to their official legal status.

The Southern Poverty Law Center (SPLC)

The SPLC is a national civil rights organization dedicated to creating a national commitment in law and policy to human rights by its website and inviting users to view special features on its Web project, Tolerance.org. It promotes and disseminates scholarship on all aspects of prejudice and discrimination, promoting tolerance, and exposing hate groups and discrimination. It provides assistance on litigation and legal matters and publishes such anti-hate and pro-tolerance tracts as: *Ten Ways to Fight Hate*, *101 Tools for Tolerance*, and *Center Information Packet*. It has been a particularly outspoken group against the Trump administration's travel ban, rescinding of DACA and DAPA, and the zero-tolerance policy. It has countered the public opinion efforts of various anti-immigrant groups and organizations and called out as hate groups those advocating and practicing anti-immigrant vigilantism. It favors comprehensive immigration reform and a path to citizenship for unauthorized immigrants.

United Farm Workers (UFW)

In 1962, Cesar Chavez cofounded, with Dolores Huerta, what became the UFW. Between 1962 and 1965, they built membership, holding the first convention of the National Farm Workers Association (NFWA) in 1962. In 1965, NFW joined with Filipino American workers of the

AFL-CIO-affiliated Agricultural Workers Organizing Committee and launched a strike against grape growers that led to a five-year effort. In 1965–1966, UFW began a national grape boycott. The United Auto Workers, then headed by Walter Reuther, supported the strike and backed the boycott. In March 1966, then Senator Robert Kennedy chaired the Senate Subcommittee on Migratory Labor and formed a close friendship and alliance with Chavez and the UFW. That year, the NFWA and the Filipino AWOC merged to form the UFW as an affiliate of the AFL-CIO. They led a national grape boycott from 1967 to 1970. In 1968, Chavez adopted the tactics of peaceful protest that had been advocated by Mahatma Ghandi, including the fast. Chavez went on a 25-day fast to demonstrate his peaceful protest and garner national support for the boycott. In 1968, the UFW campaigned for Robert Kennedy in his presidential bid. After Robert Kennedy's assassination, the UFW led a national lettuce boycott in 1970. In 1975, Chavez and the UFW led a 1,000-mile, 59-day trek to protest against the conditions under which the lettuce pickers had to work. In 1988, he began his last and longest fast in support of unauthorized immigrants. Chavez died in 1994 and President William Clinton awarded him the Medal of Freedom posthumously.

United We Dream

United We Dream is the nation's foremost organization of the Dreamer youth. It conducts campaigns powered by immigrants, people of color, and their allies determined to reject and oppose President Trump's immigration policies and to honor and celebrate immigrant and refugee resilience by defiance, and by creating undocumented-friendly classrooms and educators. It promotes schools and campuses as sanctuary places, and it demands and supports a local campaign for sanctuary cities. The organization defines sanctuary as a place promoting freedom of expression through dialogue and activism, and as a place where the dignity and integrity of every individual as a human being is respected and preserved. It organizes sanctuaries to protect individuals from deportation, preventing ICE from "infecting" local law enforcement, protecting Muslims from a religious registry, surveillance, and harassment, uniting a coalition of sanctuary places against police brutality, and opposing stop and frisk. Its various chapters and affiliated organizations are united against misogyny and to promote woman's rights. It is a major organization that has won the hearts and minds of Latino voters. It continues to push for a permanent (i.e., congressional legislative) solution to the Dreamer problem that provides a path to citizenship, and for an end to enforcement policies that have broken up so many families. It focuses on action at the state level, such as the granting of licenses and benefits from in-state tuition at state universities.

CHURCH-RELATED IMMIGRANT ADVOCACY ORGANIZATIONS

Catholic Legal Immigration Network Incorporated (CLINIC)

CLINIC promotes the dignity and protects the rights of immigrants in partnership with a dedicated network of Catholic and community legal immigration programs, including sanctuary churches. It provides research and analysis of the significant changes in immigration policy announced by the Trump administration and of proposed legislation backed by the administration. It provides summary and analysis of federal court cases, such as those concerning the travel ban. It provides a three-part guide to counter hateful anti-immigrant narratives through legislative testimony, local media work, and social media outlets. CLINIC provides a webinar series for advocates in removal orders and legal proceedings over such orders, and it issues "practice tips" for counsels involved in enhanced enforcement of border security rules and procedures. It studies and publishes a state-by-state overview of legal mechanisms to combat the unauthorized practice of immigration law to assist noncitizen victims of that practice.

Church World Service (CWS)

Founded in 1946, the CWS is the relief, development, and refugee assistance ministry of 36 Protestant, Orthodox, and Anglican denominations in the United States. It works worldwide with indigenous organizations in more than 80 countries to meet human needs and to foster self-reliance for all persons whose way is hard. One of its major programs is Immigration and Refugee Services. CWS advocates for a more liberalized immigration policy and provides relief assistance to individuals without regard to their legal status. It supports sanctuary programs and provides emergency medical assistance to undocumented immigrants. It works in coalition with other organizations to lobby for reform in immigration law towards a more fair and humanitarian way.

Hebrew Immigrant Aid Society (HIAS)

Founded in 1881, HIAS has assisted more than 4.5 million people in their quest for freedom, including the millions of Jewish refugees it helped to migrate to Israel, the United States, Canada, Latin America, Australia, New Zealand, and elsewhere. As the oldest international migration and refugee resettlement organization in the United States, HIAS played major roles in the rescue and relocation of Jewish survivors of the Holocaust and Jews from Morocco, Ethiopia, Egypt, and communist countries of Eastern Europe. It advocates on behalf of refugees and migrants on the international, national, and community levels. HIAS provides its services without regard to the legal status of the immigrant being assisted. It works with faith-based organizations and immigrant/refugee assistance, and has lobbied on behalf of legislation aimed at liberal immigration reform in favor of legalization and guest-worker programs. HIAS lobbied against the Trump administration's travel ban executive order, its policy of zero tolerance, and the separation of children from their parents at the southern border. HIAS favored the DACA and DAPA executive orders of President Obama.

Since 2013, HIAS's president and CEO is Mark Hetfield, an immigration lawyer and former INS appeals adjudicator. While in the foreign service, Hetfield was posted with the U.S. Embassy in Haiti while the country was under rule of the military junta. He processed refugee applications in-country, during which time approvals increased from 5 percent to 25 percent. In 1989 he served HIAS as a caseworker in Rome assisting Jewish refugees from the Soviet Union. Joining HIAS's Washington, D.C., office, he was senior advisor to the U.S. Commission on International Religious Freedom and directed a congressionally authorized study on the treatment of asylum seekers. He was senior vice president of programs at HIAS, and he has transformed HIAS from an agency focused on Jewish immigrants to a global agency assisting refugees of all faiths and ethnicities. HIAS is a major implementing partner of the UN Refugee Agency (UNHCIR) and the U.S. Department of Justice, assisting all who flee ethnic cleansing, violence, and other forms of ethnic, racial, and religious discrimination.

LUTHERAN IMMIGRATION AND REFUGEE SERVICE (LIRS)

LIRS states as its mission to welcome the stranger, bringing new hope and new life through its ministries for justice. It mobilizes action on behalf of uprooted people and sees to it that they receive fair and equal treatment, regardless of national origin, race, religion, culture, or legal status. LIRS advocates for just and humane solutions to migration crises and their root causes, both national and international. It works in coalition with other faith-based immigration and refugee service organizations. LIRS lobbies to enact immigration reform that is more liberal. It favors legalization and a guest-worker program. Many of its member church congregations have supported the sanctuary movement and have become sanctuary churches. It opposes Trump's travel ban and zero-tolerance policy. It supported DACA and DAPA and opposes the executive order to rescind them

Humane Borders

Humane Borders describes itself as an organization of people motivated by faith and committed to work to create a just and humane border environment. Its members respond with humanitarian assistance to those who are risking their lives and safety crossing the U.S. border with Mexico. In encourages the creation of public policies toward a humane, nonmilitarized border with legalized work opportunities for migrants to the United States, and legitimate economic opportunities in the countries of origin of migrants. Humane Borders opposes the Trump administration's travel ban, the zero-tolerance policy, and the separation of children from their parents at the southern border. It supported DACA and DAPA and opposes President Trump's rescinding of them.

Human Rights First

Human Rights First is an independent advocacy and action organization founded in 1978 as a nonpartisan, nonprofit, and international human rights organization based in New York, Washington, D.C., Houston, and

Los Angeles. It accepts no government funding. It challenges the United States to live up to its ideals—vigorously opposing, for example, the Trump administration's plans to restore waterboarding, the travel ban, and the zero-tolerance policy that implemented the separation of unauthorized immigrant children from their parents. Human Rights First promotes American leadership in the global struggle for human rights, pressing the U.S. government and private companies to respect human rights and the rule of law, demanding reform, accountability, and justice, and advocating for the rights of asylum seekers, immigrants, and refugees. It exposes and protests injustice, advocating policy solutions to ensure consistent respect for human rights. It protects the rights of refugees, combats the use of torture, and defends persecuted minorities. Human Rights First conducts campaigns to pursue specific goals so that policymakers in Washington, D.C., hear from citizen champions of human rights. For more than 35 years it has built a bipartisan coalition of frontline activists and lawyers to tackle global challenges to human rights and to demand American leadership in protecting human rights. Human Rights First believes supporting human rights is a moral obligation but also a vital national interest. In short, it believes that America is strongest when its policies and actions match its national values.

No More Deaths

No More Deaths is a coalition of diverse individuals, faith communities, and human rights organizations that work for justice in the United States by mobilizing a response to the escalating number of deaths among undocumented immigrants crossing the border in the U.S. Southwest. The coalition has established a binational network of immigrant-friendly organizations and people in the Southwest and northern Mexico (No Mas Muertes in Spanish). Its members, and affiliated organizations, participate in interventions designed to stop migrant deaths, espousing the principle that humanitarian aid is never a crime, although some of its members have been arrested, fined, and jailed for assisting undocumented migrants. It establishes movable desert camps, supports the maintenance of water stations, and regularly launches what it terms "good Samaritan patrols" that search the desert for migrants at risk and counter the vigilante groups like the Minutemen. A nonprofit organization, No More Deaths advocates on behalf of migrant-related issues, including promoting public demonstrations such as days of fast in remembrance of the lives claimed along the border and protesting the policies that caused those deaths. Several of its volunteers have been arrested for giving aid to illegal aliens, and the coalition protests to call on government to drop the charges against its members. It organizes clergy and others to contact elected officials, particularly members of Congress, in an attempt to influence immigration law reform.

OFFICE OF MIGRANT AND REFUGEE SERVICES (MRS), U.S. CONFERENCE OF CATHOLIC BISHOPS

Since the turn of the twentieth century, the Catholic Church in the United States has engaged in refugee resettlement, advocated on behalf of immigrants and asylum seekers, and provided pastoral care and services to newcomers from all over the world. Since 1970 it has helped to resettle more than one million refugees. MRS is committed to its role on behalf of immigrants, migrants, and refugees. It assists bishops in the development and advocacy of policy positions on the national and international levels, addressing immigrants' needs and conditions. MRS works with the federal government and local churches in resettling refugees admitted to the United States into caring and supportive communities. It serves its clientele without regard to their legal status, and it has worked in coalitions with other church organizations in the sanctuary movement and for passage of comprehensive immigration reform. It has spoken out strongly against the Trump administration's travel ban, expedited removal, rescinding of DACA and DAPA, and especially the zero-tolerance policy separating children and their parents at the southern border.

THINK TANK IMMIGRATION STUDY AND ANALYSIS ORGANIZATIONS

The Brookings Institution, Center on Urban and Metropolitan Policy

The Brookings Institution is an independent, nonpartisan organization devoted to research, analysis, education, and publication focused on public policy issues in the areas of economics, foreign policy, and governance. It strives to improve the performance of U.S. institutions and the quality of public policy by using social science to analyze emerging issues and to offer practical approaches to those issues in language aimed at the general public. It is one of the premier think tanks in the United States. It provides analyses through three research programs: Economic Studies, Foreign Policy Studies, and Governance Studies. Through the Center for Public Policy Education and the Brookings Institution Press, it publishes annually about 50 books and has published several landmark studies on immigration laws and issue.

Center for Immigration Studies (CIS)

CIS is an independent, nonpartisan, nonprofit research organization founded in 1985. It is a think tank devoted exclusively to research and policy analysis of economic, social, demographic, fiscal, and other impacts of immigration on the United States. It seeks to expand knowledge and understanding of the need for an immigration policy that gives first concern to broad national interests. It describes itself as pro-immigrant but favors low immigration that seeks fewer immigrants but a warmer welcome for those admitted. It publishes *Immigration Review* and is notably anti-illegal immigration.

The executive director of CIS is Mark Krikorian. He frequently testifies before Congress on immigration policy, advocating against illegal immigration and for reduced legal immigration. CIS is an ardent advocate for reduced legal immigration and for ending or greatly reducing family reunification preferences, which CIS labels "chain migration." It advocates for strict controls to reduce or eliminate illegal immigration. Krikorian, and CIS, supports the Trump travel ban and efforts by DHS to tighten border security and expedited removal of illegal aliens.

CENTER FOR MIGRATION STUDIES (CMS)

The Center for Migration Studies of New York was founded in 1964. It is one of the premier institutes for migration studies in the United States. It strives to facilitate the study of sociodemographic, historical, economic, political, legislative, and pastoral aspects of human migration and refugee movements. In 1969, it incorporated as an educational, nonprofit institute (a 501[c][3] organization). CMS brings an independent perspective to the interdisciplinary study of international migration and refugees without the institutional constraints of government analysis and special interest groups, or the profit considerations of private research firms. CMS claims to be the only institute in the United States devoted exclusively to understanding and educating the public on the causes and consequences of human mobility at both origin and destination countries. It generates and facilitates the dissemination of new knowledge and the fostering of effective policies. It publishes a leading scholarly journal in the field, the *International Migration Review*. For many years it held an annual conference in immigration policy in Washington, D.C., that brought together government officials, academic scholars of the issue, lawyers involved in immigration matters, and activists in immigration-related advocacy organizations, such as church-affiliated groups, at which this author has been a presenter or a discussion panelist.

In 2011, Don Kerwin became executive director of CMS. He is the author of *Migrant Children, Uninvited Guests, and Welcoming the Stranger* (2014). Prior to CMS, he worked for CLINIC, from 1991 to 2008, serving as its executive director for 15 years, and between 2008 and 2011, he was vice president for programs at the Migration Policy Institute, where he frequently wrote on immigration and refugee policy issues, and as an associate fellow at the Woodstock Theological Center contributing to its Theology of Migration Policy. Kerwin was a member of the American Bar Association's Commission on Immigration, a member of the Council on Foreign Relations' Immigration Task Force, a board member for the Jesuit Refugee Services–USA, a board member for the Capital Area Immigrant Rights Coalition, and on the board of directors for the Border Network for Human Rights in El Paso, Texas.

Immigration History Research Center (IHRC)

Founded in 1965, the Immigration History Research Center at the University of Minnesota is an international resource on U.S. immigration and ethnic history. It collects, preserves, and makes available archival and published resources documenting immigration and ethnicity on a national scope and is a particularly rich source of information on ethnic groups that originated in eastern, central, and southern Europe and the Near East. It sponsors academic programs and publishes biographic and scholarly works. It is directed by Professor Erika Lee, a leading scholar of Asian immigration to the United States and author of several renowned academic volumes on the subject.

Congressional Research Service (CRS)

Begun in 1914 at the insistence of Senator Robert LaFollette Sr. (R-WI) and Representative John Nelson (R-WI), the Congressional Research Service is sometimes known as the think tank of the U.S. Congress. It publishes an annual *Congressional Research Services Review*. It works exclusively for Congress, providing policy and legal analysis to committees and to members of both the U.S. House of Representatives and the Senate, regardless of political party affiliation. It is a legislative branch agency housed within the Library of Congress. Its analyses are authoritative, confidential, objective, and nonpartisan. It has recently issued research reports on immigration reform, homeland security, and on the perceived threat of terrorists entering the United States via the undocumented immigration flow. In 2018, it had a staff of 400 policy analysts. It does research reports related to immigration matters conducted by two of its research divisions: Domestic Social Policy, and Government and Finance.

Pew Hispanic Center (PHC)

Founded in 2001, the Pew Hispanic Center is a nonpartisan research organization supported by the Pew Charitable Trust. It strives to improve understanding of the U.S. Hispanic population and to chronicle the growing impact of the Latino population on the United States. Timeliness, relevance, and scientific rigor are characteristics of its work. A classic example of a think tank, it does not advocate for or take positions on policy issues. Demography, immigration, and remittances are its major research foci on unauthorized immigration matters. The Pew Forum, Hispanic Center, and Research Center data and studies are regularly reported on by the mass media, thereby influencing public opinion with respect to immigration reform issues, concerns, and proposals. Their data are widely considered among the best and most accurate related to immigration matters.

WEBSITES USED

Organizations

ACLU: www.aclu.org/about/ (accessed 8/11/2017).

American Federation of Labor–Congress of Industrial Organization (AFL-CIO): http://www.aflcio.org (accessed 8/7/2018).

American Immigration Law Foundation: https://immigration .procon.org/view.source.php?sourceID=005957 (accessed 8/5/2017).

American Refugee Committee: https://www.arcrelief.org (accessed 8/5/2018).

Border Action Network: https://borderaction.org/ (accessed 8/5/2018).

Brookings Institution, Center on Urban and Metropolitan Policy: www.brook.edu/about.htm (accessed 8/5/2018).

Bureau of Immigration and Customs Enforcement: www.ice.gov/ About; and www.ice.gov/who-we-are/ (accessed 8/5/2017 and 8/6/2017).

Catholic Legal Immigration Network (CLINIC): https:// cliniclegal.org/aboutus/ (accessed 8/6/2017).

Center for Immigration Studies: https://cis.org/About/ (accessed 8/6/2017).

Center for Migration Studies: http:/cmsny.org/About/ (accessed 8/6/2017).

Congressional Research Service (CRS): www.loc.gov/crsinfo (accessed 8/6/2017).

Church World Service: https://www.cwsglobal.org; www .immigrationadvocate.org/nonprofit/legaldirectory (accessed 8/6/2018).

Department of Homeland Security (DHS): https://www.dhs.gov/ about-dhs (accessed 8/7/2017).

Department of Justice (DOJ): https:/www.justice.gov/about (accessed 8/7/2017).

Federation for American Immigration Reform (FAIR): www.fairus.org/About/ (accessed 8/7/2017).

Government Accountability Office (GAO): www.gao.gov/about/ index.html (accessed 8/7/2017).

Hebrew Immigrant Aid Society: http:/www.hias.org (accessed 8/7/2018).

Humane Borders: http:/www.humaneborders.org (accessed 8/7/2018).

Human Rights First: https://www.humanrightsfirst.org/about www.humanrightsfirst.org/aboutus/ (accessed 8/7/2017).

Immigration History Research Center: https://cla.umn.edu/irhc (accessed 8/7/2018).

League of United Latin American Citizens: https://lulac.org (accessed 8/7/2018).

Lutheran Immigration and Refugee Service: http:/www.lirs.org (accessed 8/7/2018).

Mexican American Legal Defense Fund: http:/www.maldef.org/about (accessed 8/7/2018).

National Immigration Forum (NIF): www.immigrationforum.org/ About (accessed 8/7/2017).

National Network for Immigration and Refugee Rights: www.nnirr.org (accessed 8/7/2018).

No More Deaths: http:/forms.nomoredeaths.org/en (accessed 8/7/2018).

Office of Management and Budget (OMB): www.whitehouse.gov/omb (accessed 8/7/2017).

Office of Migrant and Refugee Services: http:/www.usccb.org/about/ migration-and-refugee-services/ (accessed 8/7/2018).

Pew Hispanic Center (PHC): www.pewhispanic.org (accessed 8/7/2017); www.pewresearch.org/ (accessed 8/7/2017); and www.pewresearch.org/staff/roberto-suro (accessed 8/7/2017).

September 11 Commission: https://9-11commission.gov (accessed 8/7/2018).

Southern Poverty Law Center: www.tolerance.org (accessed 8/7/2018).

U.S. Citizenship and Immigration Service: https://www.uscis.gov/ aboutus (accessed 8/7/2018).

U.S. Customs and Border Protection (USCBP): www.cbp.gov/about (accessed 8/7/2017).

United Farm Workers (UFW): https://ufw.org/research/history (accessed 8/7/2018).

United We Dream.org: https://actions.unitedwedream.org (accessed 6/27/2018); www.unitedwedream.org/cristina-jimenez-managing-director (accessed 6/27/2018); and www.twitter.com/UWDCristina (accessed 6/27/2018).

Urban Institute: https://www.urban.org (accessed 8/7/2018).

U.S. Census Bureau: https://www.census.gov (accessed 8/7/2018).

U.S. Commission on Civil Rights: https://www.usccr.gov (accessed 8/7/2018).

U.S. Commission on Immigration Reform: https://www.fairus.org/issue/legal-immigration/us-commission-immigration-reform (accessed 8/7/2018).

U.S. Department of Health and Human Services: https://www.dhs.gov (accessed 8/7/2018).

U.S. Department of Labor: https://www.dol.gov (accessed 8/7/2018).

U.S. Department of State: https://www.state.gov (accessed 8/7/2018).

U.S. House Committee on the Judiciary: https://judiciary.house.gov (accessed 8/7/2018).

U.S. Senate Committee on the Judiciary: https://www.judiciary.senate.gov (accessed 8/7/2018).

U.S. Social Security Administration: https://www.ssa.gov (accessed 8/7/2018).

BIOGRAPHICAL ESSAYS

This section presents biographical essays of key actors involved in the arena of immigration law and policymaking, especially with respect to the Immigration and Nationality Acts of 1952 and 1965 and its various amendments. It begins with brief profiles of presidents who were instrumental in advocating for changes in immigration law, on occasion using their executive orders to overcome resistance by the U.S. Congress that was so often stalemated on immigration reform measures. The section presents biographical sketches for seven U.S. presidents in chronological order of their terms as president: Dwight D. Eisenhower, John F. Kennedy, Lyndon B. Johnson, Ronald Reagan, George W. Bush, Barack Obama, and Donald Trump. These presidential biographies are followed by essays for seven legislators who were the primary authors/sponsors of three major immigration laws, and they are presented in chronological order of the enactment of the immigration law that they authored and for which they were the principal sponsors. Senator Pat McCarran and Representative Francis Walters sponsored the Immigration and Nationality Act of 1952. Their biographical essays are followed by those for Representative Emmanuel Celler and Senator Philip Hart, who sponsored the Immigration and Nationality Act of 1965. Three legislators were key authors of the Immigration Reform and Control Act of 1986: Senator Alan Simpson and Representatives Romano Mazzoli and Peter Rodino. Finally, the section presents biographical essays of two attorney generals who played major and controversial roles in immigration implementation: Alberto Gonzales and Jeff Sessions. They, too, are discussed in chronological order of their terms of service as attorney general.

SEVEN PRESIDENTS WHO PLAYED MAJOR ROLES IN IMMIGRATION POLICY REFORM:

All modern presidents have had contentious relations with Congress. That fact is especially true with respect to immigration lawmaking and implementation. Norms and customs associated with the modern president allow presidents to play the role of setting the legislative agenda for Congress and for the political party of which the president is titular head. Ever since President Theodore Roosevelt, the presidency has been characterized as the bully pulpit, and when presidents use that pulpit judiciously, presidents can win public support for immigration proposals. When they do so, that fact gives them a degree of leverage over Congress. Perhaps equally important to the bully pulpit to influence immigration policy is the presidential power of the veto, and often simply the threat of the veto. And in recent years particularly, in regard to immigration law and implementation, presidents have used their executive order and their proclamation powers. Richard Neustadt captured the reality of the president vis-à-vis the Congress when he asserted that "presidential power is the power to persuade."[1] Because presidents play the roles of commander-in-chief, chief legislator, and chief diplomat, presidents typically view immigration law and immigration problems from a different perspective from that of members of Congress.[2]

Dwight D. Eisenhower (1890–1969)

The president most associated with the transition in immigration law from the national origins quota system to the preference system is President Dwight David Eisenhower (1953–1961). President Eisenhower is generally ranked by historians as among the top 10 presidents in the overall impact of his presidency. Coming to the office as a World War II hero, Eisenhower certainly had the credentials to use the bully pulpit and to lead as commander-in-chief and as chief diplomat. Those characteristic roles gave him influence over a Congress mired in the increasingly inflexible national origins quota system.

Eisenhower was born in Texas in 1890. He was appointed to the U.S. Military Academy at West Point in 1911, graduating in 1915. During World War I he ran a tank training center in Gettysburg, Pennsylvania. From 1927 to 1929, he served in the War Department under General John Pershing. From 1935 to 1939, Eisenhower served under General Douglas McArthur as military advisor to the Philippines—which honed his skills as a politically astute "diplomat." That experience was invaluable for his roles in World War II. In 1942, Eisenhower was appointed major general, then commander-in-chief of the Allied forces, leading Operation Torch. In 1945 he was appointed Army chief of staff, and then Supreme Allied Commander of the North Atlantic Treaty Organization (NATO). From 1948 to 1950, he served as president of Columbia University.

In 1952, Eisenhower was elected as the 34th president of the United States, serving in that office from 1953 to 1961. As president, Ike, as he was affectionately known, favored legal immigration reform. Frustrated with congressional inaction on reform measures to end the quota system, Eisenhower set precedents by using his executive authority to use "parole power" and "mortgaging" of quotas against future quotas to enable increased immigration, notably the Hungarian Freedom Fighters, after their failed revolution in 1956. His innovative use of executive authority to influence immigration policy was followed by subsequent presidents, notably and most recently by Presidents Obama and Trump.

President Eisenhower came to office during the Cold War, and while immigration law was that established by the Immigration and Nationality Act of 1952, enacted during the presidency of Harry Truman. Eisenhower favored a more generous immigration policy than that embodied in the McCarran-Walter Act. In 1956, Ike presented a message stating his views on immigration in a column entitled "Letters from America." In it, he stated that America is a nation of immigrants. He dealt with four different aspects of immigration policy. He recommended that the Congress amend the national origin quota system by increasing quotas and allowing the pooling of unused quotas. He recommended a quota pool for each of four geographic regions—Europe, Asia, Africa, and Oceana—in which unused quota numbers in any country within a region would be assigned each year to a pool for that region. Eisenhower stated "immigration to this land has contributed greatly to the strength and character of our republic."[3]

Eisenhower advocated that America open wider the gateway to America. He successfully pushed Congress to amend the 1952 McCarran-Walter Act to redefine the definition of children contained in the 1952 act to apply to stepchildren, illegitimate children, and adopted minor-age children. When the failed Hungarian revolution in 1956 led to the foreign policy and Cold War need to do something to assist and relocate the tens of thousands of Hungarian refugees, dubbed the "Freedom Fighters,"

President Eisenhower used the "parole" authority of the 1952 act to admit more than 15,000 Hungarians, whose quota under the law was 869, and Congress followed his lead and passed the Act of July 25, 1958 to authorize the admission of the Hungarian refugees for permanent residency (72 Stat. 419). He also pressured Congress to amend the 1952 act by the Act of September 22, 1959. It provided for the entrance of many more relatives of U.S. citizens and lawfully resident aliens (73 Stat. 644).

Finally, in July 1960, Congress followed President Eisenhower's urging and passed a law to assist the resettlement of "refugee-escapees" from Communist countries (such as Cuba) who had been paroled by the attorney general (74 Stat. 504).[4] The attorney general was allowed to change the status of such refugee-escapees upon a finding by a voluntary relief agency or welfare organization recognized for that purpose by the attorney general, that such refugee-escapee can, with some assistance, become self-supporting, or is a member of a family unit capable of becoming self-supporting. The enactment of these laws indicated that the U.S. Congress was finally moving toward a willingness to end, outright, the inflexible and outmoded national origins quota system. Importantly, they also set a precedent for involving nongovernmental organizations who had been active in immigration and refugee assistance and advocacy efforts to partner with the federal government in implementing immigration policy. This precedent was especially useful later, when the Immigration Reform and Control Act of 1986 (IRCA) used what it called "Qualified Designated Entities" (QDEs) to assist in implementing the amnesty program of the 1986 law.

John Fitzgerald Kennedy (1917–1963)

John F. Kennedy (JFK) was assassinated in 1963, and his service as president (1961–1963) was therefore abruptly shortened. Like President Eisenhower, JFK is generally ranked by historians among the top 10 presidents. He certainly had a significant impact on immigration policy beyond his short term in the office. His brother, Senator Ted Kennedy, took up his mantle of leadership in immigration matters, and so Ted Kennedy is briefly profiled in a short biographical essay here as well.

John F. Kennedy (D-MA) graduated from the Choate School, studied at the London School of Economics, and also attended Princeton University. He graduated from Harvard University in 1940. That year, JFK wrote the award-winning *Why England Slept*, about the appeasement policies that led to the outbreak of World War II. He served in the Pacific during World War II and was hailed a war hero when his PT-109 boat was sunk by the Japanese and he led his crew to safe recovery.

JFK was elected to the U.S. House of Representatives in 1946 and served there until his election to the U.S. Senate in 1958. In 1956 Kennedy published his *Profiles in Courage*, which won the Pulitzer Prize in 1957. After being elected to the U.S. Senate, JFK wrote *A Nation of Immigrants* (republished in 1964), which cogently argued for rescinding the racial and ethnically biased immigration policy of the national origins quota acts and replacing the quota system with a preference system that would grant visas on a first-come, first-served basis, ending the bias for northwestern European countries and against southern and eastern European and Asian countries. JFK was elected president of the United States in 1960 and inaugurated in 1961. During his first two years as president, his administration was focused on foreign policy, most notably the Cuban Missile Crisis. The civil rights movement began to push the Kennedy administration on the civil rights issue in 1963.

John Kennedy advocated for civil rights reform, and the influence of the civil rights era impacted his position on immigration policy as markedly as did the Cold War era on the Immigration and Nationality Act of 1952. The civil rights movement agitated public opinion to question and seriously reevaluate the racial bias of much of nation's laws. Immigration did not escape that review. The passage of special acts, nonquota immigration, and refugee-escapee laws had all demonstrated that the national origin system was simply too inflexible and too biased to be continued indefinitely.

The success of the first two years of the Kennedy administration in basic economic policy, recovering from a recession that had plagued the Eisenhower administration for six of his eight years in office, worked to undercut opposition to immigration reform. Traditional supporters of the quota system, such as the American Coalition, the American Legion, the Daughters of the American Revolution, and the National Association of Evangelicals, were unorganized and largely inactive.

In July 1963, JFK submitted to Congress the bill that was to become the Immigration and Nationality Act of 1965. It fundamentally altered legal immigration law for the United States, replacing the quota system with a preference system. The 1965 act governs immigration law to this day.

Among the law's many unanticipated consequences were dramatic shifts in the nation of origin from which legal immigrants came to the United States, and resulted in huge backlogs in visas for permanent resident immigrant status. Because of its limits of 20,000 immigrants from Mexico, Central, and South American countries, which fell so far short of the demand for legal visas from the region, the Kennedy Act (as the 1965 Immigration and Nationality Act is commonly known) soon contributed to the unanticipated surge in backlogs for visas from the region, and thereby set the stage for the exponential increase in unauthorized immigration from the 1970s on. In order to garner support for his comprehensive immigration reform bill, JFK agreed to the ending of the Bracero Program (the act to do so was passed in 1964).

The percentage of persons naturalized by decades by region of birth illustrates the demographic impact of the Kennedy immigration law. From 1961 to 1970, for example, 62.4 percent of the naturalized citizens came from Europe, 20.9 percent were from the Americas, and 12.9 percent were from Asia. From 1971 to 1980, those numbers shifted dramatically: those naturalized from Europe fell to 30.8 percent, those naturalized from the Americas rose to 28.1 percent, and those from Asia shot up to 33.5 percent. For the decade 1981 to 1990, those from Europe fell even more sharply— to 15.4 percent. Those naturalized who came from the Americas rose to 26.2 percent, and those from Asia to a remarkable 48.8 percent.[5]

JFK was assassinated in Dallas, Texas, on November 22, 1963. The U.S. Congress passed the Civil Rights Act of 1964 (78 Stat. 241) and the Immigration and Nationality Act of 1965 (79 Stat. 911) as a "memorial" to the martyred president. The success of the Kennedy Act in reshaping immigration was dramatic. Between 1975 and 1980, the United States led by far all nations of the world in accepting refugees—677,000. The next nearest nation in receiving refugees during those five years was China, with 265,000.[6] Because he was so important to the legacy of JFK in immigration policy, his youngest brother, Senator Edward "Ted" Kennedy (D-MA) is briefly bio-sketched here.

Edward "Ted" Kennedy (1932–2009)

Known as the "Lion of the Senate," Kennedy was born in Boston, Massachusetts, to the prominent Kennedy family, the youngest brother of

President John F. Kennedy. Senator Edward Kennedy received his BA from Harvard in 1956, attended the Hague International Law School in 1958, and received his LL.B. from the University of Virginia Law School in 1959. Ted Kennedy worked in his brother John F. Kennedy's presidential campaign in 1960, then served as assistant district attorney for Suffolk County, Massachusetts, in 1961–1962. He was elected to the U.S. Senate in 1962, at age 30, and served in the Senate until his death in 2009. He became the single most influential member of Congress on immigration matters, from sponsoring and helping to navigate the Immigration and Naturalization Act of 1965 (commonly known as the Kennedy Act) through the U.S. Senate, and worked on every major immigration-related bill until his death in 2009. He became an icon of political progressivism and liberal thought. For example, Ted Kennedy was instrumental in the final congressional session of 1976, when Congress amended the Immigration Act of 1965 to address the problem of the long waiting period for approval of visas from Western Hemisphere countries, which created hardships for those who were otherwise qualified for preferred status. To rectify the problem, the 1976 amendment extended the preference system to Western Hemisphere nations. For a time, the 1976 act cut the waiting period for immigrants from Mexico, for example, in half.[7]

After Senator Robert Kennedy (D-NY) was assassinated in 1968, Ted Kennedy became the standard bearer of the Kennedy clan. He was elected the majority whip of the Senate in 1969. A deadly auto accident in 1969, off an unmarked bridge on Chappaquiddick Island, which killed his 28-year-old companion, ended his presidential ambitions, and he returned to the Senate. He briefly ran for the presidential nomination in 1980, losing to Jimmy Carter. Kennedy gave a hallmark convention speech that year. In 1982 he divorced his wife, Joan. He was reelected to the Senate in 1982 and 1988. In 1992 he remarried. By the 1990s, he had become the Senate's most prominent member, amassing an impressive record of bills sponsored and enacted on immigration reform (e.g. the 1976 act), criminal code reform, fair housing, public education, health care, AIDS research, and various aid to the poor programs.

Unquestionably, Ted Kennedy's most important position regarding immigration was his role on the Senate Judiciary Committee, where he advocated liberal positions on abortion, capital punishment, and busing. He maintained notable bipartisan friendships with such conservative stalwarts as Senators Nancy Kassebaum, John McCain, and Orrin Hatch. He worked to enact President George W. Bush's signature No Child Left Behind Act. After the 9/11 attacks in 2001, Ted Kennedy sponsored the bipartisan Bioterrorism Preparedness and Response Act. He was an outspoken critic of the Bush administration on civil rights and liberties matters as they impacted debate over how to control unauthorized immigration. He cosponsored the McCain-Kennedy bill to reform immigration policy in a comprehensive manner, including provisions for "earned legalization." The May 2005 bill was officially titled, "The Secure America and Orderly Immigration Act" (S. 1033). Although the bill failed, it set the stage for later bipartisan comprehensive immigration bills, such as S. 744 (2013).

Kennedy suffered a seizure in 2008 and was diagnosed with a brain tumor, which was surgically removed. He suffered another seizure in 2009, and passed away in August 2009, on Cape Cod, Massachusetts.

Lyndon B. Johnson (1908–1973)

LBJ is another president historians have ranked within the top 10. Lyndon Johnson became the 36th president on November 22, upon the assassination of President John F. Kennedy. He served as president from 1963 to 1968. LBJ's impact on civil rights policy and law, and on immigration law and its comprehensive reform, has been profound—arguably the most of any single modern president. While Senate majority leader (1955–1960), he worked productively with Republican president Dwight D. Eisenhower, and his ability to unify his party on important legislation made him one of the most effective majority leaders and an unquestioned powerful leader in Washington politics.

Born in Texas, not far from Johnson City, which his family had founded, Lyndon Johnson graduated from Southwest Texas State Teachers College in 1927. He began teaching in Houston in 1930. He was named director of the National Youth Administration in Texas in 1935 and was elected to Congress in 1938. In 1941 he lost a campaign for the U.S. Senate and went on to serve in the U.S. Navy as a lieutenant commander in the South Pacific theater. Johnson was awarded a Silver Star for that service. He was elected to the Senate in 1948, went on to serve as the Democratic whip in 1951, and became the Senate minority leader in 1953. After winning reelection to the Senate in 1954, he was elected the Senate majority leader. While majority leader, in 1954, LBJ sponsored what became known as the "Johnson Amendment." It made significant changes to the IRS tax code, essentially prohibiting tax exemption for religious organizations for either endorsing or opposing candidates for political office.

Johnson directed passage of the 1957 Civil Rights Act. He ran for the Democratic Party presidential nomination in the 1960 race but was defeated in that contest by JFK, who after a close contest with LBJ, selected Johnson as his running mate. The ticket went on to win over Republican candidate Richard Nixon, and Johnson was elected vice president in 1960. LBJ was elected president by a landslide in 1964, defeating Republican nominee Senator Barry Goldwater (R-AZ) with 61 percent of the popular vote. The landslide nature of his electoral victory enabled him to claim a true mandate.

Johnson's presidency is most noted for enactment of his "Great Society" programs of civil rights reforms, which enhanced immigrant rights, and the War on Poverty. Most notable among those legislative achievements were passage of the Civil Rights Act of 1964 (78 Stat. 241), the Voting Rights Act of 1965 (79 Stat. 437), and the Civil Rights Act of 1968 (aka the Fair Housing Act, 82 Stat. 73). His most significant impact on immigration was his ability to get the Immigration and Nationality Act of 1965 (79 Stat. 911) through the Congress and sign the bill into law, an accomplishment that JFK failed to do. The 1965 act effectively removed *de facto* discrimination against southern and eastern Europeans, Asians, and other non-northwestern European ethnic groups from American immigration policy. LBJ did so where JFK had failed for several reasons. As the former majority leader, Johnson was one of the best nose-counters in the nation, and with his landslide victory in 1964, he had more liberal/progressive Democratic noses to count than had any president since Franklin D. Roosevelt (FDR). Another factor was that he had the "martyrdom" of President Kennedy to point to and to advocate for its passage as a memorial to the slain president. Pushing the law through Congress was an important part of Johnson's civil rights emphasis and legacy.

Johnson used the bully pulpit of the office to a consummate degree in pushing for the enactment of the most ambitious policy program of progressive reforms of any modern president. He strove to pass the most legislation in his first term than did any president since FDR, wanting to match FDR's famous 100-days record. Johnson championed Medicare, Medicaid, and Head Start. Johnson also presented the first three Presidential Medal of Freedom (MOF) Awards for civil rights activism in 1964 and 1967. The MOF is the highest civilian honor the country can bestow.

As president, Johnson appointed two judges to the U.S. Supreme Court: Associate Justice Abe Fortas (1965–1969) and Associate Justice Thurgood Marshall (1967–1991), the first African American Supreme Court justice and unquestionably one of the most important justices of the court on all cases dealing with civil rights, civil liberties, and immigration matters during his long service on the court.

Johnson's presidential legacy, however, is marred by the political quagmire and growing opposition to the Vietnam War, which led him to decline to run for a second term in 1968, and he retired to his Texas ranch in 1969. He worked on his memoirs and on establishing his presidential library at the University of Texas at Austin. He died suddenly of a heart attack at his ranch, at the age of 64, on January 22, 1973.[8]

Ronald Reagan (1911–2004)

Known as the Great Communicator, Ronald Reagan served as president of the United States from 1981 to 1989. He is another president that historians have ranked among the top 10 of U.S. presidents.

Reagan was born in Illinois. He graduated from Eureka College in 1932 and began a career as a sports announcer before he signed a movie contract with Warner Brothers Studio in 1939. In 1947, he was elected president of the Screen Actors Guild, and in 1954, Reagan hosted the *General Electric Theater* television show. He campaigned for Richard Nixon for president in 1960. In 1963, he hosted the popular television program *Death Valley Days*. He was elected governor of California in 1966 and reelected to that office in 1970. He lost a bid for the presidential nomination of the Republican Party in 1976, to President Gerald Ford, before winning the nomination and the office in 1980. After winning the nomination, Reagan selected his rival for the nomination, George H. W. Bush of Texas, as his running mate.

Reagan was reelected president in 1984. The Reagan-Bush ticket defeated the Democratic ticket of former vice president Walter Mondale (D-MN) and his running mate, Representative Geraldine Ferraro (D-

NY) in one of the biggest landslides in U.S. election history. The Reagan-Bush ticket carried 49 states (all but Mondale's Minnesota), and amassed 525 electoral votes and 58.8 percent of the popular vote. His landslide victory enabled him to get much of his legislative agenda through Congress.[9]

His notable contribution to immigration reform was the establishment of the presidential task force on immigration that helped shape the debate on the Immigration Reform and Control Act of 1986 (100 Stat. 3360, November 6, 1986), which he signed into law. He established the employer sanctions approach and approved its amnesty program that legalized more than three million immigrants. Illegal immigration became a hot political issue in the 1980s as the number of alien apprehensions surged at the southwestern border with Mexico during Reagan's presidency. By 1986, when IRCA was enacted, the unauthorized alien residents were estimated at 3.2 million, and those coming from Mexico comprised 69 percent, versus those from Asia at 6 percent, and from Europe at 2 percent.[10] The Reagan administration's task force recommended the employer sanctions approach to cope with the issue, but in order to get the measure through Congress, a compromise with the Democrats included an amnesty program in the legislation. Reagan worked cooperatively with the Democratic Speaker of the House, Representative Thomas "Tip" O'Neill (D-MA, 1977–1987), and the congressional sponsors of the bill, Representatives Romano Mazzoli (D-KY, 1971–1995) and Peter Rodino (D-NJ, 1949–1989), then chair of the powerful House Judiciary Committee, and Senator Alan Simpson (R-WY, 1979–1997). The amnesty program was a success, but Republican Party opposition to it grew to the point that by, after the 2001 attacks, it was virtual political suicide for a Republican presidential candidate to advocate any provision that the party labeled amnesty, such as the various Dreamer bills and the comprehensive immigration reform bill of 2013.

Ronald Reagan retired from the presidency in 1989. In 1994, he announced that he suffered from Alzheimer's disease, and he died a much revered former president on June 6, 2004.[11]

George Walker Bush (1946–)

George W. Bush served as the 43rd president (2001–2009). He ran for president on a campaign stressing what he called "compassionate conservatism" that included espousing comprehensive immigration reform that would have provided a "path to citizenship" for unauthorized immigrants and a stance to "welcome the stranger," including Muslim immigrants and refugees. That quickly died, however, when President Bush became a wartime president after the terrorist attacks on September 11, 2001.

George W. Bush was born in New Haven, Connecticut, into the powerful Bush family. His father was former president George Herbert Walker Bush, and his brother, Jeb Bush, was elected governor of Florida and ran for the Republican nomination for president in 2016. When George W. Bush was elected president in 2000, it was only the second time in American history that a president's son went on to be elected to the office (previously, John Quincy Adams was the sixth president [1825–1829], the son of John Adams, the second president [1797–1801]). George W. Bush won the office in 2000 despite having lost the popular vote to Vice President Al Gore, but was awarded the contested Electoral College votes of Florida by the Supreme Court in a 5–4 ruling along partisan lines (*Gore v. Bush*, 531 U.S. 98, 2000). The Supreme Court's decision gave the Bush-Cheney ticket 271 ECVs to 266 for the Gore-Lieberman ticket.

George W. Bush was enrolled at Phillips Academy in Andover, Massachusetts in 1961. He worked in his father's Senate bid in 1964. Bush graduated from Yale University in 1968, and then enlisted in the Texas Air National Guard. He entered the Harvard Business School in 1973 and received an MBA from Harvard in 1975, and then returned to Midland, Texas, where he spent part of his childhood, and entered the oil business, founding an oil and gas exploration company. He married Laura Welch and they have twin daughters. A schoolteacher, Laura was credited with influencing George Bush's "compassionate conservatism" policy proposals of his governorship and immigration proposals of his later presidential campaign positions. His first foray into elective office politics was an unsuccessful run for the House of Representatives in 1978. In 1978 he also worked on his father's campaign for the presidency. He later joined a group of investors in buying the Texas Rangers baseball team in 1989. He ran for and was elected governor of Texas, serving as its 46th governor from 1995 to 2000.

After the attacks of September 11, 2001, President Bush declared a "war on terrorism," and his administration authored and Congress passed the

USA Patriot Act, of October 26, 2001. The Patriot Act granted the executive branch sweeping powers to deal with terrorism, including the controversial "enhanced interrogation" techniques that critics contended were used in a racially biased manner against Arab and Muslims, especially Muslim immigrants. Congress also passed the administration-backed law to create the new cabinet-level Department of Homeland Security in 2002 (116 Stat. 2135). An even more sweeping law, it has embroiled the DHS in many actions and controversies involving racial and ethnic profiling against Muslim Americans. Bush appointed former Pennsylvania governor Tom Ridge as the first secretary of homeland security, and later Michael Chertoff as his second secretary of DHS. The administration was noted for its crackdown on illegal immigrants and efforts to enforce expedited removal. He appointed the first director of national intelligence in an effort to control international terrorism. He pushed, unsuccessfully, for comprehensive immigration reform and a bill that would have established a guest-worker program. Bush also appointed Alberto Gonzales as attorney general, an appointment that embroiled the DOJ in immigration-related controversy.[12]

Barack Obama (1961–)

Barack Obama was the 44th president of the United States (2009–2017), the first African American to serve as president. Although it is only a short time after his presidency and therefore tentative at best to establish his ranking by historians, some recent rankings put him within the top 15. He was born in Hawaii in 1961 and raised by his grandparents. After working his way through Occidental College in Los Angeles and then transferring with a scholarship to Columbia University in New York City, he graduated in 1983 with a BA degree in political science. He moved to Chicago, where he worked with a group of churches as a community organizer to help rebuild communities devastated by high unemployment because of the closure of local steel plants. Obama went on to Harvard Law School, becoming the first African American editor of the *Harvard Law Review* and earning his JD degree.

He returned to Chicago to lead voter registration drives, to teach constitutional law at the University of Chicago, and eventually to run for the state legislature. Obama served in the Illinois State Senate

(1997–2004) where his accomplishments include being instrumental in getting the first major ethics reform law passed in 25 years, helping to get tax cuts for working-class families, and helping to the stage to pass expanded health care. As U.S. senator from Illinois (D-IL), Obama worked on bipartisan lobbying reform and transparency in government by putting federal spending online.

Obama burst on to the national political scene when giving the Democratic National Convention's keynote address in 2004. He ran for president in 2008, and after a tough primary battle with then senator Hillary Clinton (D-NY), he was elected president and sworn into office on January 20, 2009. He selected Senator Joe Biden (D-PA) as his running mate. They ran against Senator John McCain (R-AZ) and the governor of Alaska, Sarah Palin. The Obama-Biden ticket beat the McCain-Palin ticket, winning 365 ECVs to 173 ECVs, and 52.9 percent of the popular vote to 45.7 percent. Obama was reelected in 2012, this time running against Mitt Romney (former governor of Massachusetts) and Representative Paul Ryan (R-WI). The Obama-Biden ticket won 332 ECVs to 206 for Romney-Ryan, and 51.1 percent of the popular vote to 47.2 percent.

During his two terms in office, President Obama appointed two secretaries of homeland security. His first appointee was Janet Napolitano, the former governor of Arizona who served as DHS secretary from 2009 to 2013. His second was Jeh Johnson, who served from 2013 to 2017. President Obama issued two executive orders that were implemented by Johnson and the DHS, impacting unauthorized immigrants. The Deferred Action for Childhood Arrivals (DACA) was announced in 2012. The Deferred Action for Parents of Americans and Lawful Permanent Residents (DAPA) was announced in 2014. Both have been challenged in federal courts. DACA was upheld, but DAPA was put on an injunctive stay and later rescinded by President Donald Trump. But the Obama administration also set a record for deporting unauthorized immigrants, by focusing on those convicted of violent or felony crimes.

During his presidency Obama appointed two associate justices to the U.S. Supreme Court, Sonja Sotomayor (2009) and Elena Kagan (2010), both of whom have compiled strong records of progressive decisions. Both justices have been strongly critical of the Trump administration's immigration policies, albeit typically voting with the minority faction on the Supreme Court.

President Obama emphasized LGBT rights, same-sex marriage, and ended the Defense of Marriage Act, all of which earned him harsh criticism and opposition from the religious right. They also vehemently opposed his DACA and DAPA immigration policy.

President Obama is the recipient of the Nobel Peace Prize (2009), one of only four U.S. presidents so honored. He was also awarded the Profiles in Courage Award in 2017. Barack Obama is the author of three best-selling books: *Dreams of My Father* (2004), *The Audacity of Hope* (2007), and *Of Thee I Sing* (2010).[13]

Donald J. Trump (1946–)

Donald J. Trump is a multimillionaire real estate mogul and former reality television star, who was born in Queens, New York City in 1946. In 2016 he was elected as the 45th president of the United States and was sworn into office in January 2017. Donald Trump graduated from the New York Military Academy prep school and attended Fordham University and the Wharton School of the University of Pennsylvania, receiving his degree in economics in 1964. He took over his father's real estate business in 1971, building it into a real estate empire and claiming billionaire status. In 2004, he appeared as host of *The Apprentice*, becoming a reality television show celebrity

In 2012, he briefly considered running for president and was embroiled in and largely led the anti-Obama "birther" movement. He strenuously opposed President Obama's DACA and DAPA executive orders, arguing they were unconstitutional and required congressional authorization to be legal. On June 15, 2015, he announced his candidacy for the Republican Party nomination for president, running in a field of 17. On July 15, 2016, he clinched the nomination and announced his choice for vice president, Republican governor Mike Pence of Indiana. He accepted the GOP nomination on July 21, 2016. The Trump-Pence ticket ran against former secretary of state and New York senator Hillary Clinton, and Senator Tim Kaine (D-VA). Trump-Pence lost the popular vote to the Clinton-Kaine ticket 48.2 percent to 46.1 percent, by a margin of nearly three million votes, but they won the Electoral College vote 304 to 227 votes, and Trump was inaugurated President on January 20, 2017. He nominated John Kelly, a retired Marine Corps general, as secretary of the Department of Homeland Security, and Jeff Sessions as attorney general, and they in turn issued departmental rules and regulations turning back President Obama's reform policies particularly as related to immigration reform.

Trump ran a decidedly unorthodox campaign for the presidency and surprised most analysts by winning the Electoral College vote despite losing the popular vote. He ran as a popular nationalist. As a candidate for president, Trump announced that the DHS would build a border wall (which Mexico would pay for, he claimed), the extension of the southern border fence, then covering just more than 600 miles, and increased electronic surveillance along the border. In 2017, then attorney general Sessions announced that the DOJ would withhold federal funds from sanctuary cities who failed to assist the DOJ in enforcing illegal immigration policy. The DOJ launched raids to find and deport illegal aliens.

Despite having been a vigorous critic of President Obama's use of executive orders, President Trump issued several controversial executive orders that impacted homeland security, which greatly expanded the use of expedited removal of unauthorized immigrants. He rescinded President Obama's DACA and DAPA orders to protect Dreamers, although district courts placed a temporary ban on the implementation of the DACA rescinding order.

Trump ultimately issued three versions of a travel ban aimed at Muslims and refugees from the Middle East. The first two versions of the travel ban were held unconstitutional by several district and appellate courts. The third version of the executive travel ban, which added North Korea and Venezuela to the ban, was ultimately ruled constitutional, with some limitations, by the U.S. Supreme Court.

When Donald Trump rescinded the DACA and DAPA orders, he gave the Congress a few months to pass legal authorization of the policies. But when congressional leaders announced a bipartisan deal to do so, President Trump pulled back from his announced willingness to sign it. His announcement to that effect killed the effort. He ordered Sessions to begin a policy of "zero tolerance" of illegal immigration, even using it against immigrants who crossed the border illegally but who had thereby committed only a misdemeanor, to charge them as criminal aliens

from whom their children could be forcibly removed. The forced separation of some 2,500 resulted in such controversy and opposition that
President Trump reversed himself and announced that the DOJ would
no longer separate children from their parents while their immigration
proceedings and asylum requests were being adjudicated, stipulating that
such detention could be indefinite rather than complying with court rulings that specified that such detention could not be longer than 20 days.
In 2018, Trump tweeted his advocacy of the immediate deportation of
all illegal immigrants without a judicial hearing on the matter and without due process. In 2019, asylum seekers from El Salvador, Guatemala,
and Honduras crossed some 2,000 miles of Mexican territory to arrive at
the U.S.-Mexico border requesting asylum. Their numbers quickly over-
whelmed the ability of the DHS, the Customs and Border Patrol (CBP),
and the Department of Health and Human Services (DHHS) to cope
with holding so many thousands in detention. A humanitarian crisis
quickly developed at the overcrowded facilities in California, Arizona,
and Texas. Despite having announced that the DHS would no longer separate children from their parents or family members, the administration
continued to do so. These policies evoked harsh criticism in the media
and by members of Congress.

Trump attacked his critics and the media's reporting on the border crisis
(labeling the press as "fake news"). When Trump failed to get
congressional approval to allocate some $5 billion to build a border wall,
he issued a national emergency executive order to move $5 billion from
elsewhere in the budget (mostly from the Department of Defense) to build
portions of the wall or to fund replacement of sections of the border fence.
In July 2019, the Supreme Court upheld his emergency order to do so.
Trump has repeatedly used his Twitter account to advocate for the immediate deportation of all illegal immigrants without a judicial hearing on the
matter and without due process. In July 2019, he announced a new asylum
policy, stating that henceforth all asylum requests and processing had to be
done on the Mexican side of the border and that persons who traveled to
the United States to seek asylum who passed through another country to
do so would not be considered for asylum.

Trump nominated two hard-right conservative judges to the U.S.
Supreme Court, Neil Gorsuch and Brett Cavanaugh, and a sizable number
of conservative judges to federal district and appellate courts.

Trump has published nine books: *Trump: The Art of the Deal* (1987), *The America We Deserve* (2000), *Trump: How to Get Rich* (2004), *Why We Want You to be Rich* (2006), *Think Big and Kick Ass in Business* (2007), *Trump 101: The Way to Success* (2007), *Trump: Never Give Up* (2008), *Think Like a Champion* (2009), and *Time to Get Tough* (2011).[14]

KEY LEGISLATORS

Presidents can propose legislation to reform immigration or use executive orders to get around a Congress stalemated on the immigration issue, but they need members of Congress to introduce measures into the two chambers of Congress. The following biographical essays briefly highlight seven members of Congress who were the primary sponsors of bills that were enacted as major immigration reform laws: the Immigration and Nationality Act of 1952, also known as the McCarran-Walter Act; the Immigration and Nationality Act of 1965, also known as the Hart-Celler Act; and the Immigration Reform and Control Act of 1986, known as IRCA or the Simpson-Mazzoli Act. They exemplify the role that members of Congress play in the arena of immigration politics.

Authors of the Immigration and Nationality Act of 1952

Pat McCarran (1876–1954)

Pat McCarran served as Democratic senator from Nevada from 1933 to 1954. He was born in Reno, Nevada, and attended Nevada State University. He completed private law studies and was admitted to the Nevada bar in 1905, and in 1906 was elected as Nye County district attorney. McCarran was elected to the Nevada state legislature in 1903. He was associate justice of the Nevada Supreme Court from 1913 to 1917 and was its Chief Justice from 1917 to 1919. He was a member of the Nevada Board of Pardons, 1913–1919; and parole commissioner, 1913–1918. He served as chairman of the Nevada Board of Bar Examiners, 1919 to 1932. When McCarran was elected to the U.S. Senate in 1932, he was the first U.S. senator born in Nevada. He was reelected in 1938, 1944, and 1950, serving until his death in 1954. McCarran was an ardent anti-communist and sponsored the Subversive Activities Control Act of 1950, known as the McCarran Act.

He received an honorary master of arts degree from Nevada State University in 1915, and an honorary LLD from Georgetown University in 1943, and another from the University of Nevada in 1945. He served as president of the Nevada Bar Association from 1920 to 1921, and vice president of the American Bar Association from 1922 to 1923.

McCarran staunchly supported China's Chiang Kai-shek, and that association influenced his authoring of the McCarran-Walter Act, which he cosponsored with Francis Walter and which is reflected in its provision to increase controls to exclude admission and to deport dangerous aliens. The power to deny visas for ideological reasons remained in U.S. immigration law until 1976.

McCarran's primary impact on immigration matters, particularly on the 1952 law, emerged from his position as chair of the Senate Judiciary Committee from 1943 to 1953, during which time he coauthored the McCarran-Walter Act of 1952, which reaffirmed the quota system but also introduced the idea of preferences. He was a notable Cold War hawk and anti-communist and he cochaired the Joint Committee on Foreign Economic Cooperation.[15]

Francis Eugene Walter (1894–1963)

Francis E. Walter (D-PA) served in the U.S. House of Representatives from 1933 to 1952 representing two different congressional districts of Pennsylvania (because of reapportionment and redistricting): from 1933 to 1945; and from 1945 to 1952. Prior to his congressional service, Walter was admitted to the bar in 1919 and served as solicitor of Northampton County, Pennsylvania, from 1925 to 1933. He was a delegate to the Democratic National Convention in 1928.

While in the House of Representatives, Walter was a prominent member of the House Un-American Activities Committee, including serving as its chair from 1951 to 1963. Walter served on the House Judiciary Committee and he chaired the House Subcommittee on Immigration, positions that afforded him his influence on immigration matters. Like Senator Pat McCarran, Walter was a notorious and hardline anti-communist.

Walter served in the U.S. Navy in both World War I and World War II. He attended Lehigh University, George Washington University, and Georgetown University. In 1932, Walter ran for and was first elected to the U.S. House, riding in on President Franklin Delano Roosevelt's electoral coattails. He became a close ally of Speaker of the House Sam Rayburn (D-TX). Walter wanted to minimize immigration and is the noted coauthor (with Senator Pat McCarran) of the McCarran-Walter Act of 1952. He was a Director of the Pioneer Fund, noted for promoting the idea of IQ variations based on race. Impressed by the valiant and highly decorated for valor service of the Japanese Americans (the *nisei*) in World War II, Walter was a prominent advocate for the naturalization of the Japanese-born *issei*, for which he included a provision in the 1952 act that allowed for their naturalization. That provision, and the inclusion of small quotas for Asian immigrants previously barred from immigration, earned support for the 1952 bill from the Japanese American Citizens League. It awarded a tiny quota of immigrants from Asia (135 from Japan, 100 from other Asian nations). President Harry Truman vetoed the bill for its barring of admission of persons suspected of being dangerous aliens, a provision that Truman stated amounted to thought control. Congress overrode Truman's veto, and the bill became law. The provision on the bar to admission and ease of deportation of "dangerous aliens" remained in U.S. law until 1976, when Congress passed the Act of October 20, 1976 to Amend the Immigration and Nationality Act of 1965.

In 1960, Walter chaired the House Democratic caucus. As delegate to the 1960 Democratic National Convention, he opposed what he called a phony issue—the plank in the Democratic Party platform urging the abolition of the national origins quota bill, which indeed became law with the enactment of the Immigration and Nationality Act of 1965.

Francis Walter died of leukemia in 1963.[16]

Author/Sponsors of the Immigration and Nationality Act of 1965
Emanuel Celler (1888–1981)

Emanuel Celler was a representative to the U.S. House of Representatives (D-NY) from 1923 to 1973. That term, 49 years and 10 months, was the second longest in congressional history. Celler's long career reflected a lifelong interest in the plight of refugees and immigrants. During World War I, Celler served as the appeals agent for the local draft board. He ran for the U.S. Congress as a Tammany Hall Democrat.

Celler graduated from Columbia College, New York City, in 1910, and the Columbia Law School in 1912, and was admitted to the bar that year. He was a delegate to the Democratic state conventions from 1922 to 1932, and as a delegate to and member of the Platform Committee of the Democratic National Convention from 1942 to 1964.

Celler opposed the Johnson-Reed Act of 1924, and for the next four decades he advocated elimination of the national origin quota system, which he criticized as racially biased. In 1948, he cosponsored the Displaced Persons Act of June 25, 1948 (62 Stat. 1009). That law allowed 339,000 DPs to enter the United States. His most notable impact on immigration law came through his chairing the U.S. House Committee on the Judiciary when he coauthored (with Senator Philip Hart D-MI) the Immigration and Nationality Act of 1965.

After leaving the U.S. Congress in 1973, he served on the Commission on Revision of the Federal Appellate Court System, from 1973 to 1975. In 1953, he authored his autobiography: *You Never Leave Brooklyn*. He died in New York City in 1981, at the age of 93.[17]

Philip Aloysius Hart (1912–1976)

Former U.S. senator Philip Hart (D-MI) served in the Senate from 1959 until his death from cancer in 1976. The newest Senate Office Building is named after him. During his 18-year career in the Senate, he distinguished himself as an ardent supporter and floor manager of the Civil Rights Act of 1965. Hart's stellar service earned him the appellation of "The Conscience of the Senate."

Hart earned his BA from Georgetown University in 1934 and his JD from the University of Michigan in 1937. He served in the U.S. Army during World War II. Hart served on the Michigan Corporation and Securities Commission and was the director of its Office of Price Stabilization in 1951, and was the U.S. attorney for Eastern Michigan in 1952. From 1953 to 1954 he was a legal advisor to the governor of Michigan, and was its lieutenant governor from 1955 to 1958. He was elected to the U.S. Senate in 1958, where he served as assistant majority whip from 1966 to 1967. He served on numerous committees during his career in the Senate, but most notably on the Judiciary Committee and its Immigration Subcommittee. His most notable contribution to immigration law was his sponsoring and successfully seeing through Congress the Immigration and

Nationality Act of 1965 (aka the Hart-Celler Act). He retired from the Senate in 1976 and died of cancer soon thereafter.[18]

Authors/Sponsors of the Immigration Reform and Control Act of 1986 (IRCA)

Romano Mazzoli (1932–)

Romano Mazzoli (D-KY) served in the U.S. House of Representatives from 1971 to 1995. He received a BS degree from Notre Dame in 1954 and his JD from the University of Louisville in 1960. He served in the U.S. Army from 1954 to 1956, after which he worked in the law department of the L&N Railroad from 1960 to 1962. He practiced law from 1962 to 1970, at which time he was elected to the U.S. House of Representatives. He served on the Judiciary Committee, including the subcommittees Crime and Criminal Justice; Intellectual Property, and Judicial Administration; International Law, Immigration and Refugees (of which he was chair); and Small Business, SBA Legislation and the General Economy. A consistent advocate of liberal positions, in 1992 Mazzoli led the effort to give Haitian refugees protected status. From 1982 to 1986 he led the effort at immigration reform, but lost the lead to the chair of the Judiciary Committee, Peter Rodino (D-NJ) in 1985. He was chair of the Immigration Subcommittee until he lost the position to Bruce Morrison (D-CT) in 1989. Mazzoli returned as chair in 1991 when Morrison retired, and served until he retired in 1994. He was the primary sponsor of several immigration-related laws: H.R. 783, the Immigration Technical Corrections Act of 1994; H.R. 2128, the law to amend the Immigration and Nationality Act of 1965 that authorized refugee assistance for the fiscal years 1993 and 1994; H.R. 3049, the Miscellaneous and Technical Immigration and Naturalization amendments in 1991; and H.R. 14572, the Refugee Assistance Extension Act of 1986.[19]

Peter Rodino (1909–2005)

Peter Rodino (D-NJ) was a representative to the U.S. House from New Jersey. He earned his LLB from the New Jersey School of Law (now Rutgers University) in 1937. He served in the U.S. Army during World War II. He began to practice law in 1938. He was elected to the House in 1949 and served there until 1989. Rodino was the senior member of the New Jersey congressional delegation in 1971, and was assistant major-ity whip. He served on the Judiciary Committee, including as chair of its immigration subcommittee. Rodino's most notable role in immigration law reform was during the 1982–1986 efforts to enact IRCA, when he sponsored the earlier bills that ultimately became the Immigration Reform and Control Act of 1986, leading the bills through the Judiciary Commit-tee, and was instrumental in the House floor fights on the bill, helping craft some of the various compromises that made possible its passage. He was primary sponsor of H.R. 5115, the Immigration Amendment Act of 1988; and H.R. 4444, the Immigration and Nationality Act Amendments of 1986.[20]

Alan Simpson (1931–)

Alan Simpson (R-WY) was arguably, next to Senator Edward Kennedy, the most influential member of the U.S. Congress in either chamber for much of his illustrious career. Born in Denver, Colorado, Simpson earned his BS from the University of Wyoming in 1954 and his JD there in 1958. He served in the U.S. Army from 1954 to 1956 as a second lieutenant. He practiced law in Wyoming from 1959 to 1978, serving also as the city attorney for Cody, Wyoming, from 1959 to 1969. He then served in the Wyoming House of Representatives from 1964 to 1977, including a term as majority floor leader from 1976 to 1977, and as speaker pro tempore in 1977.

Simpson was elected to the U.S. Senate in 1978, serving until his retire-ment in 1997. He compiled a Senate record as a moderate conservative. One might not expect that a senator from the small state of Wyoming, not noted for having many immigrants, to become a leading senator on the issue, but perhaps it is somewhat because of that fact. Senator Simpson had no vested interest groups in his state that would lobby him in opposition to immigration reform. From 1979 to 1981, Simpson served on the Select Commission on Immigration and Refugee Policy (SCIRP), from which his interest in immigration law reform emerged. In the Senate, he coauthored several bills from 1982 to 1986, notably S. 1200 that became the Immigration Reform and Control Act, and he played a criti-cally important role in securing its passage, serving as its Senate sponsor/author. He also played a significant role in the enactment of IMMACT in 1990. Simpson served on several committees, a couple of which were and are especially important for immigration matters. He was a member of the Senate Finance Committee and its Subcommittee on Long-Term Growth, Debit and Deficit Reduction, along with Medicare Long-Term Care and Health Insurance. Simpson was a leading member of the Senate Judiciary Committee and served as chair of its Subcommittee on Immigration. It was in that capacity that Simpson had the greatest impact on immigration law. He also served on the Youth Violence Committee and as chair of the Veterans Affairs Committee and was a member of the Special Committee on Aging. Among his Senate colleagues, Simpson was noted for his sparkling sense of humor and was well respected on both sides of the aisle, a trait that became critically important for ushering through the Immigration Reform and Control Act of 1986 by negotiating key compromise provisions in the bill that ultimately secured its passage.

Senator Simpson served as Senate minority whip from 1987 to 1985 and as majority whip from 1985 to 1987. Senator Simpson retired in 1997, and for four years thereafter he taught as a visiting lecturer at the Joan Shorenstein Center on the Press, Politics and Public Policy at Harvard University's John F. Kennedy School of Government. Simpson served for two years as director of the Institute of Politics at the Kennedy School. He returned to Wyoming in 2000 as a partner in the law firm of Simpson, Kepler and Edwards. In 2001, Simpson was made honorary chairman of the Republican Unity Coalition, a gay/straight alliance. Alan Simpson is author of *Right in the Old Gazoo: A Lifetime of Grappling with the Press* (1997).[21]

Biographical Essays of Two Implementers of Immigration Law as AG of the United States and Head of the Department of Justice:

Alberto Gonzales (1955–)

Born in San Antonio, Texas, Alberto Gonzales served as U.S. attorney general from 2005 to 2007, succeeding John Ashcroft. As White House counsel to President George W. Bush (2001–2005), Gonzales was instrumental in preparing legal briefs justifying enhanced interrogation techniques and was part of the administration team that prepared the bill to establish the Department of Homeland Security. He was instrumental in drafting the Bush administration's positions on the Border Protection, Anti-Terrorism, and Illegal Immigration Control Act, and on the Real ID Act.

Gonzales was educated at the U.S. Air Force Academy (1973–1975) and earned his BA degree in political science from Rice University in 1979, and his JD from Harvard Law in 1982. Gonzales joined the law firm of Vinson and Elkins, LLP in Houston, in 1982. He also taught law as an adjunct professor at the University of Houston Law Center. Gonzales was elected to the American Law Institute in 1999. He was on the board of trustees of the Texas Bar Association from 1996 to 1999, and Board of Directors of the United Way of Texas Gulf Coast from 1993 to 1994. Gonzales was Special Legal Counsel to the Houston Host Committee for the 1990 Summit of Industrialized Nations. Gonzales served as Texas's 100th secretary of state, (1997–1999), where he was senior advisor to Governor George W. Bush and his administration's chief liaison on Mexico and immigration and border control issues. He served as an associate justice of the Supreme Court of Texas from 1999 to 2001. In 1999, Gonzales was names Latino Judge of the Year by the Hispanic National Bar Association. He served as General Counsel to Governor Bush for three years. Since leaving the attorney general's office in 2007, he has been Dean and Distinguished Professor of Law at Belmont University College of Law in Nashville, Tennessee. He has coauthored, with David Strange, *A Conservative and Compassionate Approach to Immigration Reform* (2014), and authored *True Faith and Allegiance* (2016).[22]

Sessions, Jeff (1946–)

Jeff Sessions was nominated for attorney general by President Trump in 2016, and confirmed by the U.S. Senate in 2017 by a vote of 52–47, basically along party lines, with all Republican senators voting to confirm, along with only one Democrat. He was an ardent supporter of President Trump's agenda related to immigration and to homeland security concerns—including the cutting of financial aid to sanctuary cities, the policy to separate children from their parents or family members while in detention at the southwestern border, the zero-tolerance policy of the DOJ, and strong support for the executive orders imposing travel bans.

Jeff Sessions was elected to the U.S. Senate in 1997, serving in that chamber until 2017, when President Trump appointed him attorney general. Sessions chaired the Senate Judiciary's Subcommittee on Immigration and National Interest. He was reelected to the U.S. Senate in 2008.

In 2011, he was the ranking member of the Budget Committee, and the Subcommittee on Banking. He sponsored a bill to block any funding for amnesty. He served on the Senate Armed Forces Committee, and on the Environment and Public Utility Committee. He opposed renewal of the 1965 Voting Rights Act, the Affordable Care Act, and legislation to legalize same-sex marriages.

Sessions was born in Selma, Alabama, in 1946. He received his BA degree from Huntington College in 1969 and his JD from the University of Alabama School of Law in 1973. In the mid-1970s, Sessions served in the U.S. Army Reserves, with the rank of captain.

Prior to his election to the U.S. Senate, Sessions served, as a President Reagan appointee, as the U.S. attorney for the Southern District of Alabama. While in the Senate, he was an outspoken opponent of comprehensive immigration reform and on any sort of amnesty program. He was an ardent advocate of the Patriot Acts I and II and supported creation of the Department of Homeland Security. In June 2018, Sessions reversed an immigration appeals court ruling that granted asylum to a Salvadoran woman who had been raped and beaten by her former husband, and he overturned precedent set by the Obama DOJ that allowed women with a credible threat of domestic violence to apply for asylum.

As attorney general, he announced and then implemented the "zero-tolerance" policy and defended the use of forced separation of children from their parents if they had entered the country illegally. Critics charge he instituted a DOJ policy to "slow-walk" asylum requests to further deter immigrants from Mexico and Central America (largely El Salvador, Guatemala, and Honduras). He cited Bible passages to justify the family separation policy, for which he has been widely criticized by various faith leaders and even threatened with excommunication from the Methodist Church for his implementation of the policy. Although Sessions was often at odds with and excoriated by President Trump because of his recusal on the Russian probe and Mueller investigation, Sessions was nonetheless the Trump administration's most ardent proponent of anti-illegal immigration policy and procedures; opposition to DACA and DAPA, immigration reform that would reduce family reunification preferences, which the administration called chain migration; increasing "merit-based" economic preferences; reduction of overall legal immigration; and ending the visa lottery program. He resigned as attorney general on November 7, 2018, at the request of President Trump.[23]

NOTES

1. Richard Neustadt, *Presidential Power and the Modern Presidents* (New York: The Free Press, 1990), 11.

2. Jon A. Bond, and Richard Fleisher, *The President in the Legislative Arena* (Chicago: University of Chicago Press, 1990); Brandice Canes-Wrone, *Who Leads Whom? Presidents, Policy, and the Public* (Chicago: University of Chicago Press, 2006); George C. Edwards III, *On Deaf Ears: The Limits of the Bully Pulpit* (New Haven, CT: Yale University Press, 2003); and George C. Edwards III, *The Strategic President: Persuasion and Opportunity in Presidential Leadership* (Princeton: Princeton University Press, 2009).

3. Common Council for American Unity. "Letters from America" Index No. 56-13-750, February 27, 1956.

4. These laws are excerpted in Michael LeMay and Elliott Barkan, *U.S. Immigration Laws and Issues: A Documentary History* (Westport, CT: Greenwood Press, 1999), 242–49.

5. "Persons Naturalized by Decade and Selected Region of Birth, Fiscal Years 1961–2000," in *Statistical Yearbook of Immigration and Naturalization Service*, U.S. Department of Justice, Immigration and Naturalization Service, Washington, D.C. Available at http://www.immigration.gov/graphicsshared/aboutus/statistics/00yrbk_Natz/NATZ_2000.pdf (accessed 6/30/2003).

6. Michael C. LeMay, *From Open Door to Dutch Door*. New York: Praeger Press, 1987), 122.

7. LeMay and Barkan, *U.S. Immigration Laws and Issues*, 270–72.

8. "Lyndon B. Johnson," The White House, http://www.whitehouse.gov/1600/presidents/lyndonbjohnson (accessed 12/1/2019).

9. Encyclopedia Brittanica. "United States Presidential Election of 1984." Available at: https://www.britannica.com/event/United-States-presidential-election-of-1984 (accessed 7/31/2019).

10. Michael C. LeMay, *Illegal Immigration* (Santa Barbara, CA: ABC-CLIO, 2007), 178; and U.S. Department of Justice, "INS Reporter" (Washington, DC: U.S. Government Printing Office, 1992), 144.

11. "Ronald Reagan," History.com, May 16, 2019. Available at: https://www.history.com/topics/us-presidents/ronald-reagan (accessed 7/31/2019).

12. "George W. Bush," History.com, June 7, 2019. Available at: https://www.history.com/topics/us-presidents/george-w-bush (accessed 7/31/2019).

13. "About Barack Obama," The Office of Barack and Michelle Obama, 2017. Available at: https://barackobama.com/about/ (accessed 12/1/2019).

14. "The 45th President of the United States: Donald J. Trump," https://www.donaldjtrump.com/about/ (accessed 7/31/2019).

15. Martin T. Smith, "Pat McCarran." Available at: https://nevadatrivia.com/nevada-history/pat-mccarran (accessed 8/1/2019).

16. "Walter, Francis Eugene," U.S. House of Representatives and Densho Encyclopedia, https://history.house.gov/People/Detail/23341 (accessed 8/1/2019); http://encyclopedia.densho.org/Francis%20Walter/ (accessed 8/1/2019).

17. "Emanuel Celler." Jewish Virtual Library, https://www.jewishvirtuallibrary.org/emanuel-celler (accessed 8/1/2019).

18. "Philip A. Hart," United States Senate, https://www.senate.gov/artand-history/history/common/generic/Featured_Bio_Hart.htm (accessed 8/1/2019); http://bioguide.congress.gov/scripts/biodisplay.pl?index=h000291 (accessed 8/1/2019); and https://www.govtrack.us/congress/members/philip_hart/405164 (accessed 8/1/2019).

19. "Rep. Romano Mazzoli," GovTrack and U.S. House of Representatives, https://www.govtrack.us/congress/members/romano_mazzoli/407306 (accessed 8/1/2019); and https://history.house.gov/People/Listing/M/MAZZOLI,-Romano-Louis-(M000291)/ (accessed 8/1/2019).

20. "Rep. Peter Rodino Jr.," GovTrack, https://www.govtrack.us/congress/members/peter_rodino/409344 (accessed 8/1/2019).

21. "Sen. Alan Simpson," GovTrack, https://www.govtrack.us/congress/members/alan_simpson/409923 (accessed 8/1/2019).

22. "Alberto Gonzales," The White House, https://georgewbush-whitehouse.archives.gov/government/gonzales-bio.html (accessed 8/1/2019).

23. "Jeff Sessions," Biography.com, https://www.biography.com/political-figure/jeff-sessions (accessed 8/1/2019).

Primary Documents

This section presents primary documents on immigration laws and their implementation, spanning far before the Immigration and Nationality Act of 1965 to more recent legislation. The documents present excerpts of several laws and of presidential statements concerning those laws, as well as federal court decisions.

Document 1: George Washington: Letter on America as Asylum, December 2, 1783

Shortly before resigning as commander-in-chief of the Continental Army, General George Washington, in a letter to the Volunteer Association of the Kingdom of Ireland, thanked them for their hospitality to American prisoners of war and proclaimed the idea of the new American nation as an asylum for the oppressed, an aspirational ideal that has variously influenced U.S. immigration policy ever since. The following excerpt is a key section of that letter expressing the asylum concept.

It is not an uninteresting consideration, to learn, that the Kingdom of Ireland, by a bold and manly conduct had obtained the redress of many of its grievances, and it is much to be wished that the blessings of equal Liberty and unrestrained Commerce may yet prevail ... in the meantime, you may be assured, Gentlemen, that the Hospitality and Beneficence of your Countrymen, to our Brethren who have been Prisoners of War, are neither unknown, or unregarded [sic]. The bosom of America is open to receive not only the Opulent and respected Stranger, but the oppressed and persecuted of all Nations and Religions, whom we shall welcome to participation in all our rights and privileges, if by decency and propriety of conduct they appear to merit the enjoyment.

New York, December 2, 1783

Source: George Washington papers, 1592–1943. Library of Congress.

Document 2: The Alien and Sedition Act of 1798, June 25, 1798

Responding to fears that the excesses of the French Revolution might come to the United States with immigrants, the Federalist-dominated Congress enacted the Alien and Sedition Act of 1798. Although never enforced, it reflects the degree of xenophobia present in the United States at the time. It expired after the two-year limitation of the act and was not renewed. It set a precedent, however, for granting a president sweeping enforcement powers concerning immigration.

Be it enacted by the Senate and the House of Representatives of the United States of America in Congress assembled, That it shall be lawful for the President of the United States at any time during the continuance of the act, to order all such aliens as he shall judge dangerous to the peace and safety of the United States, or shall have reasonable grounds to suspect are concerned in any treasonable or secret machinations against the government thereof, to depart out of the territory of the United States within such time as shall be expressed in such order, which order shall be served to the alien by delivering a copy thereof, or leaving the same at his usual abode, and returned to the office of the Secretary of State, by the marshal or other person to whom the same shall be directed. And in case any alien, so ordered to depart, shall be found at large within the United States after the time limited in such order for his departure, and not having obtained a license from the President to reside therein, or having obtained such license shall not have conformed thereto, every such alien shall be convicted thereof, be imprisoned for a term not exceeding three years, and shall never be admitted to become a citizen of the United States . . .

Sec. 2. *And be it further enacted*, That it shall be lawful for the President of the United States, whenever he may deem it necessary for the public safety, to order to be removed out of the territory thereof, any alien who may or shall be in prison in pursuance of this act, and to cause to be arrested and sent out of the United States such of these aliens as shall have been ordered to depart thereof and shall not have obtained a license as aforesaid, in all cases where, in the opinion of the President, public safety requires a speedy removal. And if any alien so removed or sent out of the United States shall voluntarily return thereto, such alien on conviction thereof, shall be imprisoned so long as, in the opinion of the President, the public safety may require . . .

Sec. 4. *And be it further enacted,* That the circuit and district courts of the United States, shall respectively have cognizance of all crimes and offenses against this act. And all marshals and other officers of the United States are required to execute all precepts and orders of the President of the United States issued in pursuance or by virtue of this act . . .

Sec. 5. *And be it further enacted,* That it shall be lawful for any alien who may be ordered removed from the United States, by virtue of this act, to take with him such part of his goods, chattels, or other property, as he may find convenient; and all property left in the United States by any alien, who may be removed as aforesaid, shall be, and remain subject to his order and disposal, in the same manner as if this act had not been passed.

Sec. 6. *And be it further enacted,* That this act shall continue and be in force for . . . two years.

Source: The Alien Act of June 25, 1798 (1 Stat. 570).

Document 3: Millard Fillmore: Speech on the American Party Principles, June 26, 1856

In 1855, the United States was sharply divided and the political parties took differ-ent positions on immigration. Former president Millard Fillmore, then a Whig, ran on the American Party ticket (the Know Nothing Party), which was staunchly anti-foreign. Excerpts from a speech he gave in Newburgh, New York, in which he enunciated the principles of the American Party follow.

Fellow citizens of Newburgh, Accept my cordial thanks for this hearty greeting. My friend has introduced me as the standard-bearer of the Ameri-can party, and a friend of the Union. For the former position I am indebted to the partiality of my friends, who have without my solicitation made me your standard-bearer in the contest for President, which has just com-menced; but I confess to you that I am proud of the distinction, for I am an American with an American heart. I confess that I am a devoted and unalterable friend of the Union. As an American, occupying the position I do before my countrymen, I have no hostility to foreigners. I trust I am their friend. Having witnessed their deplorable conditions in the old country, God forbid that I should add to their suffering by refusing them asylum in this. I would open wide the gates and invite the oppressed of every land to our happy country, excluding only the pauper and criminal. I would be tolerant to men of all creeds, but would expect from all faithful allegiance to our republican institution.

While I did this, I would, for the sake of those who seek an asylum on our shares, as well as for our own sake, declare as a general rule, that Americans should govern America. I regret to say that men who come fresh from the monarchies of the old world, are prepared neither by education, habits of thought, or knowledge of our institutions, to govern America.

Source: Severance, Frank H., ed. *Millard Fillmore Papers*, Vol. 2. Buffalo, NY: Buffalo Historical Society, 1907, 16.

Document 4: Chester Arthur: Veto Message of the Chinese Laborer Exclusion Bill, May 1882

In May 1882, Congress passed a new immigration act commonly known as the Chinese Exclusion Act. The act uses the term suspension rather than exclusion. President Chester Arthur vetoed the bill, objecting to its 20-year suspension as a violation of the Burlingame Treaty. His veto message illustrates the different perspectives of the president and Congress on treaty matters that affect immigration law. The following document excerpts his veto message. In response, Congress passed a new immigration act setting the time period at 10 years rather than 20.

After careful consideration of Senate bill No. 71, entitled "An act to execute certain treaty stipulations relating to Chinese," I herewith return it to the Senate, in which it originated, with my objections to its passage.

A nation is justified in repudiating its treaty obligations only when they are in conflict with great paramount interests. Even then all possible and reasonable means of modifying or changing those obligations should be exhausted before resorting to the supreme right of refusal to comply with them. These rules have governed the United States in their past intercourse with others powers as one of the family of nations. I am persuaded that if Congress can feel that this act violates the faith of the nation as pledged to China it will concur with me in rejecting this particular mode which shall meet the expectations of the people of the United States without coming into conflict with the rights of China.

The present treaty relations between that power and the United States sprang from an antagonism which arose between our paramount domestic interests and our previous relations.

The treaty commonly known as the Burlingame treaty conferred upon Chinese subjects the right of voluntary emigration to the United States for the purposes of curiosity or trade or as permanent residents, and was in all respects reciprocal as to citizens of the United States in China. It gave to the voluntary emigrant coming to the United States the right to travel there or to reside there, with all the privileges, immunities, or exemptions enjoyed by the citizens or subjects of the most favored nation.

Under the operation of this treaty it was found that the institutions of the United States and the character of its people and their means of obtaining a livelihood might be serious affected by the unrestricted introduction of Chinese labor . . .

[However,] The examination which I have made of the treaty and of the declarations which its negotiators have left on record of the meaning of its language leaves no doubt in my mind that neither contracting party in concluding the treaty of 1880 contemplated the passage of an act prohibiting immigration for twenty years, which is nearly a generation, or thought that such period would be a reasonable suspension or limitation, or intended to change the provisions of the Burlingame treaty to that extent. I regard this provision of the act as a breach of our national faith, and being unable to bring myself in harmony with the views of the Congress on this vital point the honor of the country constrains me to return the act with this objection to its passage.

Source: Messages and Papers of the Presidents. Vol. 10. New York: Bureau of National Literature, Inc., 1882, 4699–705.

Document 5: "Gentleman's Agreement": Executive Order No. 589, March 14, 1907

In March 1907, the president of the United States issued an executive order that implemented the "Gentleman's Agreement" between the United States and Japan to control the immigration of persons from Japan and Korea (then under Japanese jurisdiction). The text of Executive Order No. 589 follows.

Whereas, by the act entitled "An Act to regulate the immigration of aliens into the United States," approved February 20, 1907, whenever the President is satisfied that passports issued by any foreign government to its citizens to go to any country other than the United States or to the Canal Zone, are being used for the purpose of enabling the holders to come to the continental territory of the United States from such country or from such insular possession or from the Canal Zone; AND WHEREAS, upon sufficient evidence produced before me by the Department of Commerce and Labor, I am satisfied that passports issued by the Government of Japan to citizens of that country or Korea and who are laborers, skilled or unskilled, to go to Mexico, to Canada, and to Hawaii, are being used for the purpose of enabling the holders thereof to come to the continental territory of the United States to the detriment of labor conditions therein;

I hereby order that such citizens of Japan or Korea, to wit: Japanese and Korean laborers, skilled and unskilled, who have received passports to go to Mexico, Canada, or Hawaii, and come therefrom, be refused permission to enter the continental territory of the United States.

It is further ordered that the Secretary of Commerce and Labor be, and he thereby is, directed to take through the Bureau of Immigration and Naturalization, such measures and to make and enforce such rules and regulations as may be necessary to carry this order into effect.

Source: Executive Order no. 589, March 14, 1907. National Archives.

Document 6: Political Party Positions on Immigration for the 1928 Presidential Campaign

In the 1928 presidential campaign, both of the major political parties adopted provisions (planks of the party platforms) that supported restrictions of immigration policy. The following document excerpts their party-platform planks.

The Democratic Party Platform on Immigration

Laws which limit immigration must be preserved in full force and effect, but the provisions contained in these laws that separate husbands from wives and parents from infant children, are inhumane and not essential to the efficiency of such law.

The Republican Party Platform on Immigration

The Republican Party believes that in the interest of both native and foreign-born wage earners, it is necessary to restrict immigration. Unrestricted immigration would result in wide-spread unemployment and in the breakdown of the American standard of living. Where, however, the law works undue hardship by depriving the immigrant of the comfort and society of those bound by close family ties, such modification should be adopted as well afford relief.

We commend Congress for correcting defects for humanitarian reasons and for providing an effective system of examining prospective immigrants in their home countries.

Through the saneness and soundness of Republican rule, the American workman is paid a "real wage" which allows comfort for himself and his dependents and an opportunity and leisure for advancement. It is not surprising that the foreign workman, whose greatest ambition still is to achieve a "living wage," should look with longing toward America as the goal of his desires.

The ability to pay such wages and to maintain such a standard comes from the wisdom of the prospective legislation which the Republican Party has placed on the national statute books: the tariff which bars cheap foreign-made goods from the American market and provides continuity of employment for our workmen and fair profits for the manufacturers, and the restriction of immigration which not only prevents the gutting of our labor market, but allows to our newer immigrants a greater opportunity to secure a footing in their upward struggle.

Source: Congressional Record Press, as quoted in the Foreign Language Information Service, *Interpreter Release Clip Sheet,* 5, 15, July 5, 1928.

Document 7: The Immigration and Nationality Act of 1952, June 27, 1952

The first major amendment to the Quota Acts was passed by Congress in 1952. It is a massive, comprehensive omnibus law comprising more than 200 pages in the Code of Statutes. It codified previous immigration and naturalization laws. It maintained the basic quota system, but allowed for some new immigration quotas by revising the quotas for the Asia-Pacific Triangle. It reflected the Cold War foreign policy considerations upon U.S. immigration policy in its specific consideration for the entrance of refugees and anti-communist freedom fighters. The following document excerpts some of the major provisions of the McCarran-Walter Act, as it was more commonly known.

Title II—Immigration

Chapter 1—Selection System/Numerical Limitations

Sec. 201. (a) The annual quota of any quota area shall be one-sixth of 1 per centum of the number of inhabitants in the continental United States in 1920, which number, except for the purpose of computing quotas for the quota area within the Asia-Pacific triangle, shall be the same number heretofore determined under the provisions of section 11 of the Immigration Act of 1924, attributed by national origin to such quota areas: *Provided,* That the quota existing for Chinese persons prior to the date of the enactment of this Act shall be continued, and, except for as otherwise provided in section 202 (e), the minimum quota for any quota area shall be one hundred.

201 (c) There shall be issued to quota immigrants chargeable to any quota (1) no more immigrant visas in any fiscal year than the quota for such year, and (2) in any calendar month of any fiscal year, no more immigrant visas than 10 percentum of the quota for such year; except that during the last two months of any fiscal year immigrant visas may be issued without regard to the 10 per centum limitation contained herein . . .

201 (e) The quota numbers available under the annual quotas of each quota area proclaimed under this Act shall be reduced by the number of quota numbers which have been ordered to be deducted from annual quotas authorized prior to the effective date of the annual quotas proclaimed under this Act under—(1) section 19 (c) of the Immigration Act of 1917, as amended: (2) the Displaced Persons Act of 1948, as amended, and (3) any other Act of Congress enacted prior to the effective date of the quotas [herein] . . .

Sec. 202. (b) With reference to determination of the quota to which shall be chargeable an immigrant who is not attributable by as much as one half of his ancestry to a people or peoples indigenous to the Asia-Pacific triangle, comprising all quota areas and colonies and other dependent areas situate wholly east of the meridian sixty degrees east of Greenwich, wholly west of the meridian one hundred and sixty-five degrees west, and wholly north of the parallel twenty-five degrees south latitude—

(1) There is hereby established, in addition to quotas for separate quota areas comprising independent countries, self-governing dominions, and territories under the international trusteeship of the United Nations situate wholly within said Asia-Pacific triangle, quota of one hundred annually, which shall not be subject to the provisions of section (e);

(2) Such immigrant born within a separate quota area situate within such Asia-Pacific triangle shall not be chargeable to the Asia Pacific quota, but shall be chargeable to the quota for the separate quota area in which he was born;

(3) Such immigrant born within a colony or other dependent area situate wholly within said Asia-Pacific triangle shall be chargeable to the Asia-Pacific quota;

(4) Such immigrant born outside the Asia-Pacific triangle who is attributable by as much as one-half of his ancestry to a people or peoples indigenous to not more than one separate quota area, situate wholly within the Asia-Pacific triangle, shall be chargeable to the quota of that quota area;

(5) Such immigrant born outside the ... triangle who is attributable to one-half of his ancestry to a people or people indigenous ... to one or more colonies or other dependent areas situate wholly within the ... triangle shall be chargeable to the Asia-Pacific quota;

(c) Any such immigrant born in a colony or other component or dependent area of a governing country for which no separate or specific quota has been established ... shall be chargeable to the quota of the governing county ... except that (1) not more than one hundred persons.. shall be chargeable to the quota ... in any one year ...

Sec. 212. (d) (5) The Attorney General may in his discretion parole into the United States temporarily under such conditions as he may prescribe for emergent reasons or reasons to be deemed strictly in the public interest any alien applying for admission to the United States, but such parole of each alien shall not be regarded as an admission of the alien and when the purposes of such parole shall, in the opinion of the Attorney General, have been served the alien shall forthwith return or be returned to the custody from which he was paroled and thereafter the case shall continue to be dealt with in the same manner as that of any other applicant for admission into the United States . . .

Sec. 215. (a) When the United States is at war or during the existence of any national emergency proclaimed by the President, or, as to aliens, whenever there exists a state of war between or among two or more states, and the President shall find that the interests of the United States require that restrictions and prohibitions in addition to those provided otherwise by this section be imposed upon the departure of persons from and their entry into the United States, and shall make public proclamation thereof, it shall, until otherwise be ordered by the President or the Congress be unlawful . . . [the act then lists seven subdivisions of various restrictions and prohibitions].

Chapter 2—Nationality and Naturalization

Sec. 311. The right of a person to become a naturalized citizen of the United States shall not be denied or abridged because of race or sex or because such a person is married. Notwithstanding section 405(b), this section shall apply to any person whose petition for naturalization shall hereafter be filed, or shall have been pending on the effective date of this Act.

Sec. 312. No person except otherwise provided in this title shall hereafter be naturalized as a citizen of the United States upon his own petition who cannot demonstrate—

(1) An understanding of the English language, including the ability to read, write, and speak words in ordinary usage in the English language . . .
(2) A knowledge and understanding of the fundamentals of the history and principles and form of government of the United States.

Sec. 313. (a) Notwithstanding the provisions of section 405(b), no person shall be naturalized as a citizen of the United States—[the act lists subsections (1) through (6) which prohibit the naturalization of anarchists, communists, totalitarians, and those who believe or publish such . . .]

Sec. 316 (a) [lists and specifies how a petitioner shall be continuously residing in the United States at least five years . . .]

Sec. 337 (a) A person who has petitioned for naturalization shall, in order to be and before being admitted to citizenship, take in open court an oath (1) to support the Constitution of the United States; (2) to renounce and abjure absolutely and entirely all allegiance and fidelity to any foreign prince, potentate, state, or sovereignty of whom or which the petitioner was before a subject or citizen; (3) to support and defend the Constitution and laws of the United States against all enemies, foreign and domestic; (4) to bear true faith and allegiance the same; and (5) (A) to bear arms on behalf of the United States when required by law, or (B) to perform non-combatant service in the Armed Forces of the United States when required by law, or (C) to perform work of national importance under civilian direction when required by law . . .

Sec. 349 . . . [then specifies the conditions or actions by which a person shall lose his nationality, which includes obtaining naturalization in a foreign state . . . taking an oath of allegiance to a foreign state . . . entering into and serving in the armed forces of a foreign state unless (prior to doing so) authorized by the Secretary of State and the Secretary of Defense . . . voting in the election in a foreign state . . . making a formal renunciation of nationality before a diplomatic or consular officer of the United States in a foreign state . . . deserting the military, air, or naval forces of the United States in a time of war, if and when he is convicted thereof by court martial and as a result . . . is dismissed or dishonorably discharged from the service . . . commits any act of treason against, or attempting to overthrow, or bearing arms against the United States . . . or departing from and remaining outside the jurisdiction of the United States in time of war for the purpose of evading or avoiding . . . service in the military . . .]

Source: Congressional Record. 66 Stat. 163. Washington, DC: Government Printing Office, 1952.

Document 8: Harry S. Truman:
Veto Message of the Immigration and Nationality Bill, June 28, 1952

President Harry Truman vetoed the McCarran-Walter Act, but Congress overrode his veto and passed the act over his objections. President Truman's veto message, excerpted in the following document, emphasizes the foreign policy needs and perspectives of the president versus the racial and isolationist views of members of Congress, who in passing the bill were responding to the narrower views of their geographically small districts. He also objected to the sweeping powers it authorized for the attorney general and the president to deport or take away the citizenship on grounds not applicable to other citizens.

I return herewith, without my approval . . . the proposed Immigration and Nationality Act. In outlining my objections to this bill, I want to make it clear that it contains certain provisions that meet with my approval. This is a long and complex piece of legislation. It has 164 separate sections, some with more than 40 subdivisions. It presents a difficult problem of weighing the good against the bad, and arriving at a judgment on the whole.

H.R. 5678 is an omnibus bill which would revise and codify all of our laws relating to immigration, naturalization, and nationality.

A general revision and modernization of these laws unquestionably is needed and long overdue, particularly with respect to immigration. But this bill would not provide us with an immigration policy adequate for the present world situation. Indeed, the bill, taking all its provisions together, would be a step backward and not a step forward. In view of the crying need for reform in the field of immigration, I deeply regret that I am unable to approve H.R. 5678 . . .

I have long urged that racial or national barriers to naturalization be abolished. This was one of the recommendations in my civil rights message to the Congress on February 2, 1948. On February 19, 1951, the House of Representatives unanimously passed a bill to carry it out.

But now its most desirable provision comes before me embedded in a mass of legislation which would perpetuate injustices long standing against many other nations of the world, hamper the efforts we are making to rally the men of the East and West alike to the cause of freedom, and intensify the repressive and inhumane aspects of our immigration procedures. The price is too high, and in good conscience I cannot agree to pay it.

I want our residents of Japanese ancestry, and all our friends throughout the Far East, to understand this point clearly. I cannot take the step I would like to take, and strike down the bars that prejudice has erected against them, without, at the same time, establishing new discriminations against the peoples of Asia and approving harsh and repressive measures directed at all who seek a new life within our boundaries. I am sure the public conscience and good sense of the American people will assert themselves, and we shall be in a position to enact an immigration and naturalization policy that will be fair to all ... The bill would continue, practically without change, the national origin quota system, which was enacted into law in 1924, and put into effect in 1929. This quota system—always based upon assumptions at variance with our American ideals—is long since out of date and more than ever unrealistic in the face of present world conditions ...

The greatest vice of the present quota system, however, is that it discriminates, deliberately and intentionally, against many of the peoples of the world. The purpose behind it was to cut down and virtually eliminate immigration to this country from Southern and Eastern Europe. A theory was invented to rationalize this objective. The theory is that in order to be readily assimilable, European immigrants should be admitted in proportion to the numbers of persons of their respective national stocks already here as shown in the census of 1920. Since Americans with English, Irish and German descent were most numerous, immigrants from those three nationalities got the lion's share—more than two-thirds—of the total quota. The remaining third was divided up among all the other nations given quotas.

The desired effect was obtained. Immigration from Eastern Europe was reduced to a trickle. The quotas allotted to England and Ireland remained largely unused, as was intended. Total quota immigration fell to half or a third—and sometimes even less—of the annual limit of 354,000. People from such countries as Greece, or Spain, or Latvia were virtually deprived of any opportunity to come here at all, simply because Greeks or Spaniard or Latvians had not come here before 1920 in any substantial numbers.

The idea behind this discriminatory policy was, to put it baldly, that Americans with English or Irish names were better people and better citizens than Americans with Italian or Greek or Polish names. It was thought that people of West European origin made better citizens than Romanians or Balts or Austrians. Such a concept is utterly unworthy of our traditions and ideals. It violates the great political doctrine of the Declaration of Independence that "all men are created equal." It denies the humanitarian creed inscribed beneath the Statue of Liberty proclaiming to all nations, "Give me your tired, your poor, your huddled masses yearning to breathe free." ...

The basis of this quota system was false and unworthy in 1924. It is even worse now. At the present time, this quota system keeps out the very people we want to bring in. In its incredible to me that, in this year of 1952, we should again be enacting into law such a slur on the patriotism, the capacity, and the decency of a large part of our citizenry.

Today we entered into an alliance, the North Atlantic Treaty, with Italy, Greece, and Turkey against one of the most terrible threats mankind has ever faced. We are asking them to join with us in protecting the peace of the world. We are helping them to rebuild their defenses, and train their men, in common cause. But, through this bill, we say to their people: You are less worthy to come to this country with Englishmen or Irishmen; you Italians, who need to find homes abroad in the hundreds of thousands— you shall have a quota of 5,645; you Greeks, struggling to assist the helpless victims of a communist civil war—you shall have a quota of 308; and you Turks, you are brave defenders of the Eastern flank, but you shall have a quota of only 225! . . .

In these and many other respects, the bill raises basic questions as to our fundamental immigration and naturalization policy, and the laws and prac- tices for putting that policy into effect . . .

These conclusions point to an underlying condition which deserves the most careful study. Should we not undertake a reassessment of our immigration policies and practices in the light of the conditions we now face in the second half of the twentieth century? The great popular inter- est which this bill has created, and the criticism which it has stirred up, demand an affirmative answer. I hope the Congress will agree to a careful reexamination of this entire matter . . . To assist in this complex task, I suggest the creation of a representative commission of outstanding Amer- icans to examine the basic assumption of immigration policy, the quota system and all that goes with it, the effect of our present immigration and nationality laws, their administration, and the ways in which they can be brought into line with our national ideals and out foreign policy . . .

I very much hope that the Congress will take early action of these rec- ommendations. Legislation to carry them out will correct some of the unjust provisions of our laws, will strengthen us at home and abroad, and will serve to relieve a great deal of the suffering and tension existing in the world today. Harry S. Truman.

Source: Public Papers of the Presidents, June 25, 1952: 441–47. Washing- ton, DC: Office of the Federal Register, National Archives.

Document 9: Immigration and Nationality Act of October 3, 1965 (Re: Amending the Act of June 27, 1952)

The quota system was finally and formally ended with enactment of the Immigration and Nationality Act of 1965. It replaced the quota system with a preference system and stipulated a three-year period in which to transition from the abolished quota system to the new preference system. The law, which comprises some 20 pages in the Code of Statutes, is excerpted here, with some of its major provisions highlighted. The 1965 act is also more commonly known as the Kennedy immigration act after President John F. Kennedy, who advocated the preference system approach but was assassinated before passage of the law. It many ways, it reflected the civil rights revolutionary movement in American politics in the way the McCarran-Walter Act reflected the Cold War era of American politics. In replacing the national origin quota system with a preference system, the 1965 law enshrined into law the value and the primacy of family reunification over ethnic, foreign policy, or racial considerations.

Be it enacted by the Senate and the House of Representatives of the United States of America in Congress assembled, That section 201 of the Immigration and Nationality Act ... be amended to read as follows:

Sec. 201. (a) Exclusive of special immigrants defined in section 101 (a) (27), and of the immediate relatives of United States citizens specified in subsection (b) of this section, the number of aliens who may be issued immigrant visas or who may otherwise acquire the status of an alien lawfully admitted to the United States for permanent residence, or who may, pursuant to section 203 (a) (7) enter conditionally, (i) shall not in any of the first three quarters of any fiscal year exceed a total of 45,000 and (ii) shall not in any fiscal year exceed a total of 170,000.

(b) The 'immediate relatives' referred to in subsection (a) of this section will mean the children, spouses, and parents of citizens of the United States. *Provided,* That in the case of parents, such citizen must be at least twenty-one years of age ...

(c) During the period from July 1, 1965, through June 30, 1968, the annual quota of any quota area shall be the same as that which existed for that area on June 30, 1965 ...

(d) Quota numbers not issued or otherwise used during the previous fiscal year, as determined in accordance with subsection (c) hereof, shall be transferred to an immigration pool. Allocation of numbers from the pool and from national quotas shall not together exceed in any fiscal year the numerical limitations in subsection (a) of this section. The immigration pool shall be made available to immigrants otherwise admissible under the provisions of this Act who are unable to obtain prompt issuance of a preference visa due to oversubscription of their quotas, or subquotas as determined by the Secretary of State . . .

(e) The immigration pool and the quota areas shall terminate June 30, 1965. Thereafter immigrants admitted under the provisions of this Act who are subject to numerical limitations of subsection (a) of this Act will be admitted in accordance with the percentage limitations and in the order of priority specified in section 203.

Sec. 2, Section 202 of the Immigration and Nationality Act . . . is amended to read as follows:

(a) No person shall receive any preference or priority or be discriminated against in the issuance of an immigrant visa because of his race, sex, nationality, place of birth, or place of residence, except as specifically provided in section 101 (a) (27), section 201 (b), and section 203. *Provided,* That the total number of immigrant visas and the number of conditional entries made available to natives of any single foreign state . . . shall not exceed 20,000 in any fiscal year . . .

(b) Each independent country, self-governing dominion, mandated territory, and territory under the international trusteeship of the United Nations, other than the United States and its outlying possessions, shall be treated as a separate foreign state for the purposes of the numerical limitation set forth in the proviso to subsection (a) of this section when approved by the Secretary of State. All other inhabited lands shall be attributed to a foreign state specified by the Secretary of State. For the purposes of this Act the foreign state to which an immigrant is chargeable shall be determined by birth within such foreign state . . .

Sec. 3. Sec. 203 of the Immigration and Nationality Act . . . is amended as follows:

Sec. 203 (a) Aliens who are subject to the numerical limitations ... shall not be allotted visas or their conditional entry authorized, as the case may be as follows:

(1) Visas shall be first made available, in a number not to exceed 20 per centum of the number specified in section 201 (a) (ii), plus visas not required to be classes specified in paragraph (1), to qualified immigrants who are spouses, unmarried sons or daughters of citizens of the United States.

(2) Visas shall next be made available, in a number not to exceed 20 per centum of the number specified in section 201 (a) (ii), plus visas not required to be classes specified in paragraph (1), to qualified immigrants who are spouses, unmarried sons or unmarried daughters of an alien admitted for permanent residence.

(3) Visas shall be next made available, in a number not to exceed 10 per centum ... to qualified immigrants who are members of the professions, or who because of their exception ability in the sciences or arts will substantially benefit prospectively the national economy, cultural interests, or welfare of the United States.

(4) Visas shall next be made available, in a number not to exceed 10 per centum ... to qualified immigrants who are the married sons or married daughters of citizens of the United States.

(5) Visas shall next be made available, in a number not to exceed 10 per centum of the number specified ... to qualified immigrants who are the brothers or sisters of citizens of the United States.

(6) Visas shall next be made available, in a number not to exceed 10 per centum of the number specified ... to qualified immigrants who are capable of performing specified skilled or unskilled labor, not of a temporary or seasonal nature, for which a shortage of employable and willing persons exist in the United States.

(7) Conditional entries shall next be made available by the Attorney General, pursuant to such regulations as he may prescribe and in a number not to exceed six per centum ... to aliens who satisfy an Immigration and Naturalization Service officer, (A) that (i) because of persecution or fear of persecution on account of race, religion, or political opinion, have fled (I) from any Communist or Communist-dominated country or area, or (II) from any country within the general area of the Middle East, and (ii) are unable

or unwilling to return to such country or area on account of race, religion, or political opinion, and (iii) are not nationals of the countries or areas in which their application for conditional entry was made; or (B) that they are persons uprooted by catastrophic natural calamity as defined by the President who are unable to return to their usual place of abode. For the purpose of foregoing the term "general area of the Middle East" means the area between and including (1) Libya on the west, (2) Turkey on the north, (3) Pakistan on the east, and (4) Saudi Arabia and Ethiopia on the South ...

(8) Visas authorized in paragraphs (1) through (6) and less the conditional entries and visas made available pursuant to paragraph (7), shall be made available to other qualified immigrants strictly in the chronological order in which they qualify. Waiting lists of applicants shall be maintained in accordance with regulations prescribed by the Secretary of State. No immigrant visa shall be issued to a nonpreference immigrant under this paragraph, or to an immigrant with a preference under paragraph (3) or (6) of this subsection, until the consular officer is in receipt of a determination made by the Secretary of Labor in pursuant to the provisions of section 212 (a) (14).

(9) A spouse or child as defined in section 101 (b) (1) (A), (B), (C), (D), or (E) shall, if not otherwise entitled to an immigrant status and the immediate issuance of a visa, or to conditional entry under paragraph (1) through (8) be admitted to the same status, and the same order of consideration provided in subsection (b), if accompanying, or following his spouse or parent. ...

Sec. 8. Section 101 of the Immigrant and Nationality Act ... is amended as follows:

(a) Paragraph (27) of subsection (a) is amended to read as follows: (27) The term "special immigrant" means—(A) an immigrant who was born in any independent foreign country of the Western Hemisphere or in the Canal Zone and the spouse and children of any such immigrant, if accompanying, or following to join him ...

(B) an immigrant lawfully admitted for permanent residence, who is returning from a temporary visit abroad;

(C) an immigrant who was a citizen of the United States and may, under section 324 (a) or 327 of title III, apply for reacquisition of citizenship;

(D) (i) an immigrant who continuously for at least two years immediately preceding the time of his application for admission ... has been, and who seeks to enter the United States solely for the purpose of carrying on the vocation of minister of a religious denomination, and whose services are needed by such religious denomination having a bona fide organization in the United States, and (ii) the spouse or child of any such immigrant, if accompanying or following to join him; or

(E) an immigrant who is an employee, or an honorably retired former employee, of the United States Government abroad, and who has performed faithful service for a total or fifteen years or more, and his accompanying spouse and children ...

Sec. 21. (a) There is hereby established a Select Commission of Western Hemisphere Immigration ... to be composed of fifteen members. The President shall appoint the Chairman of the Commission and four other members thereof. The President of the Senate, with the approval of the majority and minority leaders of the Senate, shall appoint five members from the membership of the Senate. The Speaker of the House of Representatives, with the approval of the majority and minority leaders of the House, shall appoint five members from the membership of the House. Not more than three members appointed by the President of the Senate and the Speaker of the House of Representatives respectively, shall be members of the same political party ...

(b) The Commission shall study the following matters:

(1) Prevailing and projected demographic, technological, and economic trends as they pertain to the Western Hemisphere;

(2) Present and projected unemployment in the United States, by occupations, industries, geographic areas, and other factors in relation to immigration from the Western Hemisphere;

(3) The interrelationships between immigrants, present and future, and existing and contemplated national and international program and projects of Western Hemisphere nations, including program and projects for economic and social development;

(4) The operation of immigration laws of the United States as they pertain to Western Hemisphere nations, including adjustment of status for Cuban refugees . . .;

(5) The implication of the foregoing with respect to the security and international relations of Western Hemisphere nations; and

(6) Any other matters which the Commission believes to be germane to the purposes for which it was established.

Source: Congressional Record. 79 Stat. 911. Washington, DC: Government Printing Office, 1965.

Document 10: Lyndon B. Johnson: Remarks at the Signing of the Immigration and Nationality Act of 1965, October 3, 1965

President Lyndon B. Johnson gave an address at the foot of the Statue of Liberty on October 3, 1965, while signing the Immigration Act of 1965. In his remarks, excerpted here, President Johnson downplays the expected impact of the new law, stating it is not a revolutionary bill. In fact, however, the new law did in many ways remake America. It had a profound impact on the demographics of the United States. It set in motion the waves of undocumented immigration from Mexico and Central America, and it enabled a huge wave of immigration from Asia and Latin America.

This bill that we will sign today is not a revolutionary bill. It does not affect the lives of million. It will not reshape the structure of our daily lives, or really add importantly to either our wealth or our power. Yet it is still one of the most important acts of this Congress and of this administration. For it does repair a very deep and painful flaw in the conduct of the American nation . . .

This bill says simply that from this day forth those wishing to immigrate to America shall be admitted on the basis of their skills and their close relationship to those already here. The fairness of this standard is so self-evident that we may well wonder that it has not always been applied. Yet the fact is that for over four decades the immigration policy of the United States has been distorted by the harsh injustice of the national origins system. This system violated the basic principle of American democracy—the principle that values and rewards each man on the basis of his merit as a man. It [the quota system] has been un-American in the highest sense, because it has been untrue to the faith that brought thousands to these shores before we were a country. Today, with my signature, this system is abolished.

Asylum for Cuban Refugees

So it is in that spirit that I declare this afternoon to the people of Cuba that those who seek refuge here in America will find it. The dedication of America to our traditions as an asylum for the oppressed is going to be upheld. I have directed the Departments of State and Justice and Health, Education, and Welfare to immediately make all the necessary arrangements to permit those in Cuba who seek freedom to make an orderly entry into the United States of America.

Our first concern will be with those Cubans who have been separated from their children and parents and their husbands and their wives and that are now in this country. Our next concern is with those who are imprisoned for political reasons . . . And I will send to the Congress tomorrow a request for supplementary funds of $12,600,000 to carry forth the commitment that I am making today . . .

And so we Americans will welcome these Cuban people. For the tides of history run strong, and in another day they can return to their homeland to find it cleansed of terror and free from fear . . . And today we can all believe that the lamp of this grand old lady is brighter today—and the golden door that she guards gleams more brilliantly in the light of an increased liberty for the people from all the countries of the globe. Thank you very much.

Source: The Papers of the Presidents, Lyndon B. Johnson, 1965. Vol. 2. Washington, DC: U.S. Government Printing Office, 1966, 1037–40.

Document 11: The Refugee Act, March 17, 1980

In 1980 Congress dealt with the refugee crises which strained the 20,000-per-country limit of the 1965 act. The Refugee Act of 1980 systematized refugee policy, incorporated the UN definition of refugees, and allowed for 50,000 persons annually to enter as refugees. The following document presents excerpts of some key provisions of the Refugee Act of 1980.

Be it enacted by the Senate and House of Representatives of the United States of America in Congress assembled, That this Act may be cited as the "Refugee Act of 1980."

Sec. 101 (a) The Congress declares that it is the historic policy of the United States to respond to the urgent needs of persons subject to persecution in their homelands, including where appropriate, humanitarian assistance for their care and maintenance in asylum areas, efforts to promote opportunities for resettlement or voluntary repatriation, aid for necessary transportation and processing, admission to this country of refugees for special humanitarian concern to the United States, and transitional assistance to refugees in the United States. The Congress further declares that it is the policy of the United States to encourage all nations to provide assistance and resettlement opportunities to refugees to the fullest extent possible.

(b) The objectives of this Act are to provide permanent and systematic procedures for the admission to this country of refugees of special humanitarian concern to the United States, and to provide comprehensive and uniform provisions for the effective resettlement and absorption of those refugees who are admitted.

Sec. 201 (a) Section 101 (a) of the Immigration and Nationality Act ... is amended by adding after paragraph (41) any person who is outside any country of such person's nationality, or, in the case of a person having no nationality, is outside any country in which such person last habitually resided, and who is unable or unwilling to return to, and is unable or unwilling to avail himself or herself of the protection of, that country, because of persecution or a well- founded fear of persecution on account of race, religion, nationality, membership in a particular social group, or political opinion, or (B) in such special circumstances as the President after appropriate consultation ... may specify ... The term "refugee" does not include any person who ordered, incited, assisted, or otherwise participated in the persecution of any person on account of race, religion, nationality, membership in a particular social group, or political opinion. ...

Sec. 207. (a) (1) Except as provided in subsection (b), the number of refugees who may be admitted under this section in fiscal year 1980, 1981, or 1982, may not exceed fifty thousand unless the President determines, before the beginning of the fiscal year and after appropriate consultation ... that admission of a specific number of refugees in excess of such number is justified by humanitarian concerns or is otherwise in the national interest ... [the Act then specifies several provisions regarding consultation].

(3) The refugee status of any alien (and of the spouse or child of the alien) may be terminated by the Attorney General pursuant to such regulations as the Attorney General may prescribe if the Attorney General determines that alien was not in fact a refugee within the meaning of subsection 101 (a) (42) at the time of the alien's admission ...

(4) (d)(1) Before the start of each fiscal year the President shall report to the Committees of the Judiciary in the House of Representatives and the Senate regarding the foreseeable number of refugees who will be in need of resettlement during the fiscal year and the anticipated allocation of refugee admission during the fiscal year ...

Sec. 208 (a) The Attorney General shall establish a procedure for an alien physically present in the United States or at a land border or port of entry, irrespective of such alien's status, to apply for asylum, and the alien may be granted asylum at the discretion of the Attorney General if the Attorney General determines that such alien is a refugee within the meaning of section 101(a)(42)(a) ...

Sec. 209. (b). Not more than five thousand of the refugee admissions authorized under section 207 (a) in any fiscal year may be made available by the Attorney General, in the Attorney General's discretion and under such regulations as the Attorney General may prescribe, to adjust to the status of an alien lawfully permitted for permanent residence the status of any alien granted asylum who—(1) applies for such adjustment; (2) has been physically present in the United States for at least one year after being granted asylum; (3) continues to be a refugee in the meaning of section 101(a)(42)(a) or a spouse or child of such refugee; (4) is not firmly resettled in any foreign country; and (5) is admissible ...

301. (a) The President shall appoint, by and with the advice and consent of the Senate, a United States Coordinator of Refugee Affairs ... The Coordinator shall have the rank of Ambassador-at-Large.

Source: The Refugee Act of 1980. Public Law 96-212. *U.S. Statutes at Large* 94 (1980): 102.

Document 12: Ronald Reagan: Statement on U.S. Immigration and Refugee Policy, July 30, 1981

In 1981, the nation continued to debate both refugee and immigration policy. President Ronald Reagan appointed a special task force within his administration to study these problems and recommend policy alternatives. President Ronald Reagan's statement on those issues follows.

Our nation is a nation of immigrants. More than any other country, our strength comes from our own immigrant heritage and our capacity to welcome those from other lands. No free and prosperous nation can by itself accommodate all those who seek a better life or flee persecution. We must share this responsibility with other countries.

The bipartisan select commission, which reported this spring, concluded that the Cuban influx to Florida made the United States sharply aware of the need for more effective immigration policies and the need for legislation to support those policies.

For these reasons, I asked the Attorney General last March to chair a Task Force on Immigration and Refugee Policy. We discussed the matter when President Lopez Portillo visited me last month, and we have carefully considered the views of our Mexican friends. In addition, the Attorney General has consulted with those concerned in Congress and in affected States and localities and with interested members of the public.

The Attorney General is undertaking administrative action and submitting to Congress, on behalf of the administration, a legislative package, based on eight principles. These principles are designed to preserve our tradition of accepting foreigners to our shores, but to accept them in a controlled and orderly fashion.

We shall continue America's tradition as a land that welcomes peoples from other countries. We shall also, with other countries, continue to share in the responsibility of welcoming and resettling those who flee oppression.

At the same time, we must ensure adequate legal authority to establish control over immigration, to enable us, when sudden influxes of foreigners occur, to decide to whom we grant the status of refugee or asylee; to improve our border control; to expedite (consistent with fair procedures and our Constitution) return of those coming here illegally; to strengthen enforcement of our fair labor standards and laws; and to penalize those who would knowingly encourage violations of our laws. The steps we take to further these objectives, however, must be consistent with our values of individual privacy and freedom.

We have a special relationship with our closest neighbors, Canada and Mexico. Our immigration policy should reflect this relationship.

We must also recognize that both the United States and Mexico have historically benefited from Mexicans obtaining employment in the United States. A number of our States have special labor needs, and we should take these into account.

Illegal immigrants in considerable numbers have become productive members of our work force. Those who have established equities in the United States should be recognized and accorded legal status. At the same time, in doing so, we must not encourage illegal immigration.

We shall strive to distribute fairly, among the various localities of this country, the impacts of our national immigration and refugee policy, and we shall improve the capability of those agencies of the Federal Government that deal with these matters.

We shall seek new ways to integrate refugees into our society without nurturing their dependence on welfare.

Finally, we recognize that immigration and refugee problems require international solutions. We will seek greater international cooperation in the resettlement of refugees, and, in the Caribbean Basin, international cooperation to assist accelerated economic development to reduce motivations for illegal immigration.

Immigration and refugee policy is an important part of our past and fundamental to our national interest. With the help of the new Congress and of the American people, we will work towards a new and realistic immigration policy, a policy that will be fair to our own citizens while it opens the door to opportunity for those who seek a new life in America.

Source: The Papers of the Presidents, Ronald Reagan, 1981. Vol. 1. Washington, DC: U.S. Government Printing Office, 1982, 676–77.

Document 13: *INS v. Chadha et al.*, 1983

In 1983, the U.S. Supreme Court rendered a decision on immigration that had importance beyond the immediate issue in immigration law. In INS v. Chadha et al., a class action suit filed against the INS over its deportation proceedings, the court ruled that a U.S. House of Representative's use of the legislative veto of the executive branch's rules and regulations (of the INS) in the 1965 Immigration and Nationality Act was unconstitutional. The following text presents a summary of the Chadha decision.

Decision: One-house congressional veto provisions in 244(c) (1) of the Immigration and Nationality Act held unconstitutional.

Summary:

An immigration judge suspended an alien's deportation pursuant to 244(c) (2) of the Immigration and Nationality Act (8 U.S.C.S 1254 (c)(1). The United States House of Representatives passed a resolution vetoing the suspension pursuant to 244 (c)(2), which authorizes one House of Congress to invalidate the decision of the executive branch to allow a particular deportable alien to remain in the United States. The immigration judge reopened the deportation proceedings to implement the House order, and the alien was ordered deported. The Board of Immigration Appeals dismissed the alien's appeal, holding that it had no power to declare unconstitutional an Act of Congress. The United States Court of Appeals for the Ninth Circuit held that the House was without constitutional authority to order the alien's deportation and that 244 (c)(2) violated the constitutional doctrine of separation of powers (634 F2nd 408).

On appeal, the United States Supreme Court affirmed. In the opinion of Chief Justice Burger, joined by Justices Brennan, Marshall, Blackmun, Stevens, and O'Connor, it was held that the legislative veto provision of 244 (c)(2) was unconstitutional since the one-house veto was legislative in purpose and effect and subject to the procedures set out in Article I of the Constitution requiring passage by a majority of both Houses and presentment to the president.

Justice Powell, concurring in the judgment, expressed the view that the case should be decided on a narrower ground and declared that when Congress finds that a particular person does not satisfy the statutory criteria for permanent residence it has assumed a judicial function in violation of the principle of separation of powers.

Justice White dissented, expressing the view that the legislative veto is an important if not indispensable political invention and that neither

Article I nor the doctrine of separation of powers is violated by the mechanism.

Justice Rehnquist joined by Justice White, dissenting, expressed the view that 244 (c)(2) was not severable from the rest of the statute.

Source: *INS v. Chadha et al.*, 462 U.S. 919 (1983).

Document 14: The Immigration Reform and Control Act of 1986

The Immigration Reform and Control Act of 1986 (IRCA) had a long, tangled history in its path through the U.S. Congress. In 1986, a joint conference committee finally agreed on a compromise package of provisions that enabled it to be enacted into law. The following document excerpts several major provisions of IRCA. Much of IRCA is still relevant, and reaction to its amnesty provisions drive Republican opposition to anything even resembling amnesty in current immigration reform proposals.

Title 1—Control of Illegal Immigration

SEC. 101. CONTROL OF UNLAWFUL EMPLOYMENT OF ALIENS

In general, It is unlawful for a person or other entity to hire, or to recruit or refer for a fee, the employment in the United States

(A) Any alien, knowing the alien is an unauthorized alien . . .

(B) An individual without complying with the requirements of subsection (b).

Continuing employment—It is unlawful for a person or other entity, after hiring an alien for employment in accordance with paragraph (1), to continue to employ the alien in the United States knowing the alien is (or has become) an unauthorized alien with respect to such employment.

Defense—a person or entity that establishes that it has complied in good faith with the requirements of subsection (b) with respect to the hiring, recruiting, or referral for employment of an alien in the United States has established an affirmative defense that the person or entity has not violated paragraph (1) (A) with respect to such hiring, recruiting, or referral.

Use of Labor through Contract—A person or other entity who uses a contract, subcontract, or exchange, entered into, renegotiated, or extended after the date of the enactment of this section, to obtain the labor of an alien in the United States, knowing that the alien is an unauthorized alien, with respect to performing such labor, shall be considered to have hired the alien for employment in the United States in violation of paragraph (1)(A).

Use of State Employment Agency Documentation—A person or entity shall be deemed to have complied with the requirements of subsection (b) with respect to the hiring of an individual who was referred for such employment by a State employment agency.

Employment Verification System—The requirements referred to [above] are, in the case of a person or other entity hiring, recruiting, or referring an individual for employment in the United States, the requirements specified in the following three paragraphs:

(1) Attestation after Examination of Documentation—
   (A) In General—the person or entity must attest, under penalty of perjury and on a form established by the Attorney General be regulation, that it has verified that the individual is not an unauthorized alien by examining—
       (i) a document described in subparagraph (B), or
       (ii) a document codified in subparagraph (C) and (D).
   (B) Documents Establishing Both Employment Authorization and Identity—A document described in this subparagraph is an individual's—
       (i) United States passport;
       (ii) Certificate of United States Citizenship;
       (iii) Certificate of naturalization;
       (iv) Unexpired foreign passport, if the passport has an appropriate, unexpired endorsement of the Attorney General authorizing the individual's employment in the United States; or
       (v) Resident alien card or other alien registration, if said card contains a photograph of the individual, and is evidence of authorization of employment in the United States.
   (C) Documents Evidencing Employment Authorization—A document described [above] is
       (i) A social security account number card;

(ii) Certificate of birth in the United States or establishing United States nationality at birth;

(iii) Other documents evidencing authorization of employ-ment in the United States which the Attorney General finds, by regulation, to be acceptable for the purposes of this section.

(D) Documents Establishing Identity of an Individual—A docu-ment described in this subparagraph is an individual's

(i) Driver's license or similar document issued for the pur-pose of identification by a State, if it contains a photo-graph of the individual;

(ii) In the case of individuals under 16 years of age or in a State which does not provide for issuance of an identifi-cation document,

(iii) Documentation of personal identity of such type as the Attorney General finds, by regulation, provides a reliable means of identification . . .

(3) Definition of Unauthorized Alien—the term "unauthorized alien" means with respect to the employment of an alien at a particular time, that the alien is not at the time either (A) an alien lawfully admitted for permanent residence, or (B) authorized to be so employed by this Act or by the Attorney General.

Deferral of Enforcement with Respect to Seasonal Agricultural Services—

(A) In General—it is unlawful for a person or entity (including a farm labor contractor) or an agent of such a person or entity, to recruit an unau-thorized alien (other than an alien described in clause (iii)), who is outside the United States to enter the United States to perform seasonal agricul-tural service.

(ii) Exception—Clause (i) shall not apply to an alien who the person or entity reasonably believes to meet the requirements of section 210(a)(2) of this Act (relating to the performance of seasonal agricultural services).

General Accounting Office Reports—

In General—

Beginning one year after the date of enactment of this Act, and at inter-vals of one year thereafter for a period of three years after such date, the Comptroller General of the United States shall prepare and transmit to the Congress and to the task for established under subsection (k) a report describing the results of a review of the implementation and enforcement of this section during the preceding twelve month period, for the purpose of determining if—

(A) such provisions have be carried out satisfactorily;

(B) a pattern of discrimination has resulted against citizens or nationals of the United State or against eligible workers seeking employment; and

(C) an unnecessary regulatory burden has been created for employers hiring such workers.

REVIEW BY TASK FORCE—

(1) Establishment of Task Force—The Attorney General, jointly with the Chairman of the Commission on Civil Rights and the Chairman of the Equal Employment Opportunity Commission, shall establish a task force to review each report of the Comptroller General.

(2) Recommendations to Congress—If the report transmitted includes a determination that the implementation of this section has resulted in a pattern of discrimination in employment (against others than unauthorized aliens) on the basis of national origin, the task force shall, taking into consideration any recommendations in the report, report to Congress recommendations for such legislation as may be appropriate to deter or remedy such discrimination.

TERMINATION DATE FOR EMPLOYER SANCTIONS—

(1) If report of widespread discrimination and Congressional Approval —the provisions of this section shall terminate 30 days after receipt of the last report required to be transmitted under subsection (j), if—

(A) The Comptroller General determines and so reports . . . that a widespread pattern of discrimination has resulted against citizens or nationals of the United States or against eligible workers seeking employment solely from the implementation of this section, and

(B) There is enacted, within such period of 30 calendar days, a joint resolution stating in substance that the Congress approves the findings of the Comptroller General contained in such report. . . .

(2) Senate Procedures for Consideration—Any joint resolution referred to in clause (B) of paragraph (1) shall be considered in the Senate in accordance with subsection (n) . . .

Increased Authorization of Appropriations for INS and EOIR—In addition to any other amounts authorized to be appropriated, in order to carry out this Act, there are authorized to be appropriated to the Department of Justice—

(1) For the INS, for FY 1987, $12,000,000 and for FY 1988, $15,000,000 . . . to provide for an increase in the border patrol personnel . . . so that the average level of such personnel in each fiscal year 1987 and 1988 is at least 50 percent higher than such level for fiscal year 1986. . . .

Title II—Legalization

SEC. 201—LEGALIZATION OF STATUS
Temporary Resident Status—
The Attorney General shall adjust the status of an alien to that of an alien lawfully admitted for temporary residence if the alien meets the following requirements:

(1) Timely Application—

    (A) During Application Period—Except as provided in subparagraph (B), the alien must apply for such adjustment during the 12 month period beginning on a date (not later than 180 days after the date of enactment of this section) designated by the Attorney General . . .

(2) Continuous Lawful Residence Since 1982—

    (A) In General—The alien must establish that he entered the United States before January 1, 1982, and that he has resided continuously in the United States in an unlawful status since such date and through the date the application is filed under this subsection.

    (B) Nonimmigrants—In the case of an alien who entered the United States as a nonimmigrant before January 1, 1982, the alien must establish that the alien's period of authorized stay as a nonimmigrant expired before such date through the passage of time or the alien's unlawful status was known to the Government as of such date.

Subsequent Adjustment to Permanent Residence and Nature of Temporary Resident Status—

(1) Adjustment to Permanent Residence—The Attorney General shall adjust the status of any alien provided lawful temporary resident status under subsection (a) to that of an alien lawfully admitted for permanent residence if the alien meets the following requirements:

    (A) Timely Application After One Year's Residence—The alien must apply for such adjustment during the one-year period beginning with the nineteenth month that begins after the date the alien was granted such temporary status.

    (B) Continuous Residence—The alien must establish that he has continuously resided in the United States since the date the alien was granted such temporary resident status.

    (C) Admissible as Immigrant—The alien must establish that he or she—

        (i) is admissible to the United States as an immigrant . . . and

        (ii) has not been convicted of any felony or three or more misdemeanors committed in the United States.

Basic Citizenship Skills—The alien must demonstrate that he or she either—

(1) meets the requirements of section 312 (relating to minimal understanding of ordinary English and a knowledge and understanding of the history and government of the United States), or (II) is satisfactorily pursuing a course of study (recognized by the Attorney General) to achieve an understanding of English and such knowledge and understanding of the history and government of the United States . . .

Temporary Disqualification of Newly Legalized Aliens from Receiving Certain Public Welfare Assistance—

(1) In General—During the five year period beginning on the date an alien was granted lawful temporary resident status under subsection

(a) except as provided in paragraph (2) and (3), the alien is not eligible for—

   (i) Any program of financial assistance furnished under Federal law;

  (ii) medical assistance under a State plan approved under Title XIX of the Social Security Act; and

 (iii) assistance under the Food Stamp Act of 1977; and State or political subdivision therein may, to the extent consistent with paragraph (A) and paragraph (1) and (3), provide that an alien is not eligible for the programs of financial assistance or for medical assistance described in subparagraph (A) (ii) furnished under the law of that State or political subdivision.

Title III—Reform of Legal Immigration
Part A—Temporary Agricultural Workers

SEC. 301. H-2A AGRICULTURAL WORKERS

(a) Providing New "H-2A" Nonimmigrant Classification for Temporary Agricultural Labor—Paragraph (15) (H) of section 101 (a) (8 USC 1101 (a) is amended by striking out "to perform temporary services or labor," in clause (ii) and inserting in lieu thereof," (a) to perform agricultural labor or services, as defined by the Secretary of Labor in regulations and including agricultural labor defined in section 3121 (g) of the Internal Revenue Code of 1954 and agriculture as defined in section 3 (f) of the Fair Labor Standards Act of 1938 . . . or a temporary or seasonal nature, or (b) to perform other temporary service or labor."

Source: The Immigration Reform and Control Act of 1986. Public Law 99-603. *U.S. Statutes at Large* 100 (1986): 3360.

Document 15: *Jean v. Nelson,* 1986

In another class action suit brought against the INS, Jean v. Nelson, *the issue concerned the denial of parole by the INS to undocumented Haitian aliens who were ruled as "economic refugees" and therefore excluded from parole status.*

A federal district court ruled in favor of the Haitians on the basis that the INS deci-
sion to detain the aliens without parole was made on the basis of race and national
origin, and was thus in violation of the equal protection clause of the Fifth Amend-
ment. The Supreme Court affirmed the judgment of the appeals court, which
although rejecting the constitutional claim, accorded relief on the basis of INS
regulation, remanding the case to the district court to ensure that the INS exercised
its discretion in parole decisions in a nondiscriminatory manner. The following
document presents a summary of the Supreme Court's decision in the Jean v.
Nelson *case.*

Decision: Court of Appeals held to have improperly reached constitutional issue in deciding case challenging INS' denial of parole to undocumented Haitian aliens.

Summary:

The named representative of a class of undocumented and unadmitted
aliens from Haiti brought suit against the Commissioner of the Immigration and Naturalization Service (INS) in a Federal District Court, alleging
in part that they have been detained without parole by the INS officials on
the basis of race and national origin, in violation of the equal protection
guarantee of the Fifth Amendment to the United States Constitution.
The District Court rejected the constitutional claim (544 F. Supp. 973),
but a panel of the United States Court of Appeals for the Eleventh Circuit
held that the Fifth Amendment's equal protection guarantee applied to
the parole of unadmitted aliens for parole. After a rehearing en banc, the
Court of Appeals held that the Fifth Amendment did not apply to the
consideration of unadmitted aliens for parole. Although rejecting the constitutional claim, the Court of Appeals accorded relief based on the applicable INS regulation (8 CFR 212.5), remanding to the District Court to
ensure that the INS exercised its discretion in making parole decisions in
an individualized and nondiscriminatory manner (727 F2d 957).

On certiorari, the United States Supreme Court affirmed the judgment
remanding the case to the District Court. In the opinion of Justice
Rehnquist, and joined by Justices White, Blackmun, Powell, Stevens,
and O'Connor, it was held that the Court of Appeals should not have
reached and decided the parole question on constitutional grounds, since
the applicable statute and regulations were factually neutral and since the
INS' parole discretion thereunder did not extend to consideration of race
or national origin.

Justice Marshall, joined by Justice Brennan, dissented, expressing the view that there was no principled way to avoid making the constitutional issue and that aliens have a Fifth Amendment right to parole decisions free from invidious discrimination based on race or national origin.

Source: Jean v. Nelson, 472 U.S. 846 (1986).

Document 16: The Immigration Act of 1990 (IMMACT), November 29, 1990

In 1990, Congress moved to enact reforms of the legal immigration law and process, amending the 1965 act as it was further amended in 1976 and 1986. Known as IMMACT, it set new ceilings for worldwide level of immigration, redefined the preference system with respect to family reunification, and added the so-called "diversity immigrants" (also known as the Kennedy provision after its chief advocate, U.S. senator Edward Kennedy), introduced in IRCA as a temporary measure. It established a Commission on Legal Immigration Reform, what came to be called "The Jordan Commission" after its chair, Representative Barbara Jordan (D-TX). Some key provisions of this rather lengthy act are excerpted here.

Sec. 201 (a) In General—Exclusive of aliens described in subsection (b), aliens born in a foreign state or dependent area who may be issued immigrant visas or who may otherwise acquire the status of an alien lawfully admitted to the United States for permanent residence are limited to:

(1) Family-sponsored immigrants described in section 203(a) ... in a number not to exceed in any fiscal year the number specified in subsection (c) for that year, and not to exceed in any of the first three years of any fiscal year 27 percent of the worldwide level under such subsection for all such fiscal year;

(2) Employment-based immigrants described in subsection 203 (b) ... in a number not to exceed in any fiscal year the number specified in subsection (d) for that year, and not to exceed in any of the first three quarters of any fiscal year 27 percent of the worldwide level under such subsection for all of each fiscal year; and

(3) For fiscal years beginning with fiscal year 1995, diversity immigrants described in section 203 (c) ... in a number not to exceed in any fiscal year the number specified in subsection (e) for that year,

and not to exceed in any of the first three quarters of any fiscal year 27 percent of the worldwide level under such subsection for all such fiscal year.

(2)(A)(i) Immediate Relatives—for the purpose of this subsection, the term "immediate relatives" means the children, spouses, and parents of a citizen of the United States, except that, in the case of parents, such citizen be at least 21 years of age. In the case of an alien who was the spouse of a citizen of the United States at least two years at the time of the citizen's death, and was not legally separated from the citizen at the time of the citizen's death, the alien shall be considered, for the purpose of this subsection, to remain an immediate relative after the date of the citizen's death but only if such spouse files a petition under section 204(a)(1)(A) within 2 years after such date and only until the date the spouse remarries.

(c) Worldwide Level of Family Sponsored Immigrants—(1)(A) The worldwide level of family-sponsored immigrants under this section for a fiscal year is, subject to paragraph (B) equal to; (i) 480,000 minus (ii) the number (if any) computed under paragraph (2), plus (iii) the number, if any, computed under paragraph (3).

(B)(i) For each of fiscal years 1992, 1993, and 1994, 465,000 shall be substituted for 480,000 in subparagraph (A)(i).

(ii) In no case shall the number computed under subparagraph (A) be less than 226,000 . . .

(c) Worldwide Level of Employment-Based Immigrants—(1) The worldwide level of employment-based immigrants under this subsection for a fiscal year is equal to—

(A) 140,000 plus (B) the number computed under paragraph (2).

(2) The number computed under this paragraph for a fiscal year is the difference (if any) between the maximum number of visas which may be issued in section 203(a) . . . during the previous fiscal year and the number of visas issued under that section during that year.

(d) Worldwide Level of Diversity Immigrants—the worldwide level of diversity immigrants is equal to 55,000 for each fiscal year.

Sec. 102. Per Country Levels.

Sec. 202 (8 U.S.C. 1152) is amended—(1) by amending subsection (a) to read as follows:

(a) Per Country Level—(1) Nondiscrimination—Except as specifically provided in paragraph (2) and in section 101(a)(27), 201(b) (2) (A)(1), and 203, no person shall receive any preference or priority or be discriminated in the issuance of an immigrant visa because of a person's race, sex, nationality, place of birth, or place of residence.

(2) Per Country Levels for Family-Sponsored and Employment-Based Immigrants—Subject to paragraph (3) and (4), the total number of immigrant visas made available to natives of any single foreign state or dependent area under subsection (a) and (b) of section 203 in any fiscal year may not exceed 7 percent (in the case of a single foreign state) or 2 percent (in the case of a dependent area) of the total number of such visas made available under such subsection in that fiscal year.

Subtitle B—Preference System

Part I—Family-Sponsored Immigrants
Sec. 111. Family-sponsored immigrants.
Sec. 203 (8 U.S.C. 1153) is amended—

(1) By re-designating subsection (b) and (e) as subsection (d) through (g) respectively and inserting the following: (a) Preference Allocation for Family-Sponsored Immigrants—Aliens subject to the worldwide level specified in section 201(c) for family-sponsored immigrants shall be allotted visas as follows:

    (1) Unmarried sons and daughters of citizens … in a number not to exceed 23,400 plus any visas required for the class specified in paragraph (4).

    (2) Spouses and unmarried sons and daughters of permanent resident aliens … shall be allocated visas in a number not to exceed 114,200 plus the number (if any) by which such worldwide level exceeds 226,000 plus any visas not required for the class specified in paragraph (1); except to aliens described in subparagraph (A).

    (3) Married sons and married daughters of immigrants—in a number not to exceed 23,400, plus any visas not required to the classes specified in paragraphs (1) and (2).

(4) Brothers and sisters of citizens—in a number not to exceed 65,000, plus any visas not required for the classes specified in paragraphs (1) through (3) . . .

(c) Legalized Alien Defined—in this section the term "legalized alien" means an alien lawfully admitted for temporary or permanent residence who was provided—

(1) Temporary or permanent residence status under section 210 of the Immigration and Nationality Act,

(2) Temporary or permanent residence status under section 245 (A) of the Immigrant and Nationality Act, or

(3) Permanent residence status under section 202 of the Immigration Reform and Control Act of 1986.

Part 2. Employment-Based Immigrants.

Sec. 121. Employment-Based Immigrants (a) In General—Section 203 (8 U.S.C. 1153) is amended by inserting after subsection (a), as inserted by section 111, the following new subsection:

(b) Preference Allocation for Employment-Based Immigrants—Aliens subject to a worldwide level specified in section 201(d) for employment-based immigrants in a fiscal year shall be allocated visas as follows:

(1) Priority Workers—Visas shall first be made available in a number not to exceed 40,000, plus any visas not required for the classes specified in paragraphs (4) and (5), to qualified immigrants who are aliens described in any of the following subparagraphs (A) through (C).

(A) Aliens with extraordinary ability—in sciences, arts, education, business, or athletics which have been demonstrated by sustained national or international acclaim and whose achievements have been recognized in the field through extensive documentation.

(B) Outstanding Professors and Researchers.

(C) Certain Multinational Executives and Managers.

(2) Alien members of Professions holding advanced degrees or aliens of exceptional ability . . .

(3) Skilled workers, professionals, and other workers . . .

(4) Certain special immigrants—Visas shall be made available, in a number not to exceed 10,000 to qualified special immigrants described in section 101 (a)(27) ... of which not more than 5,000 may be made available in any fiscal year to special immigrants described in subclause (II) or (III) of section 101(a)(27) (C)(ii).

(5) Employment Creation—

(A) In General—Visas shall be made available in a number not to exceed 10,000 to qualified immigrants seeking to enter the United States for the purpose of engaging in a new commercial enterprise—(i) which the alien has established, (ii) in which such alien has invested ... or is actively in the process of investing, capital in an amount not less than the amount specified in subparagraph (C), and (iii) which will benefit the United States and create full-time employment for not fewer than 10 United States citizens or aliens lawfully admitted for permanent residence or other immigrants lawfully authorized to be employed in the United States (other than the immigrant and the immigrant's spouse, sons, or daughters).

Part 3 – Diversity Immigrants

Sec. 121. Diversity Immigrants.

Sec. 203, as amended by sections 111 and 121 of this Act, is further amended by inserting after subsection (b) the following new subsection:

(c) Diversity Immigrants—(1) In General—Except as provided in paragraph (2), aliens subject to the worldwide level specified in section 201 (e) for diversity immigrants shall be allotted visas each fiscal year as follows:

(A) Determination of Preference Immigration—The Attorney General shall determine for the most recent previous 5 year period for which data are available, the total number of aliens who are natives of each foreign state and who (1) were admitted or otherwise provided lawful permanent resident status ... and (ii) were subject to the numerical limitations of section 201(a) ... or who were admitted or otherwise provided lawful permanent residence status as an immediate relative or other alien described in section 201(b)(2) status as an immediate relative or other alien described in section 201(b)(2) ... (iv) Redistribution of Unused Visa Numbers—If the Secretary of State estimates that the number of immigrant visas to be issued to natives in any region for the fiscal year under this paragraph is less than the number of immigrant visas made available to such natives under this paragraph for the fiscal year, subject to clause (v), the excess visa numbers shall be made available to natives (other than the natives of a high-admission state) of the other regions in proportion to the percentages otherwise specified in clauses (ii) and (iii).

Subtitle C—Commission and Information

Sec. 141. Commission of Legal Immigration Reform.

(a) Establishment and Composition of Commission—(1) Effective October 1, 1991, there is established a Commission on Legal Immigration Reform ... which shall be composed of 9 members appointed as follows:

  (A) One member who shall serve as Chairman, to be appointed by the President.

  (B) Two members to be appointed by the Speaker of the House of Representatives who shall select such members from a list of nominees provided by the Chairman of the Subcommittee on Immigration ... of the Committee on the Judiciary of the House.

  (C) Two members to be appointed by the Minority Leader of the House who shall select such members form a list of nominees provided by the ranking member of the Subcommittee on Immigration ... of the Committee on the Judiciary of the House.

  (D) Two members to be appointed by the Majority Leader of the Senate from a list provided by the Chairman of the Subcommittee on Immigration and Refugee Affairs of the Committee on the Judiciary of the Senate.

  (E) Two members appointed by the Minority Leader of the Senate.

Title III—Family Unity and Temporary Protected Status [covers temporary stay of deportation and work authorization for certain eligible immigrants; defines the term "legalized alien"; granting of status by the Attorney General and under what conditions—such as armed conflict, certain natural disasters like earthquakes, floods, drought, epidemic, or other environmental disaster in a state] . . .

Sec. 303—Special Temporary Protected Status for Salvadorans.

Title IV [details the administration of Naturalization]

Source: The Immigration Act of 1990 (IMMACT). Public Law 101–649. U.S. Statutes at Large 104 (1990): 4983.

Document 17: California's Proposition 187, November 1994

Despite national legislation intended to curb the illegal immigration flow, such as IRCA and IMMACT, the unauthorized migration flow continued virtually unabated, resulting in political pressure to do something about it. States that received the largest immigration, both legal and unauthorized, such as California, Florida, and Texas, sued the federal government in their respective federal district courts for the estimated billions of dollars state and local governments had to bear related to illegal immigrants and their children. In 1994, California attempted to deal with the illegal migration legislatively, in an attempt to reduce the draw of its economy services, and to send a message to Congress, by passing an anti-immigration measure known as Proposition 187, the "Save Our State" initiative. The following document excerpts key sections of Proposition 187.

Section 1: Findings and Declaration

The People of California find and declare as follows: That they have suffered and are suffering economic hardship by the presence of illegal aliens in the state. That they have suffered and are suffering personal injury and damage by the criminal conduct of illegal aliens in the state. That they have a right to the protection of their government from any person or persons entering this country unlawfully.

Therefore, the People of California declare their intention to provide for cooperation between their agencies of state and local government with the federal government, and to establish a system of required notification by and between such agencies to prevent illegal aliens in the United States from receiving benefits or public services in the State of California.

Section 2. Manufacture, Distribution, or Sale of False Citizenship or Resident Alien Documents: Crime and Punishment.

Section 113. Is added to the Penal Code, to read: Any person who manufactures, distributes or sells false documents to conceal the true citizenship or resident alien status of another is guilty of a felony and shall be punished by imprisonment in the state prison for five years or by a fine of twenty-five thousand dollars.

Section 3: Use of False Citizenship or Resident Alien Documents: Crime and Punishment.

Section 114. Is added to the Penal Code, to read: Any person who uses false documents to conceal his or her true citizenship or resident alien status is guilty of a felony, and shall be punished by imprisonment in a state prison for five years or by a fine of twenty-five thousand dollars.

Section 4. Law Enforcement Cooperation with the INS

Section 834b is added to the Penal Code, to read: (a) Every law enforcement agency in California shall fully cooperate with the United States Immigration and Naturalization Service regarding any person who is arrested if he or she is suspected of being present in the United States in violation of federal immigration laws,. (b) With respect to any such person who is arrested, and suspected of being present in the United States in violation of federal immigration laws, every law enforcement agency shall do the following:

(1) Attempt to verify the legal status of such person as a citizen of the United States, an alien lawfully admitted as a permanent resident, an alien lawfully admitted for a temporary period of time or as an alien who is present in the United States in violation of immigration laws. The verification process may include, but shall not be limited to, questioning the person regarding his or her date and place of birth and entry into the United States, and demanding documentation to indicate his or her legal status.

(2) Notify the person of his or her apparent status as an alien who is present in the United States in violation of federal immigration laws and inform him or her that, apart from any criminal justice proceedings [sic] he or she must obtain legal status or leave the United States.

(3) Notify the Attorney General of California and the United States Immigration and Naturalization Service of the apparent illegal status and provide any additional information that may be requested by any other public entity.

(c) Any legislative, administrative, or other action by a city, county, or other legally authorized local governmental entity with jurisdictional boundaries, or by a law enforcement agency, to prevent or limit the co-operation required by subdivision (a) is expressly prohibited.

Section 5: Exclusion of Illegal Aliens from Public Social Services.

Section 10001.5 is added to the Welfare and Institutions Code to read: (a) In order to carry out the intention of the People of California that only citizens of the United States and aliens lawfully admitted to the United States may receive the benefits of public social services and to ensure that all persons employed in the providing of those services shall diligently pro-tect public funds from misuse, the provisions of this section are adopted. (b) A person shall not receive any public social service to which she may not otherwise be entitled until the legal status of that person has been veri-fied as one of the following:

(1) A citizen of the United States.
(2) An alien lawfully admitted as a permanent resident.
(3) An alien lawfully admitted for a temporary period of time.

(c) If any public entity in this state to whom a person has applied for public social services determines or reasonably suspects, based on the infor-mation provided to it, that the person is an alien in the United States in violation of federal law ... the services will not be provided and the INS will be notified.

Section 6. Exclusion of Illegal Aliens from Publicly Funded Health Care.

Chapter 1.3 of the Health and Safety Code to read: (a) In order to carry out the intention of the People of California that, excepting emergency medical care required by federal law, only citizens of the United States and aliens lawfully admitted to the United States may receive the benefits of publicly-funded health care, and to ensure that all persons employed in providing those services shall diligently protect public funds from misuse, the provisions of this section are adopted ... (c) If any publicly-funded health care facility in this state from whom a person seeks health care services, other than emergency medical care as required by federal law, determines or reasonably suspects, based on information provided it, that the person is an alien in the United States in violation of federal law ... [service will not be provided and the INS will be notified] ...

Section 7: Exclusion of Illegal Aliens from Public Elementary and Secondary Schools.

Section 48215 Is added to the Education Code to read: (a) No public elementary or secondary school shall admit, or permit the attendance of, any child who is not a citizen of the United States, an alien lawfully admitted as a permanent resident, or a person who is otherwise authorized under federal law to be present. ...

(b) Commencing January 1, 1995, each school district shall also have verified the legal status of each parent or guardian of each child enrolling in the school district for the first time ...

(c) By January 1, 1996, each school district shall also have verified the legal status of each parent or guardian of each child referred to ...

(d) Each school district shall provide information to the State Superintendent of Public Instruction, the Attorney General of California and the United States Immigration and Naturalization Service regarding any enrollee or pupil, or parent or guardian, attending a public elementary or secondary school in the school district determined or reasonably suspected to be in violation of federal immigration laws within forty-five days after becoming aware of an apparent violation ...

Section 8. Exclusion of Illegal Aliens from Public Postsecondary Educational Institutions.

Section 66010.8 is added to the Education Code to read: (a) No public institution of postsecondary education shall admit, enroll, or permit the attendance of any person who is not a citizen of the United States, an alien lawfully admitted as a permanent resident, in the United States, or a person who is otherwise authorized under federal law to be present in the

United States..(c) Commencing with the first term or semester that begins after January 1, 1996, and at the end of each term or semester thereafter, each public postsecondary educational institution shall verify the status of each person enrolled or in attendance at that institution.

Section 9. Attorney General Cooperation with the INS.

Section 53609.65 is added to the Government Code, to read: Whenever the state or a city, or a county, or any other legally authorized local government entity with jurisdictional boundaries reports the presence of a person who is suspected of being present in the United States in violation of federal immigration laws to the Attorney General of California, that report shall be transmitted to the United States Immigration and Naturalization Service. The Attorney General shall be responsible for maintaining on-going and accurate records of all such reports, and shall provide any additional information that may be requested by any other government entity.

Section 10. Amendment and Severability.

In the event that any portion of this act or the application thereof to any person or circumstances is held invalid, that invalidity shall not affect any other provision or application of the act, which can be given effect without the invalid provision or application, and to that end the provisions of this act are severable.

Source: LULAC et al. v. Wilson et al. 908 F. Supp. 755 (C.D. Cal. 1995): 7887–91.

Document 18: *LULAC et al. v. Wilson et al.*, 1995

Section 10 of Proposition 187 anticipated a federal court challenge to the law's constitutionality and it was immediately brought to court by the League of United Latin American Citizens. The federal district court ruled most of the law unconstitutional. What follows is a summary of the LULAC v. Wilson decision.

Summary:
Public interest groups and individual citizens, in consolidated actions, brought suit for declaratory and injunctive relief to bar California Governor, Attorney General, and other state actors from enforcing provisions

of the voter-approved California initiative measure requiring state personnel to verify immigration status of persons with whom they come into contact, report persons in the United States unlawfully to state and federal officials, and deny those persons social services, health care, and education benefits. On plaintiff's motion for summary judgment, the District Court, Pfaelzer, J. held that: (1) classification, notification, cooperation and reporting provisions of the measure had direct and substantial effect on immigration, so as to be preempted by federal immigration law; (2) initiative's denial of public benefits based on federal determination of immigration status was not impermissible regulation of immigration; (3) provision excluding illegal aliens from public elementary and secondary schools was preempted by federal law as being prohibited by equal protection clause of Fourteenth Amendment; (4) verification components of the measure prohibiting public postsecondary education to persons not authorized under federal law to be in the United States were permissible; (5) provisions of measure criminalizing making and using false documents to conceal true citizenship or resident alien status were legitimate exercise of state's police power; (6) provisions denying public social services to illegal immigrants as applied to federally funded programs administered by the state that awarded benefits regardless of immigration status conflicted with and was preempted by federal law; (7) provisions of measure prohibiting public postsecondary educational institutions from admitting, enrolling or permitting attendance of persons not authorized under federal law to be in the United States were not preempted by federal law; and (8) criminal penalties contemplated by provision criminalizing the manufacture, distribution, sale or use of false documents to conceal immigration status were not preempted by federal law. Motions granted in part and denied in part.

Source: *908 F. Supp. 755* (C.D.Cal. 1995).

Document 19: Executive Order 13780— Protecting the Nation from Foreign Terrorist Entry into the United States, 2017

President Donald Trump issued several versions of executive orders imposing a travel ban during his first term in office. The text below is excerpted from Executive Order 13780, the first version of the travel ban.

By the authority invested in me as President by the Constitution and the laws of the United States of America, including the Immigration and Nationality (INA), 8 U.S.C. 1101 *et seq*, and section 301 of title 3, United States Code, and to protect the Nation from terrorist activities by foreign nationals admitted to the United States, it is hereby ordered as follows:

Section 1. Policy and Purpose. (a) It is the policy of the United States to protect its citizens from terrorist attacks, including those committed by foreign nationals. The screening and vetting protocols and procedures associated with the visa-issuance process and the United States Refugee Admissions Program (USRAP) play a crucial role in detecting foreign nationals who may commit, aid, or support acts of terrorism and in preventing those individuals from entering the United States. It is therefore the policy of the United States to improve the screening and vetting protocols and procedures associated with the visa-issuance process and the USRAP.

(b) On January 27, 2017, to implement this policy, I issued Executive Order 13769 (Protecting the Nation from Foreign Terrorist Entry into the United States).

(i) Among other actions, Executive Order 13769 suspended for 90 days the entry of certain aliens from seven countries: Iran, Iraq, Libya, Somalia, Sudan, Syria, and Yemen. These are countries that had already been identified as presenting heightened concerns about terrorism and travel to the United States. Specifically, the suspension applied to countries referred to in, or designated under, section 217(a)(12) of the INA, 8 U.S.C. 1187 (a)(12), in which Congress restricted use of the Visa Waiver Program for nationals of, and aliens recently present in, (A) Iraq or Syria, (B) any country designated by the Secretary of State as a state sponsor of terrorism (currently, Iran, Syria, and Sudan), and (C) any other country designated as a country of concern by the Secretary of Homeland Security, in consultation with the Secretary of State and the Director of National Intelligence. In 2016, the Secretary of Homeland Security designated Libya, Somalia, and Yemen as additional countries of concern for travel purposes, based on consideration of three statutory factors related to terrorism and national security: "(I) whether the presence of an alien in the country or area increases the likelihood that the alien is a credible threat to the national security of the United States; (II) whether a foreign terrorist organization has a significant presence in the country or area; and (III) whether the country or area is a safe haven for terrorists." 8 U.S.C. 1187(a)(12)(D)(ii). Additionally, Members of Congress have expressed concerns about screening and vetting procedures following recent terrorist attacks in this country and in Europe.

(ii) In ordering the temporary suspension of entry in subsection (b)(i) of this section, I exercised my authority under Article II of the Constitution and under section 212(f) of the INA, which provides in relevant part: "Whenever the President finds that the entry of any aliens or of any class of aliens into the United States would be detrimental to the interests of the United States, he may by proclamation, and for such period as he shall deem necessary, suspend the entry of all aliens or any class of aliens as immigrants or nonimmigrants, or impose on the entry of aliens any restrictions he may deem to be appropriate." 8 U.S.C. 1182(f). Under these authorities, I determined that, for a brief period of 90 days, while existing screening and vetting procedures were under review, the entry into the United States of certain aliens from seven identified countries—each afflicted by terrorism in a manner that compromised the ability of the United States to rely on normal decision-making procedures about travel to the United States—would be detrimental to the interests of the United States. Nonetheless, I permitted the Secretary of State and the Secretary of Homeland Security to grant case-by-case waivers when they determined that it was in the national interest to do so.

(iii) Executive Order 13769 also suspended the USRAP for 120 days. Terrorist groups have sought to infiltrate several nations through refugee programs. Accordingly, I temporarily suspended the USRAP pending a review of our procedures for screening and vetting refugees. Nonetheless, I permitted the Secretary of State and the Secretary of Homeland Security to jointly grant case-by-case waivers when they determined that it was in the national interest to do so.

(iv) Executive Order 13769 did not provide a basis for discriminating for or against members of any religion. While that order allowed for prioritization of refugee claims from members of persecuted religious minority groups, that priority applied to refugees from every nation, including those in which Islam is a minority religion, and applied to minority sects within a religion. That order was not motivated by animus toward any religion, but was instead intended to protect the ability of religious minorities—whoever they are and wherever they reside—to avail themselves of the USRAP in light of their particular challenges and circumstances.

(v) (c) The implementation of Executive Order 13769 has been delayed by litigation. Most significantly, enforcement of critical provisions of that order has been temporarily halted by court orders that apply nationwide and extend even to foreign nationals with no prior or substantial connection to the United States. On February 9, 2017, the United States Court of Appeals of the Ninth Circuit declined to stay or narrow one such order pending the outcome of further judicial proceedings, while noting that the "political branches are far better equipped to make appropriate distinctions" about wo should be covered by a suspension of entry or of refugee admissions.

(d) Nationals from the countries previously identified under section 217 (a)(12) of the INA warrant additional scrutiny in connection with our immigration policies because the conditions in these countries present heightened threats. Each of these countries is a state sponsor of terrorism, has been significantly compromised by terrorist organizations, or contains active conflict zones. Any of these circumstances diminishes the foreign government's willingness or ability to share or validate important information about individuals seeking to travel to the United States. Moreover, the significant presence in each of these countries of terrorist organizations, their members, and others exposed to those organizations increases the chance that conditions will be exploited to enable terrorist operatives or sympathizers to travel to the United States. Finally, once foreign national from these countries are admitted to the United States, it is often difficult to remove them, because many of these countries typically delay issuing, or refuse to issue, travel documents. . . .

Section 2. Temporary Suspension of Entry for Nationals of Countries of Particular Concern During Review Period. (a) The Secretary of Homeland Security, in consultation with the Secretary of State and the Director of National Intelligence, shall conduct a world-wide review to identify whether, and if so what, additional information will be needed from each country to adjudicate an application by a national of that country for a visa, admission, or other benefit under the INA in order to determine that an individual is not a security or public-safety threat. The Secretary of Homeland Security may conclude that certain information is need from particular countries even if it is not needed from every country . . .

Sec. 3: Scope and Implementation of Suspension. (a) Scope. Subject to the exceptions set forth in subsection (b) of this section and any waiver under subsection (c) of this section, the suspension of entry pursuant to section 2 of this order shall apply only to foreign nationals of the designated countries who: (i) are outside the United States on the effective date of this order; (ii) did not have a valid visa at 5:00 p.m. eastern standard time on January 27, 2017; and (iii) do not have a valid visa on the effective date of this order . . .

Sec. 4. Additional Inquiries Related to Nationals of Iraq. An application by any Iraqi national for a visa, admission, or other immigration benefit should be subjected to thorough review, including, as appropriate, consultation with a designee of the Secretary of Defense and use of the additional information has been obtained in the context of the close U.S.-Iraqi security partnership, since Executive Order 13769 was issued, concerning the individuals suspected of ties to ISIS or other terrorist organizations and individuals coming from territories controlled or formally controlled by ISIS . . .

Sec. 5. Implementing Uniform Screening and Vetting Standards for All Immigration Programs . . .

Sec. 6. Realignment of the U.S. Refugee Admissions Program for Fiscal Year 2017. (a) The Secretary of State shall suspend travel of refugees into the United States under the USRAP, and the Secretary of Homeland Security shall suspend decisions on applications for refugee status, for 120 days after the effective date of this order, subject to waivers pursuant to subsection (c) of this section . . .

Sec. 7. Rescission of Exercise of Authority Relating to the Terrorism Grounds of Inadmissibilty.

Sec. 8. Expedited Completion of the Biometric Entry-Exit Tracking System. (a) The Secretary of Homeland Security shall expedite the completion and implementation of a biometric entry-exit system for in-scope travelers to the United States, as recommended by the National Commission on Terrorist Attacks Upon the United States ...

Sec. 12. Enforcement. (a) The Secretary of State and the Secretary of Homeland Security shall consult with appropriate domestic and international partners, including countries and organizations, to ensure efficient, effective, and appropriate implementation of the actions directed by this order ...

Sec. 13. Revocation. Executive Order 13769 of January 27, 2017, is revoked by the effective date of this order.

Sec. 14. Effective Date. This order is effective at 12:01 a.m., eastern daylight time on March 16, 2017.

Sec. 16. General Provisions ... (c) This order is not intended to, and does not, create any right or benefit, substantive or procedural, enforceable at law or in equity by any party against the United States, its departments, agencies, or entities, its officers, employees, or agents, or any other person.

Sec. 17. Severability. (a) If any provision of this order, or the application of any provisions to any person or circumstance, is held to be invalid, the remainder of this order and the application of its other provisions to any other person or circumstances shall not be affected thereby ...

Signed: Donald J. Trump, The White House, March 6, 2017.

Source: Trump, Donald. Executive Order Protecting the Nation from Foreign Terrorist Entry into the United States. March 6, 2017. The White House.

Document 20: *Trump v. Hawaii*, Supreme Court Case 17-965, Syllabus

A second and third version of President Trump's travel ban executive order was issued, and the final version was ruled constitutional by the U.S. Supreme Court in June 2018. The Supreme Court's syllabus of that ruling, in Trump v. Hawaii, decided on June 26, 2018, is presented as follows.

TRUMP, PRESIDENT OF THE UNITED STATES, ET AL. V. HAWAII, ET AL.

CERTIORARI TO THE UNITED STATES COURT OF APPEALS FOR THE NINTH CIRCUIT.

No. 17-965. Argued April 25, 2018—Decided June 26, 2018.

In September 2017, the President issued Proclamation No. 8645, seeking to improve vetting procedures for foreign nationals traveling to the United States by identifying ongoing deficiencies in the information needed to assess whether nationals of particular countries present a security threat. The Proclamation placed entry restrictions on the nationals of eight foreign states shoes systems for managing and sharing information about their nationals the President deemed inadequate. Foreign states were selected for inclusion based on a review undertaken pursuant to one of the President's earlier Executive Orders. As part of that review, the Department of Homeland Security (DHS), in consultation with the State Department and intelligence agencies, developed an information and risk assessment "baseline." DHS then collected and evaluated data for all foreign governments, identifying those having deficient information-sharing practices and presenting national security concerns, as well as other countries "at risk" of failing to meet the baseline. After a 50-day period during which the State Department made diplomatic efforts to encourage foreign governments to improve their practices, the Acting Secretary of Homeland Security concluded that eight countries—Chad, Iran, Iraq, Libya, North Korea, Syria, Venezuela, and Yemen—remained deficient. She recommended entry restrictions for certain nationals from all those countries but Iraq, which had a close cooperative relationship with the U.S. She also recommended including Somalia, which met the information-sharing component of the baseline standards but had other special risk factors, such as a significant terrorist presence. After consulting with multiple Cabinet members, the President adopted the recommendations and issued the Proclamation.

Invoking his authority under 8 U.S.C. 1182(f) and 1185(a), he determined that certain restrictions were necessary to "prevent the entry of those foreign nationals about whom the United States Government lacks sufficient information" and "elicit improved identity-management and information-sharing protocols and practices from foreign governments." The Proclamation imposes a range of entry restrictions that vary based on the "distinct circumstances" in each of the eight countries. It exempts lawful permanent residents and provides case-by-case waivers under certain circumstances. It also directs DHS to assess on a continuing basis whether the restrictions should be modified or continued, and to report to the President every 180 days. At the completion of the first such review period, the President determined that Chad had sufficiently improved its practices, and he accordingly lifted restrictions on its nationals.

Plaintiffs—the State of Hawaii, three individuals with foreign relatives affected by the entry suspension, and the Muslim Association of Hawaii—argue that the Proclamation violates the Immigration and Nationality Act (INA) and the Establishment Clause. The District Court granted a nationwide preliminary injunction barring enforcement of the restrictions. The Ninth Circuit Court affirmed, concluding that the Proclamation contravened two provisions of the INA: 1182(f), which authorizes the President to "suspend the entry of all aliens or any class of aliens" whenever he "finds" that their entry "would be detrimental to the interests of the United States," and 1152(a)(1)(A), which provides that "no person shall . . . be discriminated against in the issuance of an immigrant visa because of the person's race, sex, nationality, place of birth, or place of residence." The court did not reach the Establishment Clause claim.

Held:

1. This Court assumes without deciding that plaintiffs' statutory claims are reviewable, notwithstanding consular nonreviewability or any other statutory nonreviewability issue . . .

2. The President has lawfully exercised the broad discretion granted to him under 1182(f) to suspend the entry of aliens into the United States . . .

(a) By its terms, 1182(f) exudes deference to the President in every clause. It entrusts to the President the decisions whether and when to suspend entry, whose entry to suspend, for how long, and on what conditions. It his vests the President with "ample power" to impose entry restrictions in addition to those elsewhere enumerated in the INA . . . The Proclamation falls well within this comprehensive delegation. The sole prerequisite set forth in 1182(f) is that the President "find" that the entry of the covered aliens "would be detrimental to the interests of the United States." The President has undoubtedly fulfilled that requirement here. He first order DHS and other agencies to conduct a comprehensive evaluation of every single country's compliance with the information and risk assessment baseline. He then issued a Proclamation with extensive findings about the deficiencies and their impact. Based on that review, he found that restricting entry of aliens who could not be vetted with adequate information was in the national interest.

Even assuming that some form of inquiry into the persuasiveness of the President's findings is appropriate, but see *Webster v. Doe,* 486 U.S. 592, 600, plaintiffs ' attacks on the sufficiency of the findings cannot be sustained. The 12–page Proclamation is more detailed than any prior order issued under 1182(f). Ans such a searching inquiry is inconsistent with the broad statutory text and the deference traditionally accorded to the President in this sphere. See, e.g. *Sale, 509 U.S., at 187-188.*

The Proclamation comports with the remaining textual limits in 1182(f). While the word "suspend" often connotes a temporary deferral, the President is not required to prescribe in advance a fixed end date for the entry restriction. Like its predecessors, the Proclamation makes clear that its "conditional restrictions" will remain in force only so long as necessary to "address" the identified "inadequacies and risks" within the covered nations. Finally, the Proclamation properly identifies a "class of aliens" whose entry is suspended, and the word "class" comfortably encompasses a group of people linked by nationality . . .

(b) Plaintiffs have not identified any conflict between the Proclamation and the immigration scheme reflected in the INA that would implicitly bar the President from addressing deficiencies in the Nation's vetting system. The existing grounds of inadmissibility and the narrow Visa Waiver Program do not address the failure of certain high-risk countries to provide a minimum baseline of reliable information. Further, neither the legislative history of 1182(f) nor historical practice justifies departing from the clear text of the statute . . .

(c) Plaintiffs' argument that the President's entry suspension violates 1182(a)(1)(A) ignores the basic distinction between admissibility determinations and visa issuance that runs throughout the INA. Section 1182 defines the universe of aliens who are admissible into the United States (and therefor eligible to receive a visa). Once 1182 sets the boundaries of admissibility, 1152(a)(1)(A) prohibits discrimination in the allocation of immigrant visas based on nationality or other traits. Had Congress intended in 11582(1)(A) to constrain the President's power to determine who may enter the country, it could have chosen language directed to that end. Common sense and historical practice confirm that 1152(a)(1)(A) does not limit the President's delegated authority under 1183(f). Presidents have repeatedly exercised their authority to suspend entry on the basis of nationality. And on plaintiffs' reading, the President would not be permitted to suspend entry from any particular foreign state in response to an epidemic, or even if the United States were on the brink of war . . .

(3) Plaintiffs have not demonstrated a likelihood of success on the merits of their claim that the Proclamation violates the Establishment Clause . . .

(a) The individual plaintiffs have Article III standing to challenge the exclusion of their relatives under the Establishment Clause. A person's interest in being united with his relatives is sufficiently concrete and particularized to form the basis of an Article III injury in fact. Cf, e.g. *Kerry v. Din, 576 U.S. ___.___. pp. 24–26.*

(b) Plaintiffs allege that the primary purpose of the Proclamation was religious animus and that the President's stated concerns about vetting protocols and national security were but pretexts for discrimination against Muslims. At the heart of their case is a series of statements by the President and his advisers both during the campaign and since the President assumed office. The issue, however, is not whether to denounce the President's statements, but the significance of those statements in reviewing a Presidential directive, neutral on its face, addressing a matter within the core of executive responsibility. In doing so, the Court must consider not only the statements of a particular President, but also the authority of the Presidency itself . . .

(c) The admission and exclusion of foreign nationals is a "fundamental sovereign attribute exercised by the Government's political departments largely immune from judicial control." *Fiallo v. Bell* 430 U.S. 787, 792. Although foreign nationals seeking admission have no constitutional right to entry, this Court has engaged in a circumscribed judicial inquiry when the denial of a visa allegedly burdens the constitutional rights of a U.S. citizen. That review is limited to whether the Executive gives a "facially legitimate and bona fide" reason for its actions, *Kleindienst v. Mandel,* 408 U.S. 754, 769, but the Court need not define the precise contours of that narrow inquiry in this case. For today's purposes, the Court assumes that it may look behind the face of the Proclamation to the extent of applying rational basis review, i.e., whether the entry policy is plausibly related to the Government's stated objective to protect the country and improve vetting processes. Plaintiffs' extrinsic evidence may be considered, but the policy will be upheld so long as it can reasonably be understood to result from a justification independent on unconstitutional ground . . .

(d) On the few occasions where the Court has struck down a policy as illegitimate under rational basis scrutiny, a common thread has been that the laws at issue were "divorced from any factual context from which [the Court] could discern a relationship to legitimate state interests." *Romer v. Evans*, 517 U.S. 620, 635. The Proclamation does not fit that pattern. It is expressly premised on legitimate purposes and says nothing about religion. The entry restrictions on Muslim-majority nations are limited to countries that were previously designated by Congress or prior administrations as posing national security risks. Moreover, the Proclamation reflects the results of a worldwide review process, undertaken by multiple Cabinet officials and their agencies. Plaintiffs challenge the entry suspension based on their perception of its effectiveness and wisdom, but the Court cannot substitute its own assessment of the Executive's predictive judgement on such matters . . .

Three additional features of the entry policy support the Government's claim of a legitimate national security interest. First, since the President introduced entry restrictions in January 2017, three Muslim-majority countries—Iraq, Sudan, and Chad—have been removed from the list. Second, for those countries still subject to entry restrictions, the Proclamation includes numerous exceptions for various categories of foreign nationals. Finally, the Proclamation creates a waiver program open to all covered foreign nationals seeking entry as immigrants or nonimmigrants. Under these circumstances, the Government has set forth a sufficient national security justification to survive rational basis review.

878 F. 3d 662, reversed and remanded.

Roberts, C.J., delivered the opinion of the Court, in which Kennedy, Thomas, Alito, and Gorsuch, JJ. Joined. Kennedy, J., and Thomas, J. filed concurring opinions. Breyer, J. filed a dissenting opinion, in which Kagan, J. joined. Sotomayor, J. filed a dissenting opinion, in which Ginsburg, J., joined.

Source: Trump v. Hawaii, No. 17-965, 585 U.S. ___ (2018).

GLOSSARY

Absconders people who had been ordered deported but failed to leave.

Adjustment to immigrant status a procedure whereby a nonimmigrant must apply for a change of status to lawful permanent resident if an immigrant visa is available for his or her country. The alien is an immigrant as of the date of the adjustment. It was used extensively for Cuban and Vietnamese refugees, and for Hungarian Freedom Fighters.

Advocacy the support given by the sanctuary movement to unauthorized immigrants involving attendance at immigration court hearings, and accompanying individuals to mandatory check-ins with the Department of Homeland Security.

Alien is a person who is not a citizen or national of a given nation-state.

Amnesty is a legal pardoning of a person who entered the United States illegally or is otherwise in nonlegal status, thereby changing his or her legal status to legal resident alien. It was used extensively by IRCA to cover more than three million persons.

Apprehensions refers to the physical control or temporary detainment of a person who is not lawfully in the United States, which may or may not result in an arrest.

Biometric identification is the use of DNA, fingerprints, iris scans, facial recognition technology, voice imprints to identify someone as an anti-terrorist screening procedure and to attempt to identify unauthorized immigrants.

Biometrics involves the use of fingerprints, facial recognition technology, and iris scans as a way of accurately identifying people in a quick and efficient manner.

Border card is a card allowing a person living within a certain zone of the U.S. border to legally cross back and forth for employment purposes without a passport or visa.

Border Patrol is the law enforcement arm of the Department of Homeland Security.

Brain drain refers to the flow of talented migrants from lesser developed to developed countries.

Chain migration occurs when one family member first enters the United States as a legal, permanent resident and then brings in many family members (extended, not just nuclear family members). It can also refer to immigrant groups coming who are not related but come from the same place or origin and settle in the same place in the United States, for example, drawn by ethnic or religious association in the home country.

Conundrum is a confusing or difficult problem or question.

DACA is an acronym for Deferred Action for Childhood Arrivals; a program of the Obama administration's DHS that protected Dreamer children from deportation as unauthorized immigrants.

DAPA is an acronym for Deferred Action for Parental Accountability.

De facto is a Latin phrase meaning "by action."

De jure is a Latin phrase meaning something being done "by law."

Deportation is a legal process by which a nation sends individuals back to their countries of origin after refusing them legal residence.

Devolution is the transfer or delegation of power to a lower level, especially by a central government to local or regional administration.

Dream Act is an acronym for Development, Relief, and Education for Alien Minors; a proposed law that would provide a path to citizenship for unauthorized immigrants brought to the United States as minor children.

Due process of law is the constitutional limitation on government behavior to deal with an individual according to prescribed rules and procedures.

Earned legalization is a proposal to allow unauthorized immigrants to change their status to that of legal permanent resident by paying fines and satisfying stipulated conditions akin to those who came as authorized permanent resident aliens.

Earned residency is a path to get a green card and the right to stay in the United States but not a path to citizenship. It involves paying taxes, learning English, and committing no substantial crime.

Emigrant is a person who voluntarily leaves his or her country of birth for permanent resettlement elsewhere.

Employer sanctions are a provision of the 1986 Immigration Reform and Control Act that provided legal penalties (fines and/or prison) for knowingly hiring an illegal alien.

Equal protection of the law is the constitutionally guaranteed right that all persons be treated the same before the law.

Executive orders are actions issued by a president, assigned numbers and published in the federal register, akin to laws passed by Congress, that direct members of the executive branch to follow a new policy or directive.

Exempt is an individual or class or category of individuals to whom a certain provision of the law does not apply.

Expedited removal is a stipulation in law changing the procedures by which persons in the United States without legal status may be deported with fewer judicial protections to do so.

Expulsion is the decision of a sovereign nation to legally compel an individual to permanently leave its territory.

Globalization is a tide of economic, technological, and intellectual forces that is integrating a global community.

Green card is a document issued by the DHS that certifies an individual as a legal immigrant entitled to work in the United States.

Guest-Worker Program is a program enabling the legal importation of workers for temporary labor in specified occupations.

H-1B Visa is a category of temporary visa issued to a nonimmigrant allowing employers who will employ guest-workers temporarily in a specialty occupation or field for a stipulated period of time.

Illegal aliens are individuals who are in a territory without documentation permitting permanent residence.

Immediate relatives are spouses, minor children, parents, grandparents, and brothers and sisters of a U.S. citizen or permanent resident alien.

Immigrant is an alien admitted to the United States as a lawful permanent resident.

Inadmissibles are persons encountered at ports of entry who are seeking lawful admission into the United States but are determined to be inadmissible, individuals presenting themselves to seek humanitarian protection under U.S. laws, and individuals who withdraw their application for admission and return to their countries of origin with a short timeframe.

Inclusion is an individual's or group's engagement with the process or organization that recognizes the individual or group by conferring membership or by providing resources such as entitlement or protests; it provides a sense of security, stability, and predictability understood primarily as an ability to plan for the future.

Investor immigrant is an individual permitted to immigrate based upon the promise to invest $1 million in an urban area or $500,000 in a rural area to create at least 10 jobs.

Lone-wolf terrorist is a person perpetrating a terrorist act or plot who is inspired by but not associated with an international terrorist group or organization, such as al Qaeda or ISIS.

Naturalization is the legal act of making an individual a citizen who is not born a citizen.

Nonimmigrant is an alien seeking temporary entry into the United States for a specific purpose other than permanent settlement—such as a foreign government official, tourist, student, temporary worker, or cultural exchange visitor.

Overstayers are persons who enter the United States on a temporary visa who then stay beyond the time specified in their visa at which they are to voluntarily depart the United States; and because they overstay, their status becomes unauthorized/illegal.

Passport is a legal identification document issued by a sovereign nation-state attesting to the nationality of an individual for the purpose of international travel.

Patriotic assimilation is the adoption, by the newcomer, of American civic values and the American heritage as one's own.

Permanent resident is a noncitizen who is allowed to live permanently in the United States, who can travel in and out of the country without a visa, and who can work without restriction; such person is allowed to accumulate time toward becoming a naturalized citizen.

Political incorporation is a model that holds that for a minority community to witness an effective response to its needs, minority leaders must come to occupy positions of government authority.

Prosecutorial discretion is a privilege given to the prosecuting attorney in deciding whether to prosecute or to plea bargain, recommend parole, and so on.

Protocol is an international agreement governing the understanding and procedures that member states who are parties to a treaty agreed upon for a given purpose, as in the UN protocols regarding the status and treatment of refugees.

Pull factor is an aspect of the receiving nation that draws immigrants for resettlement.

Push factor is an event that compels large numbers of persons to emigrate—that is, leave their country of origin for permanent resettlement elsewhere.

Racial profiling is a pattern of behavior of police officers based on racial appearance.

Refugee is a qualified applicant for conditional entry into the United States whose application could not be approved because of an adequate number of preference visas.

Requests for detention are requests by the DHS that a local or state law enforcement agency hold an individual beyond the point at which they would otherwise be released.

Requests for notification are requests that state or local law enforcement notify ICE of a pending release during the time that a person is otherwise in custody under state or local authority.

Sabbatarian is a religious law, norm, or customary practice as to which day, Saturday or Sunday, a religious group/denomination/cult/sect holds to be the holy day.

Sanctuary city is a city in the United States that follows certain procedures that shelter illegal immigrants that may be by "de jure" or "de facto" action. The designation has no legal meaning and is most commonly used for cities that do not permit municipal funds or resources to be applied in furtherance of enforcement of federal immigration laws; that is, they do not allow police or municipal employees to inquire about one's immigrant status.

Stakeholder is a person or organization with an interest or concern in something, especially a business; or one who is involved or is affected by a policy or course of action.

Unauthorized immigrants are those who come undocumented or break or overstay the conditions of their visas and become illegal immigrants without the status of permanent resident alien.

Undocumented immigrants are individuals who enter the United States without inspection or paper documentation allowing them to enter and to reside in the United States and to legally work while doing so.

Unfunded mandates are requirements by the federal government upon state and local governments without offsetting funding for their implementation.

Visa is a legal document issued by a consular or similar state department official allowing a person to travel to the United States for either permanent or temporary reasons—such as immigrant, student, tourist, government representative, business, or cultural exchange.

Xenophobia is an unfounded fear of foreigners.

ANNOTATED BIBLIOGRAPHY

INTRODUCTION

This chapter presents an annotated list of the major sources of information that the reader is encouraged to consult. It begins with print sources, including brief annotations of 100 books on the subject. The list includes those published since 2000, but also contains some published earlier to provide a historical context in order to help the reader to better grasp the rich complexities of the subject. The chapter also provides a brief annotated list of some of the major scholarly journals that publish original research articles relative to immigration reform and the 1965 act. For its nonprint sources, it annotates some feature-length films and a few shorter videos that dramatically depict the issues and people involved in the immigration debate over reform attempts tried or proposed for both laws and policies. The nonprint sources put real "faces" to the numbers and statistics presented in the previous chapter or often used in debates over immigration reform. In doing so, the nonprint sources highlight the human interest aspects of this controversial topic.

SELECTED PRINT RESOURCES

Books

Alienkoff, T. Alexander, and Douglas Klusmeyer, eds. *From Migrants to Citizens: Membership in a Changing World.* Washington, DC: Brookings Institution, 2000.
    This edited collection presents a scholarly discussion of the incorporation of immigrants with a multifaceted view of naturalization and immigration law and policy.

Allport, Alan, and John Ferguson, eds. *Immigration Policy*, 2nd ed. New York: Chelsea House, 2009.

This edited volume uses the point/counterpoint approach to present a thorough discussion of the complex topic of U.S. immigration policy and law. Among its wide range of issues covered, it examines controversies such as the comparative cost/benefits associated with undocumented immigration whose numbers rose exponentially in part as a result of the 1965 act. The editors refrain from taking a position, allowing the reader to decide after reading arguments for both sides of a controversy.

Anderson, Stuart. *Immigration*. Westport, CT: Praeger, 2010.

Anderson presents a penetrating and extensive study of the difficulty involved with enacting and then implementing border control policy to resolve undocumented immigration, focusing on the southern border with Mexico, and by extension, with Central American countries.

Armey, Dick, and Matt Kibbe. *Give Us Liberty: A Tea Party Manifesto*. New York: William Morrow, 2010.

A polemic, this manifesto is aimed at tea party activists, but it is useful to anyone seeking to understand what the tea party movement is all about, what it is fighting for, and what is next for the movement. The two authors have been leaders of the movement and of its advocacy organization, Freedom Works. They believe in limited government and individual liberty, and this is their national call to action. The movement's activists are among the strongest voices for strict immigration control, for the crackdown at the border approach to immigration law, and vehemently oppose any "amnesty" programs.

Arnold, Kathleen R., ed. *Anti-Immigration in the United States: A Historical Encyclopedia*. Westport, CT: Greenwood Press, 2011.

This two-volume set is one of the first to address recent anti-immigration sentiment. Arnold organizes the topic alphabetically, using the encyclopedia approach. She puts current anti-immigrant attitudes in context by covering major historical periods, and covers relevant concepts, leading figures, and the most important groups within the anti-immigration movement.

Ashcroft, John. *Never Again: Securing America and Restoring Justice*. Nashville, TN: Center Street Publishing, 2006.

This is a provocative book by the former and quite controversial attorney general. In it, Ashcroft tells the "behind the scenes, untold story" of the war on terror in the post-9/11 United States. He shares his perspective on the dangers to and within the United States from outside forces and explains what he did to repair serious flaws and failures in U.S. security. He has several recommendations pertaining to immigration law and the failure to keep international terrorists out of the country.

Bakken, Gordon, and Alexandra Kindell. *Encyclopedia of Immigration and Migration in the American West*. Los Angeles: Sage Publications, 2006.
This two-volume set takes an encyclopedic look at the ethnic groups crossing the plains, landing at the ports, and crossing the northern and southern borders. It contains focused biographies, community history, and economic enterprises and uses a variety of demographic data.

Barone, Michael. *Shaping Our Nation: How Surges in Migration Transformed America and Its Politics*. New York: Crown Forum, 2013.
This comprehensive and engaging book examines the long history of immigration and how past surges in immigration influenced American culture, politics, policies, and society.

Bean, Frank, George Vernez, and Stephanie Bell-Rose, eds. *Immigration and Opportunity: Race, Ethnicity, and Employment in the U.S.* New York: Russell Sage, 1999.
This book is comprised of an array of essays from leading sociologists and demographers that collectively provides a systematic account of the sundry ways in which immigration impacts the labor market experiences of the native-born.

Bean, Frank D., and Gillian Stevens. *America's Newcomers: Immigrant Incorporation and the Dynamics of Diversity*. New York: Russell Sage, 2003.
In this book, a leading demographer and a language specialist examine the factors influencing the gradual incorporation of immigrants and their children, and the variety of aspects that collectively influence their rate of incorporation.

Beck, Roy H. *The Case against Immigration*. New York: Norton, 1996.
This polemic is a thorough articulation of all of the arguments and data that the author can marshal against high levels of immigration. It well represents the views of many if not most of the politicians and the leadership of the anti-immigration and especially the anti-undocumented immigrant political and social movement that have become organized in American politics, largely in response to the increase in undocumented immigration as an unanticipated consequence of the 1965 immigration reform act.

Benton-Cohen, Katherine. *Inventing the Immigration Problem: The Dillingham Commission and Its Legacy*. Cambridge, MA: Harvard University Press, 2018.

In this comprehensive historical work, the author argues that the Dillingham Commission's legacy still influences U.S. immigration policy a century later. Her book is a timely reminder that immigrants shape the present and the future of America. She anchors the development of immigration law into both a global context and in domestic conflicts over race, ethnicity, and religion. She demonstrates immigration law is a mixture of suspicion and celebration of migrants that remains at the core of current conflicts over these issues and perceived problems.

Brewer, Stewart. *Borders and Bridges.* Westport, CT: Praeger Securities International, 2006.

The author examines the complex relationship between the United States and Latin American nations with an introduction to the most important events in the diplomatic, military, social, and economic history of that often stormy relationship.

Brotherton, David, and Philip Kretsedemas, eds. *Keeping Out the Others: A Critical Introduction.* New York: Columbia University Press, 2008.

The authors provide a historical analysis of recent immigration enforcement in the United States. They show how anti-immigration tendencies gather steam for decades. They provide contributions from social scientists, policy analysts, legal experts, community organizers, and journalists. The editors critically examine the discourse that has framed the debate over immigration enforcement. The book explores the politics and practices of deportation and frames the issues in constitutional law and defense of civil liberties. The book draws on theories of structural inequality and institutional discrimination.

Brunet-Jailly, Emmanuel, ed. *Border Disputes: A Global Encyclopedia.* Westport, CT: Greenwood Press, 2015, 3 vols.

This three-volume set covers 80 current international border disputes and conflicts using social science studies, political science, human geography, and related subjects. It analyzes the conflicts as territorial, positional, or functional. It provides key legal rulings and primary documents on the important resolutions of various border disputes. It profiles key organizations' relationships to those disputes and to specific border-dispute commissions.

Bryne-Hessick, Carisa, and Gabriel Chin, eds. *Strange Neighbors: The Role of States in Immigration Policy.* New York: New York University Press, 2014.

This book explores the complicated and complicating role of the states in immigration policy and its enforcement. Some contributors explicate the dangers of in-state regulation of immigration policy. Two of the contributors support it, and others offer empirically based examination of state efforts to regulate immigration within their borders. The book demonstrates the wide state-to-state disparities in locally administered immigration policy and laws. It is a timely and spirited discussion on the issue.

Calavita, Kitty. *Inside the State: The Bracero Program, Immigration and the INS*. New York: Routledge Press, 1992.
　　In an authoritative narrative history, Calavita presents one of the best examinations of the Bracero Program, offering insights into temporary worker programs and the many problems inherently associated with that approach. It helps the reader better understand the entrenched opposition to any proposals that include any large-scale guest-worker program in future comprehensive immigration reform.

Chomsky, Aviva. *Undocumented: How Immigration Became Illegal*. Boston: Beacon Press, 2014.
　　Using legal, social, economic, and historical context, the author, an immigration rights activist, shows how "illegality" and "undocumented" are concepts created to exclude and exploit. She probes how U.S. policy assigns this status on Mexican and Central American migrants to the United States. The book blends historical narrative with human drama and with what it means to be undocumented in legal, social, economic, and historical contexts. It highlights the complex, contradictory, and ever-shifting natures of status in America.

Cieslik, Thomas, David Felsen, and Akis Kalaitzdis. *Immigration: A Documentary and Reference Guide*. Westport, CT: Greenwood Press, 2008.
　　Three respected authorities on immigration and international affairs examine the contemporary realities of immigration enmeshed as it is in complex economics, human rights, and national security issues.

Cohen, Steve, Beth Humphries, and Ed Mynott, eds. *From Immigration Controls to Welfare Controls*. New York: Routledge, 2001.
　　This edited collection examines theoretical, political, and practical aspects of the connection between immigration controls and internal welfare controls. Topics include forced dispersal of asylum seekers, local authority and voluntary sector regulations, nationalism, racism, class and fairness, strategies of resistance to such controls, and U.S. controls. It includes discussion of the role of welfare workers as immigration control enforcers.

Cornelius, W. A., and Ricardo A. Montoya. *America's New Immigration Law: Origins, Rationales and Potential Consequences*. San Diego: Center for U.S./Mexican Studies, University of California, 1983.

This study of Mexico-U.S. relations examines the social and economic impact of Mexican immigrants on receiving communities, especially on health care, education, and labor-market participation.

Craig, Richard. *The Bracero Program: Interest Groups and Foreign Policy.* Austin: University of Texas Press, 1971.

This is one of the early scholarly analyses of the controversial Bracero Program. It focuses on the interest groups for and against the program, and how they shaped the program's implementation and relationship to broader foreign policy concerns. Although it is dated, some of the interest groups discussed are involved in today's immigration reform politics, and the insights relating immigration to foreign policy provide relevant context for current relations and foreign policy arguments.

Daniels, Roger. *Coming to America: A History of Immigration and Ethnicity in American Life,* 2nd ed. New York: Harper, 2002.

In this second edition, the eminent historian offers a brief but insightful history of immigration and ethnicity and their impact on U.S. society, adding a timely new chapter on immigration during the age of globalization. It includes new appendixes with more recent statistics (up to 2000). It is an engrossing study of U.S. immigration from colonial times to the end of the twentieth century by a noted historian of Asian Americans and immigration.

Daniels, Roger. *Not Like Us: Immigrants and Minorities in America, 1890–1924.* Chicago: Ivan Dee, Rowman and Littlefield Group, 1998.

Daniels examines the conditions of immigrants, Native Americans, and Black Americans during this critical era of American history. He shows how these groups experienced as much repression as "advances" during the Progressive Era. He covers immigration law from the enactment of the Chinese Exclusion laws to the Quota Act of 1924. He details the ethnic strife and race riots of the era.

Daniels, Roger. *Guarding the Golden Doors.* New York: Hill and Wang, 2005.

Daniels gives a detailed analysis of immigration policy and how and why it changed as it did over time, focusing on the years 1882–2000. He provides an enlightening historical context to the current debate over comprehensive immigration reform and the impact on the flow of immigration as a result of the 1965 immigration and naturalization act.

Daniels, Roger, and Otis Graham. *Debating American Immigration, 1882 to the Present.* Lanham, MD: Rowman and Littlefield, 2001.

Two prominent historians present competing interpretations of past, present, and future immigration policy and American attitudes toward immigrants and immigration. They include supporting primary documents, and each offers recommendations for future policies and legal remedies for immigration law problems.

Eastman, Cari Lee Skogberg. *Immigration: Examining the Facts*. Santa Barbara, CA: ABC-CLIO, 2016.

This book explores the myths and truths regarding U.S. immigration. It provides an impartial understanding of the true state of U.S. immigration policy. It refutes falsehoods, misinformation, and exaggerations on the topic, while confirming the validity of other assertions. It analyzes specific claims about immigration in the media and public discourse. It identifies the origins of the claims and offers empirical data to consider their veracity. It presents a host of statistical data in an easy-to-read format.

Ferris, Elizabeth G., ed. *Refugees and World Politics*. New York: Praeger, 1985.

The editor provides a thorough collection of essays on the refugee crisis up to the early 1980s. It is an important source of data to that point in time, and many of its issues and problems remain relevant today.

Foner, Nancy. *In a New Land: A Comparative View of Immigration*. New York: New York University Press, 2005.

In this study of comparative immigration, Foner, a leading immigration scholar, draws on the rich history of American immigrants with statistical and ethnographic data. She compares new immigrants with past influxes of Europeans to the United States across cities and regions in the United States and over different periods of time. She offers a comprehensive assessment and analysis that focuses on race, ethnicity, gender, and transnational connections.

French, Laurence A. *Running the Border Gauntlet*. Westport, CT: Praeger, 2010.

French traces the long history of racial, political, religious, and class conflicts that result from America's contentious immigration policies. It is a lucid narrative account accessible to college students and the general public and, as such, provides a historical context to the current debates over immigration reform.

Gans, Judith, Elaine M. Replogie, and Daniel J. Tichenor, *Debates on Immigration*. Los Angeles: Sage Publications, 2012.

This is an issue-based and solid reference guide that examines immigration policy in the United States and the impassioned debates about the scope and nature of restrictionist policy. After an introductory essay, it uses a collection of original essays in the point/counterpoint style exploring the multiple sides of this complex topic.

Gomez, Laure. *Manifest Destinies*. New York: New York University Press, 2007.
Gomez, a law professor and American studies scholar at the University of New Mexico, presents this narrative history of Mexican Americans in the context of race relations and racism in the United States and discusses the racial identity, legal status, and colonization patterns of Mexican Americans.

Hampshire, David. *U.S. Immigration Handbook*. Bath, UK: Survival Books, 2010.
This handbook is aimed at persons planning to live and work in the United States. It details how to get a visa and a green card (work-authorization card), a survey of all 50 states, immigration history and pertinent demographics, both immigrant and nonimmigrant visas, a discussion of the process for naturalization, and miscellaneous but useful information for the potential immigrant. It includes a reference section of relevant resources.

Haugen, David. *Immigration*. Boston: Greenhaven/Cengage, 2009.
Using an opposing-viewpoints approach, Haugen explores immigration through a wide range of views by respected experts in the pro-con format. His book is presented in an accessible style aimed at general readers and undergraduate-level students.

Hayes, Patrick J., ed. *The Making of Modern Immigration: An Encyclopedia of People and Ideas*. Santa Barbara, CA: ABC-CLIO, 2012.
This library reference volume is a comprehensive examination of the legal immigration system of the United States using the encyclopedia format of alphabetical entries covering the major government actors and interest group stakeholders, as well as the key concepts of immigration law.

Hernandez, Kelly. *Migra! A History of the U.S. Border Patrol*. Berkeley: University of California Press, 2010.
Hernandez presents a narrative history of the U.S. Border Patrol from its beginnings in 1924 as a small, peripheral law enforcement outfit to its emergence as a large, professional police force. She mines lost and largely unseen primary documents and records stored in garages, closets, and an abandoned factory, as well as those in U.S. and Mexican archives. She details how the U.S. Border Patrol translated the mandate for comprehensive migrant control into a project of policing Mexicans in the U.S.-Mexico borderland.

Hutchinson, E. P. *Legislative History of Immigration Policy, 1798–1965*. Philadelphia: University of Pennsylvania Press, 1981.

The most comprehensive and authoritative examination of immigration laws from the early republic to the 1965 reform.

Information Plus. *American Immigration: An Encyclopedia of Political, Social, and Cultural Change*. Farmington Hills, MI: Thomson/Gale, 2014.
This library reference volume presents a narrative history of American immigration, with tables, figures, and analysis of immigration to the United States on current immigration issues, laws, and policies.

Information Plus. *Immigration and Illegal Aliens: Blessing or Burden?* Farmington Hills, MI: Thomson/Gale, 2006.
This is one of a series of brief but thorough monographs that focuses on the undocumented immigrants issue viewed from a variety of perspectives. It presents many graphs, figures, and tables of data that touch upon every aspect of the illegal immigration issue. It presents the pros and cons on all sides of the issue and offers a solid historical perspective, as does every volume in the series.

Kellas, James. *The Politics of Nationalism and Ethnicity*, 2nd ed. London: Palgrave Macmillan Press, 1998.
Kellas reviews the key theoretical approaches to the study of nationalism within a wide range of disciplines. He presents multinational case studies to illuminate the power of nationalism and ethnicity in politics. He evaluates the strategies of accommodation that have developed in various attempts to cope with ethnic conflict.

Keller, Morton. *America's Three Regimes: A New Political History*. New York: Oxford University Press, 2016.
This narrative history is a sweeping view of American political history. The author divides that history into what he terms "three regimes," each of which lasted decades. He portrays the steady evolution of American politics, government, and law. The regimes are: Deferential and Republican, colonial to 1820s; Party and Democratic, 1830s to 1930s; and Populist and Bureaucratic, 1930s to the present.

Kennedy, John F. *A Nation of Immigrants*. New York: Harper Perennial, 2008 (Reissued on its 50th anniversary).
This new release of the former president's book details then senator Kennedy's passion for immigration reform. He notes the many contributions to American culture made by immigrants. He describes the discrimination that they faced, which resonates with the current anti-immigration movement. The rhetoric and reasoning of the current anti-immigrant movement

reads the same as that of the 1950s and 1960s; only the targets of their xeno-phobic fears change. With an introduction to the new edition written by Edward Kennedy, this edition details what became of President John F. Kennedy's immigration reform—the 1965 act—passed in no small measure as a memorial to the assassinated president.

Kivisto, Peter, and Thomas Faist. *Beyond a Border: Causes and Consequences of Contemporary Immigration*. Los Angeles: Sage Publications, 2010.

This is a comprehensive look at both legal and illegal immigration to America. It focuses on both push and pull factors driving the immigration process. It covers both undocumented and visa overstayers, and shows the relationship of problems in the legal immigration system to the unauthorized immigration flow.

Krauss, Erick, and Alex Pacheco. *On the Line: Inside the Border Patrol*. New York: Citadel Press, 2004.

This book offers an "insider's" look at the Border Patrol, presented in journal-istic style. It portrays the difficult tasks, numerous resource problems, suc-cesses, and shortcomings of the controversial agency.

Lamm, R. D., and G. Imhoff. *The Immigration Time Bomb*. New York: Truman Talley Books, 1985.

Published prior to the enactment of IRCA, this polemic marshals every argu-ment and all the data it can muster to show the costs or detrimental effects of large-scale immigration, in particular those used to promote policy reforms to "control" the illegal immigration flow. The arguments presented here con-tinue to be used by anti-immigration and especially anti-illegal immigration entities today, and they give a historical perspective to the Republican Party's intransigent position on any and all immigration reform that in their view constitutes "amnesty."

Lee, Erika. *At America's Gates: Chinese Immigration During the Exclusion Era, 1882–1943*. Chapel Hill: University of North Carolina Press, 2003.

In this award-winning book, Lee examines the Chinese Exclusion acts and how those laws changed the course of American history. She details stories of both the immigrants and the immigrant officials devoted to keeping them out. She shows how the laws transformed the lives of Chinese Americans, their patterns of immigration, identities, and families. She shows how those laws recast America from an immigrant welcoming nation into a gatekeeping nation using immigrant identification, border enforcement, surveillance, and deportation policies that are reflected powerfully in current immigration policy and law.

Lee, Erika. *The Making of Asian America: A History*. New York: Simon and Schuster, 2016.

> Lee's volume is a sweeping and comprehensive examination of the history of Asian Americans and of their role in American life. She is one of the preeminent scholars of the subject, and her expertise shows throughout this engaging historical narrative. Lee shows how Asian immigrants and their descendants have remade American Asian life. Published 50 years after passage of the Immigration and Nationality Act of 1965, Lee's inspiring stories are epic and eye-opening, illuminating the complicated history of race and immigration and of their place in today's world.

LeMay, Michael C. *The American Political Party System: A Reference Handbook*. Santa Barbara, CA: ABC-CLIO, 2017.

> This Contemporary World Issues volume examines the rise and development of political parties in the United States from the founding era to 2016. It links the various political parties that took positions on immigration, pro and con, and demonstrates how their positions on the issue influenced their development, and how the parties and their policy positions in turn influenced the flow of immigration over some 200 years of American history.

LeMay, Michael C. *Doctors at the Borders: Immigration and the Rise of Public Health*. Westport, CT: Praeger, 2015.

> This monograph is a detailed historical narrative that examines the rise of U.S. public health from the early 1800s to 2014. It uses primary documents and copious data to trace the efforts of the U.S. Marine Hospital Service, the precursor of the U.S. Public Health Service, to effectively and efficiently screen the millions of immigrants entering the nation to prevent the spread of pandemic contagious diseases.

LeMay, Michael C., ed. *The Gatekeepers: Comparative Immigration Policy*. Westport, CT: Praeger, 1989.

> This monograph provides a historical overview of U.S. immigration policy making since 1820. It discusses the waves of immigration and distinguishes four phases of immigration policymaking that dominated historical eras in reaction to preceding waves, employing a door analogy to characterize each era of immigration policy.

LeMay, Michael C. *Guarding the Gates: Immigration and National Security*. Westport, CT, and London: Praeger Security International, 2006.

> This monograph is a historical narrative analysis of the inherent linkage between immigration policy and national security policy, from the founding era of American politics to the post-9/11 attacks and enactment of laws

rushed through the Congress in response to the threat of international terrorism and the fears that terrorists would enter the nation through the undocumented immigrant flow.

LeMay, Michael C. *Illegal Immigration: A Reference Handbook*, 1st ed. Santa Barbara, CA: ABC-CLIO, 2007.

This library reference volume in the Contemporary World Issues series examines both undocumented and visa overstayer forms of unauthorized immigration to the United States, concentrating on the post-1965 exponential rise in
such immigration. It covers the history of the issue and discusses the main
problems and controversies of the subject. It profiles the major stakeholders,
both governmental and nongovernmental, on all sides of the issue. It presents
tables of data and excerpts of key laws and court cases on the issue. It presents
an extensive annotated list of the key resources, both print and nonprint, to
alert the readers to the basic literature necessary for further examination of
the subject.

LeMay, Michael C. *Illegal Immigration: A Reference Handbook*, 2nd ed. Santa
Barbara, CA: ABC-CLIO, 2015.

This second edition of a library reference volume of the Contemporary
World Issue series updates the examination of the unauthorized immigration
issue to 2015. It details the historical background, major controversies, and
issues, profiles the key actors and organizations involved in the issue, surveys
the scholarly literature on the subject, and offers a useful chronology of the
issue from 1965 to 2015.

LeMay, Michael. *The Perennial Struggle: Race, Ethnicity, and Minority Group Relations in the United States*, 3rd ed. Upper Saddle River, NJ: Prentice-Hall, 2009.

This basic textbook on ethnic and minority group politics in the United
States has extensive coverage of the major immigrant groups that came to
the United States, and the effects of immigration laws and policies, the struggle to cope with minority status, and discrimination against them. It presents
a conceptual framework to better understand the political incorporation process of ethnic, religious, and racial minority groups into American culture,
politics, and society.

LeMay, Michael C., ed. *Transforming America: Perspectives on Immigration*, 3 vols.
Santa Barbara, CA: ABC-CLIO, 2013.

This three-volume set presents original essays by 30 leading authorities on the
subject written from various disciplinary perspectives. It covers immigration
from 1820 to 2012. It offers a thorough view of immigration to the United
States in all of its complexities.

LeMay, Michael. *U.S. Immigration: A Reference Handbook*. Santa Barbara, CA: ABC-CLIO, 2004.

This library reference volume examines legal immigration from 1965 to 2004, using the standard format of the Contemporary World Issues series of the publisher. It is an objective presentation of the topic, allowing the reader to reach his or her own conclusions. It has a chapter offering tables of data and figures, as well as excerpts from primary documents, including synopses of court cases and laws on the issue.

LeMay, Michael C., and Elliott Robert Barkan, eds. *U.S. Immigration and Naturalization Laws and Issues: A Documentary History*. Westport, CT: Greenwood Press, 1999.

This unique volume by two leading authorities on the subject summarizes and presents excerpts from primary sources, containing 150 documents covering all major laws and court cases concerning U.S. immigration and naturalization law from colonial times to 1990.

Lew-Williams, Beth. *The Chinese Must Go: Violence, Exclusion, and the Making of the Asian American*. Cambridge, MA: Harvard University Press, 2018.

Princeton University historian Beth Lew-Williams examines the social consensus that gave rise to the Chinese Exclusion laws of the 1880s and 1890s. She details how the expansion of citizenship came to a halt, denying entire classes of people the right to naturalize based solely on racism. She shows how immigration laws created the very idea that the Chinese were inassimilable aliens. She argues persuasively how that concept hurts the United States to this day.

Loucky, James, Jeanne Armstrong, and Larry J. Estrada, eds. *Immigration in America Today: An Encyclopedia*. Westport, CT: Praeger, 2006.

This book offers an interdisciplinary overview of complex immigration-related issues using alphabetically arranged entries that define key terms and concepts, provide a historical background, and suggest future trends in immigration and in the proposals to reform immigration policy.

Lutton, Wayne, and John Tanton. *The Immigration Invasion*. Petoskey, MI: The Social Contract Press, 1994.

A largely polemic book, it marshals virtually all the arguments the authors can think to bring to the immigration debate discourse from the perspective that immigration is too open and needs to be dramatically restricted.

Marshall, Ray. *Immigration for Shared Prosperity: A Framework for Comprehensive Reform*. Washington, DC: Economic Policy Institute, 2007.

This insightful book by a prominent economist and former U.S. secretary of labor explains what provisions he maintains are essential in any comprehensive immigration reform package, emphasizing immigration's importance to the vibrancy of the U.S. economy. Although written a decade ago, its insights are relevant for the current debate over comprehensive immigration reform.

Massey, Douglas, Rafael Alarcon, Jorge Durand, and Humberto Gonzalez. *Return to Aztlan: The Social Process of Immigration from Western Mexico.* Berkeley: University of California Press, 1987.

The authors provide a thorough and many-viewed examination of Mexican immigration to the United States, both legal and unauthorized, focusing on the southwestern United States (the mythical Aztlan of the book's title).

Massey, Douglas, Jorge Durand, and Nolan Malone. *Beyond Smoke and Mirrors: Immigration in an Era of Economic Integration.* New York: Russell Sage, 2003.

The authors provide a fresh perspective on Mexican migration history by systematically tracing the predictable consequences of highly unsystematic policy regimes. They focus on post-9/11 immigration policy actions by marshalling new and compelling evidence to expose the flagrant contradiction of allowing the free flow of goods and capital, but not of people, and they argue persuasively for much-needed policy reforms.

Meier, Matt S., and Margo Gutiérrez. *Encyclopedia of the Mexican American Civil Rights Movement.* Westport, CT: Greenwood Press, 2000.

Using an encyclopedia format, the authors present a reliable, accessible, and broad coverage of the persons, events, movements, and concepts that have informed the Mexican American civil rights movement. It is a thorough review of this ethnic group's experiences of the American way of life.

Merino, Noel. *Illegal Immigration.* Boston: Greenhaven/Cengage, 2012.

The author presents a comprehensive discussion of unauthorized immigration using a reference volume format to organize discussion of the issues involved. The book demonstrates why enacting comprehensive immigration reform is politically so difficult and why policy designed to cope with the unauthorized flow is so fraught with unanticipated consequences.

Miller, Debra. *Immigration.* Boston: Greenhaven/Cengage, 2014.

Miller uses the library reference volume format to present to readers an exhaustive examination of legal immigration and its complexities that contribute to the current public policy stalemate.

Motomura, Hiroshi. *Americans in Waiting: The Lost Story of Immigration and Citizenship in the United States.* New York: Oxford University Press, 2006.

Motomura provides an in-depth look at Chinese and Japanese Americans and their struggles to secure citizenship rights from a nation that had institutional racism infusing its immigration and naturalization policy and law. In doing so, the book provides lessons relevant to the current policy positions targeting Muslim immigrants.

Motomura, Hiroshi. *Immigration Outside the Law*. New York: Oxford University Press, 2014.
An immigration history scholar examines the complex issue of unauthorized immigration and why it reflects gaps and problems with legal immigration law and policy. He demonstrates that fixing the illegal immigration problem requires reform of legal immigration, providing an argument for comprehensive immigration reform.

Muller, Thomas, and Thomas Espanshade. *The Fourth Wave*. Washington, DC: Urban Institute Press, 1985.
This groundbreaking book was among the first and most thoroughly analytical examinations of the post-1965 wave of immigrants to the United States. It contributed significantly to renewing the scholarly debate over large-scale immigration and its costs and benefits to the United States.

Navarro, Armando. *Mexican Political Experience in Occupied Aztlan*. Lanham, MD: Altamura Press, 2005.
Navarro provides a critical look at the Hispanic/Latino, and especially the Mexican immigrants' struggle with American politics and their minority status as largely the result of racial attitudes. He demonstrates that the attitudes of the past decade profile the policy attitudes and prescriptions of the Republican Party in the era of Trumpism.

Nelson, Michael. *Resilient America: Electing Nixon in 1968, Channeling Dissent, and Dividing Government*. Lawrence: University Press of Kansas, 2014.
Nelson's insightful book on the 1968 presidential election explains why it was a reordering of party coalitions, groups, and regions that helped set a hardening and widening partisan and ideological divide. It shows how the election was a watershed event that provides insights for our current political environment.

Ngai, Mae. *Impossible Subjects: Illegal Aliens and the Making of Modern America*. Princeton, NJ: Princeton University Press, 2014.
In this beautifully written historical narrative, Ngai traces the origins of "illegal alien" in American law and society, explaining its how and why. She details how it profoundly affected ideas and practices about U.S. citizenship, race, and state authority. She shows how the national origins system remapped

America by creating new categories of racial differences and by emphasizing America's contiguous land borders and the efforts to control them.

Ngai, Mae, ed. *Major Problems in American Immigration History: Documents and Essays*. Boston: Wadsworth/Cengage, 2011.

This excellent collection of essays and documents explores the themes of political and economic forces that cause immigration. It details the alienation and uprootedness caused by relocation. It treats difficult questions of citizenship and assimilation, using primary sources, and the interpretations of distinguished historians while allowing readers to draw their own conclusions.

O'Leary, Anna Ochoa, ed. *Undocumented Immigrants in the United States: An Encyclopedia of Their Experience*. Santa Barbara, CA: Greenwood, 2014.

This two-volume reference work uses the encyclopedia format to address the dynamic lives of undocumented immigrants. It shows how their experiences are a key part of the nation's demographic and sociological evolution. It supplies extensive and comprehensive coverage of a complex topic by consolidating the insights of scholars who have examined the subject over many years.

Orreniris, Pia and Madelaine Zavodny. *Beyond the Gold Door: U.S. Immigration in a New Era of Globalization*. Washington, DC: American Enterprise Institute Press, 2010.

The authors document how recent immigration reforms have resulted in an inefficient patchwork system that shortchanges high-skilled immigrants and poorly serves the American public. They propose a radical overhaul of current immigration policy stressing economic competitiveness and long-term growth favoring employment-based immigration over the family reunification preference system established by the 1965 act.

Papademetrious, Demetrios, and Mark J. Miller, eds. *The Unavoidable Issue*. Philadelphia: Institute for the Study of Human Issues, 1984.

This volume is an impressive array of essays discussing all of the major issues of U.S. immigration policy and the need for reforms in law and policy. It is a particularly good review of the topic for the 1965–1980 period, but it provides a historical perspective useful to understanding the complexity of the issue for today's immigration policy debate.

Payan, Tony. *The Three U.S.-Mexico Border Wars: Drugs, Immigration, and Homeland Security*. Westport, CT: Praeger, 2006.

The book examines the post-9/11 responses to the attacks as felt in the most affected area—the U.S.-Mexico border, and the effects resulting from these three "wars"—on drugs, immigration, and terror. He shows how these three areas of law are linked inexorably in the border region, affecting the lives of all who live there.

Perea, Juan, ed. *Immigrants Out! The New Nativism and the Anti-Immigrant Impulse in the United States.* New York: New York University Press, 1997.

Perea provides a collection of 18 original essays by leading immigration scholars. The volume approaches the complex subject using interdisciplinary perspectives to examine current nativism in light of past waves. It examines the relationship between the races and the perception of a national immigration crisis resulting from those largely racially based attitudes toward immigration. It gives a historical perspective as to why today's national populism contains racial undertones that make comprehensive immigration reform so difficult to achieve.

Pfaelzer, Jean. *Driven Out: The Forgotten War against Chinese Americans.* Berkeley: University of California Press, 2008.

Pfaelzer tells the story of thousands of Chinese immigrants who were violently herded into railroad cars, steamers, or logging rafts to be marched out of towns or killed, from the Pacific Coast to the Rocky Mountains. Using primary documents including local and national laws and several court cases, she chronicles the Chinese immigrants' campaign against what they called the "Dog Tag Law," and launching what she calls "the largest organized act of civil disobedience in the United States," against "ethnic cleansing." She offers a new understanding—in geography, chronology, and cast of characters—of the civil rights movement. Her groundbreaking book records over 100 roundups, pogroms, expulsions, and ethnic cleansings used by white Westerners to drive the Chinese out of their communities from 1850 to 1906. She details how they used warnings, arson, boycotts, and outright violence to achieve their goals to do so.

Portes, Alejandro and Reuben G. Rumbaut, eds. *Ethnicities: Children of Immigrants in America.* New York: Russell Sage, 2001, 2 vols.

These two volumes present the findings of an extensive examination of the "political incorporation" of second-generation immigrants. This collection of essays detail that while assimilation was in the past a relatively homogeneous linear process, it is now a segmented one.

Powell, John. *Encyclopedia of North American Immigration.* New York: Facts on File, 2005.

This narrative history shows how, for good or bad, immigration has shaped and transformed the United States. It covers the magnitude and diversity of migration to North America. It is a solid, one-volume encyclopedia with more than 300 A–Z entries, and an extensive bibliography of resources for further research.

President's Commission on Immigration and Naturalization. *Whom Shall We Welcome?* Washington, DC: U.S. Government Printing Office, 1953.

This report of the President's Commission examines in detail emigration and U.S. immigration law. The commission was established by President Harry Truman. It recommended that the national origins quota system be abolished because the system discriminated against potential southern and eastern European immigrants, as well as Asia and the Pacific/Oceanic regions whose immigrants were limited to 100 persons a year. The report set in motion a long public debate over immigration law that culminated in the Immigration and Nationality Act of 1965 that finally abolished the restrictive national origins quota system.

Salomone, Rosemary. *True American: Language, Identity, and the Education of Immigrant Children.* Cambridge, MA: Harvard University Press, 2010.

The author uses the heated debate over how best to educate immigrant children as an approach to explore what national identity means in an age of globalization, transnationalism, and dual citizenship. She addresses the myths that bilingualism impedes success, that English is under threat, or that today's immigrants are more reluctant to learn English than were immigrants of the past. She provides a vivid narrative of the history of bilingual education.

Salyer, Lucy E. *Laws Harsh as Tigers: Chinese Immigrants and the Shaping of Modern Immigration Law.* Chapel Hill: University of North Carolina Press, 1995.

In her award-winning book, Salyes analyzes the popular and legal debates about immigration law and its enforcement policies during the height of the nativist movement of the early twentieth century. She links Asian immigrants on the West Coast with European immigrants on the East Coast. She discusses their sophisticated and often successful legal challenges to exclusionary immigration laws. Salyer shows, however, that by 1924, immigration law diverged from constitutional norms and that the Bureau of Immigration emerged as an exceptionally powerful organization, largely free from the constraints imposed on other government agencies. Her book offers a powerful lesson for today's approach to immigration law and its enforcement policies.

Samito, Christian. *Becoming American Under Fire.* Ithaca, NY: Cornell University Press, 2009.

Samito provides a rich account of how African American and Irish American soldiers in the Civil War influenced the modern vision of citizenship that developed during the war. They helped define the legal meaning and political practices of American citizenship as embodied in the Constitution and U.S. laws. Citizenship determines official membership in the country and helps define the duties and rights they enjoy, defines inclusion and exclusion in a community, as well as personal identities and collective patriotism.

Schrag, Peter. *Not Fit for Our Society: Nativism and Immigration.* Berkeley: University of California Press, 2010.

This historical narrative covering 300 years of U.S. history is a timely, thoughtful, and extensive look at anti-immigration attitudes in the United States from the founding to the present, emphasizing periodic spasms, the long history of ambivalence and inconsistency with strands of welcome and rejection.

Select Commission on Immigration and Refugee Policy. *Final Report.* Washington, DC: U.S. Government Printing Office, 1981.

The SCIRP was a joint Presidential/Congressional Commission established in 1979 by President Jimmy Carter, Senator Edward Kennedy (then chair of the Senate Judiciary Committee), and Representative Joshua Eilberg (then chair of the House Judiciary's Subcommittee on Immigration). The massive (400-page-plus) report's recommendations shaped the debate from 1982 to 1986 and the enactment of IRCA. Many of its recommendations influenced subsequent immigration debates since then (such as IMMACT) as well.

Stolarik, M. Mark, ed. *Forgotten Doors: The Other Ports of Entry to the United States.* Philadelphia: Balch Institute Press, 1988.

A comparative study of seven other ports of entry than New York from the early nineteenth century to the 1980s.

Strobel, Christoph. *Daily Life of the New Americans: Immigration since 1965.* Westport, CT: Praeger, 2010.

This is a detailed historical narrative that is an engaging look at the daily life of the new immigrants (post 1965). It provides an extensive chronology of events of the main events in recent immigration history. It offers a helpful historical perspective to better understand the politics of today's debates over immigration policy reform.

U.S. Commission on Immigration Policy. *U.S. Refugee Policy: Taking Leadership.* Washington, DC: U.S. Government Printing Office, 1997.

The commission held more than 40 hearings. This report presents the Jordan Commission's recommendations for a comprehensive and coherent U.S. refugee policy. It features data on Russian Jews, Iraqis, Kurds, Hmong, Somalis, and Yugoslavians. It suggested changes to the refugee resettlement program.

U.S. Commission on Immigration Policy. *Becoming American: Immigration and Immigration Policy*. Washington, DC: U.S. Government Printing Office, 1997.

> After 40 hearings and both domestic and foreign on-site visits, the Commission released this report in June 1997. It focuses on the goals of Americanization, setting out recommendations to help orient immigrants to their new communities, to learn English and civics, and to reinforce the integrity of the naturalization process, including a chapter titled "A Credible Framework for Immigration Policy."

Waters, Mary C., Reed Ueda, and Helen B. Marrow, eds. *The New Americans: A Guide to Immigration Since 1965*. New York: Russell Sage/Harvard University Press, 2007.

> This volume focuses on the wave of immigrants to the United States that began with and is influenced by laws and policies since 1965. It is written by an interdisciplinary group of scholars, who discuss immigration law and policy, refugees, unauthorized immigrants, naturalization, and the economic impact of immigration on religion, education, and family relations.

Wolbrecht, Christina, and Rodney E. Hero. *The Politics of Democratic Inclusion*. Philadelphia: Temple University Press. 2005.

> This book is an innovative examination of the complexity of the incorporation process for immigrants, explaining the "inclusion" or "incorporation" approach to the issue instead of the linear "assimilation" approach. It provides useful insights to better understand the process as it affects Muslims and Hispanics in post-9/11 America. It also provides the reader a useful counterpoint to view the arguments of the current nativist and populist strain in U.S. politics, which essentially views today's immigrants as unable to assimilate as did past immigrant groups.

Wood, Andrew Grant, ed. *The Borderlands: An Encyclopedia of Culture and Politics on the U.S.-Mexico Divide*. Westport, CT: Greenwood Press, 2008.

> This volume presents a broad collection of essays from multidisciplinary backgrounds. It uses the encyclopedia format to examine complex issues around migration flows, legal and unauthorized, across the U.S.-Mexico border.

Zolberg, Aristide. *A Nation by Design: Immigration Policy in the Fashioning of America*. Cambridge, MA: Russell Sage Foundation at Harvard University Press, 2008.

> The late Harvard professor explores American immigration policy from the colonial period to the present, discussing how it has been used as a tool of nation building. It covers policy at the local and state levels and profiles the

vacillating currents of opinions on immigration throughout American history. It examines legal, unauthorized, and asylum-seeking immigration, and how opinion varies so greatly among them.

Zucker, Norman, and Naomi Flink Zucker. *The Guarded Gate: The Reality of American Refugee Policy*. New York: Harcourt Brace Jovanovich, 1987.

The authors examine U.S. policy toward refugees as it emerged and was amended over a 40-year period. They show how refugee policy was and is shaped by foreign relations with both allies and adversaries abroad. They link refugee and asylum policy to domestic immigration history. They trace the history of restrictive policy of the national origins system, and the U.S. failure to respond to the Holocaust during the interwar and World War II years. They show how refugee policy continued to discriminate during the post– World War II years in favor of refugees fleeing communist countries and against those fleeing authoritarian regimes.

Zuniga, Victor, and Ruben Hernandez-Leon, eds. *New Destinations: Mexican Immigration in the United States*. New York: Russell Sage, 2005.

This book is an eclectic array of essays on the new Mexican immigration to the United States. It includes a discussion of both legal and unauthorized immigration matters. It examines census data to discern the historical evolution of Mexican immigration to the United States, discussing the demographic, economic, and legal factors that led to recent moves to areas beyond where their predecessors had settled. They conclude that undocumented immigrants did a better job than did their documented peers of the past in incorporating into the local culture. The book examines paternalism and xenophobic aspects of local residents toward the new immigrants. It details the strong work ethic of the new migrants and provides hopeful examples of their progress toward incorporation. It is one of the first scholarly assessments of the new settlements and experiences in the Midwest, Northeast, and the Deep South, and of the largest immigrant group in the United States from the perspectives of demographers, sociologists, folklorists, anthropologists, and political scientists.

Leading Scholarly Journals

American Demographics

Published 10 times per year, this peer-reviewed journal is an outlet for multidisciplinary articles of original research dealing with all aspects related to demography as well as occasional articles and reflective essays on migration, legal and unauthorized immigration, and an annually published useful resource guide.

American Journal of Sociology

This is a peer-reviewed quarterly journal of sociology that frequently publishes articles concerning assimilation, incorporation, integration, social trends, and policies regarding migration, both legal and unauthorized immigration. It also reviews books on immigration-related topics.

Annual Review of Sociology

This quarterly peer-reviewed academic journal has been published since 1975. It covers significant developments in the field of sociology including theoretical and methodological developments, as well as current research in the major subfields. Review chapters typically cover social processes, institutions and culture, organizations, political and economic sociology, stratification, demography, social policy, historical sociology, and major developments in other regions of the world.

Citizenship Studies

This peer-reviewed journal, published by Taylor and Francis in print and online, publishes internationally recognized scholarly work on contemporary issues of citizenship, human rights, and democratic processes. It is an interdisciplinary journal covering politics, sociology, history, anthropology, and cultural studies. It features aspects of citizenship such as gender, equality, migration, and borders.

Columbia Law Review

Published eight times per year, the law review frequently has case reviews and analytical articles and original essays dealing with immigration law matters.

Demographics

This peer-reviewed journal of the Population Association of America publishes scholarly research of interest to demography from a multidisciplinary perspective, with an emphasis on social sciences, geography, history, biology, statistics, business, epidemiology, and public health

Ethnohistory

This is a peer-reviewed quarterly publication and the official journal of the American Society for Ethnohistory. It contains articles of original research, commentaries, review essays, and useful book reviews.

Geographical Review

The quarterly, official journal of the American Geographical Society publishes research on all topics related to geography, including ones dealing with legal and unauthorized immigration, immigration reforms, and the incorporation of immigrants. It also publishes book reviews in each issue.

Georgetown Immigration Law Journal

This quarterly law review is the most specifically related law journal dealing with U.S. immigration law, current developments in law, and reform-related matters concerning all three branches of the U.S. government. It frequently focuses on unauthorized immigration. It contains case reviews, articles, notes and commentaries, and workshop reports devoted to the topic.

Harvard Law Review

Arguably the most influential law journal, this law review is published eight times per year. It contains original articles, case reviews, essays, commentaries, and book reviews that occasionally are on topics related to U.S. immigration law and its reform.

International Migration

This quarterly is an intergovernmental publication featuring documents, conference reports, and articles dealing with international migration topics. It regularly features articles dealing with revisions in laws affecting emigration and immigration matters. It provides a useful international context to American immigration law reform issues.

International Migration Review (IMR)

The leading quarterly journal in the field of migration, *IMR* contains current research articles, book reviews, documents, and bibliographies. It is a publication of the Center for Migration Studies in New York.

International Social Sciences Journal

This quarterly journal is published by Blackwell Publishers for UNESCO. It regularly contains articles concerning international migration, refugee and asylum issues, and their impact on societies and social systems and other topics related to UNESCO.

Journal of American Ethnic History

This peer-reviewed scholarly journal has been published since 1981 for the Immigration and Ethnic History Society. It addresses various aspects of North American immigration, including emigration, race and ethnic relations, immigration policies and the processes of incorporation, integration, and acculturation. Each issue contains articles, review essays, and book reviews. It features occasional scholarly forums and "research comments." It occasionally publishes special issues on a specific theme.

Journal of American Studies

Published three times per year, this multidisciplinary, scholarly refereed journal is multinational with articles on politics, economics, and geography and, in each issue, book reviews that often relate to immigration matters.

Journal of Economic Issues

This peer-reviewed scholarly economics journal covers all aspects of economic issues, including original research on immigration and migration, with a focus on the economic impact of migration and on labor market issues. Each issue has book reviews of related matters as well.

Journal of Economic Perspectives

This journal of the American Economic Association publishes occasional symposium issues and, regularly, original scholarly articles, features, and economic analysis on a variety of public policy issues, including both legal and unauthorized immigration, and book reviews on related matters.

Journal of Ethnic and Migration Studies

This peer-reviewed academic journal produces 16 issues per year and has been published since 1998. It features original research on all forms of migration and its consequences, with articles about ethnic conflict, discrimination, racism, nationalism, citizenship, and policies of integration. An international journal, it publishes comparative research in Europe, North America, and the Asian-Pacific.

Journal of Intercultural Studies

This journal presents international research related to intercultural studies across national and disciplinary boundaries. One issue per year is thematic. It examines common issues across a range of disciplinary perspectives. Peer-reviewed research, theoretical papers, and book reviews are included in each issue.

Journal of International Refugee Law

This quarterly publishes articles on refugee law and policy matters, including legislation, documentation, and abstracts of recent publications in the field.

Journal of Migration and Human Security

A publication of the Center for Migration Studies of New York, this is an online, peer-reviewed public policy academic journal focusing on the broad scope of social, political, and economic dimensions of human security. It publishes an annual bound volume of its articles.

Journal of Social Policy

This British journal publishes original research articles about all aspects of social policy. Published since 1972 by Cambridge University Press, it is international and interdisciplinary. It contains relevant book reviews in each issue.

Migration News

This monthly newsletter is published by the University of California, Davis. It concerns all manner of topics related to migration, with particular emphasis on how unauthorized immigration impacts U.S. society, both positively and negatively.

Migration World

This journal publishes articles and information about migration and refugee problems worldwide. It is a readable and accessible publication that is a good source for school and college reports.

Patterns of Prejudice

This journal provides a forum for exploring the historical roots and contemporary varieties of demonization of "the other." It probes language and social construction of race, nation, color, and ethnicity as well as the linkages between these categories. The journal discusses issues and the policy agenda that impact asylum issues, unauthorized immigration, hate crimes, Holocaust denial, and citizenship.

Perspectives on Politics

Published since 2003, this journal is an official publication of the American Political Science Association. It is a peer-reviewed scholarly quarterly aimed at nurturing political science within the public sphere. It is released both in print and online. It occasionally has featured articles on inclusion and exclusion and on public policy debates about immigration, both legal and unauthorized.

Political Research Quarterly

This peer-reviewed quarterly scholarly journal publishes original research on all aspects of politics. It is published on behalf of the Western Political Science Association by the University of Utah. Published since 1948, it was renamed in 1992. It features articles on public policy, race, and ethnicity

Political Science Quarterly

This scholarly, peer-reviewed quarterly discusses public and international affairs. It is nonpartisan, with scholarly articles devoted to the study and analysis of government, politics, and international affairs, with original articles, essays, thematic review essays, and book reviews.

Public Opinion Quarterly

This peer-reviewed academic journal is published by Oxford University Press for the American Association for Public Opinion Research. This social science interdisciplinary journal has been published since 1937, and is one of the most often cited journals of its kind. Its original research studies concern the analyses of public opinion on all sorts of political topics.

Refugee Reports

This is a monthly report of information and documents concerning refugees and the legislation, policies, and programs that affect them. A year-end statistical issue is published every December and is considered an authoritative source on data on refugees, their treatment and problems in refugee camps, and on their migration to asylum locations.

Refugee Survey Quarterly

This quarterly lists abstracts of the many publications concerning refugees, including a selection of "country reports" and one on human rights-related legal documents.

Review of Politics

This peer-reviewed academic journal publishes articles on political theory, public law, comparative politics, and international relations. Founded in 1939, it is published by the University of Notre Dame. Each issue has book reviews of recent academic books on politics. It has occasional symposium issues organized around a specific theme.

Sociological Forum

This peer-reviewed quarterly is published by Wiley-Blackwell for the Eastern Sociological Society. Founded in 1986, it publishes original research on comparisons in the study of immigrant integration, on belonging and "othering," and on critical ethnographies on immigrants and refugees to the United States.

Sociological Perspectives

Published by Sage since 1957, it is the official journal of the Pacific Sociological Association. It regularly features original research articles on social processes related to economic, political, and historical issues. Published six times per year, it has "up to the minute" articles within the field of sociology.

Social Science Quarterly

Published for the Southwestern Social Science Association by Blackwell, this interdisciplinary quarterly has articles of original research, review essays, book reviews, and occasional symposium issues. It contains articles dealing with U.S. immigration and illegal immigration policy as well as issues related to the incorporation of immigrants and their children into U.S. society.

NONPRINT SOURCES

Films

America 101. 2005. 86 minutes, color. Fabia Films.

The documentary film traces the trials and tribulations of two Mexican brothers who get smuggled over the border in an attempt to find their American dream.

Backyard (*El Traspatio*). 2009. 122 minutes, color. Tarazod films, Tardon/Berman Productions.

This feature-length film stars Jimmy Smits. It tells the true story of the border town of Juarez, Mexico, where since the mid-1990s, thousands of women have gone missing or turned up as sunburned corpses in the Sonora Desert.

Beyond Borders: The Debate over Human Migration. 2007. 51 minutes, color. Brian Ging Films.

The debate covered in this documentary is between Noam Chomsky and Jim Gilchrist, and it presents both sides of the controversy over illegal immigration to the United States and what can or should be done to address the problem.

Coyote. 2007. 94 minutes, color. Side Street Productions

Filmed in Los Angeles, this documentary feature-length film is directed by Brian Petersen. It tells the tale of two young Americans who decide to begin smuggling immigrants into the United States for profit. It is in Spanish and English.

Crossing Over. 2009. 113 minutes, color. MGM/The Weinstein Company.

This is an independent crime film drama starring Harrison Ford, Ashley Judd, Ray Liotta, and Jim Sturgess. It presents a multi-character canvas showing how immigrants of different nationalities struggle to achieve legal status in Los Angeles.

Dying to Get In: Undocumented Immigration at the U.S.-Mexico Border. 2005. 40 minutes, color. Films for the Humanities and Sciences.

> This documentary film by Christopher Deufert and directed by Brett Tolley traces the experiences and insights of Tolley, who embedded himself with a group of Mexicans crossing the U.S.-Mexico border. It presents their story as they make their way in a harrowing journey across the border.

From the Other Side. 2002. 99 minutes, color. Icarus Films.

> This multiple award–winning documentary film dramatizes how technology developed by the U.S. military is being used to stem the flow of unauthorized immigrants in the San Diego area, and how the success there is forcing the desperate, unauthorized immigrants to hazard crossing the dangerous deserts of Arizona. It is directed by renowned documentary filmmaker Channel Ackerman.

The Golden Cage: A Story of California's Farmworkers. 1990. 29 minutes, color. Filmmakers Library.

> Sort of a modern version of *The Grapes of Wrath*, this documentary video presents a moving and vivid portrait of contemporary farmworkers using historical footage, newspaper clippings, and black-and-white stills to trace the history of the United Farm Workers Union from the 1960s to 1990. It shows the tactics used by many companies to evade using union labor. It offers candid interviews with legal and illegal migrant workers, growers, doctors, and others.

Human Contraband: Selling the American Dream. 2002. 22 minutes, color. Films for the Humanities and Sciences.

> This ABC News program investigates the lucrative trade in smuggling into Mexico desperate human beings from all over the world, but mostly from Central America, who view Mexico as the back door to the United States. INS officials discuss multilateral efforts to combat such smuggling and unauthorized, undocumented entry into the United States.

Illegal Americans. 2002. 45 minutes, color. Films for the Humanities and Sciences.

> This CBS News documentary examines the hazardous enterprise of immigrants coming to the United States illegally, focusing on their desperate plight. It examines their living conditions in detention centers and the growing strains they place on U.S. cities, and it looks at those who provide assistance to the unauthorized immigrants. It shows how they manage to evade capture, the sweatshops that employ and exploit them, and the efforts of some who attempt to beat the system by using false IDs and marriages of convenience.

Immigrant Nation: The Battle for the Dream. 2010. 96 minutes, color.
This documentary film won an award at the Oaxaca Film Fest. It portrays the story of the modern immigrant rights movement and its struggle as seen through the eyes of a single mother, Elvira Arellano, who fought against her forced deportation and separation from her American-born child.

Laredoans Speak: Voices on Immigration. 2011. 75 minutes, color. Border Town Pictures.
Featuring veteran actor Pepe Serana, this documentary is directed by Victor Martinez. It takes the viewers through the issues involved in the pro-and-con debate over undocumented immigration as seen through the eyes of the citizens of Laredo, Texas.

Legacy of Shame: Migrant Labor; an American Institution. 2002. 52 minutes, color. Films for the Humanities and Sciences.
This CBS News documentary is a follow-up to the 1960 award-winning film *Harvest of Shame*. It documents the ongoing exploitation of migrant labor in the United States by highlighting efforts made to protect them. It investigates pesticide risks, uneven enforcement of employment and immigration regulations, and virtual peonage conditions. It covers the efforts of rural legal services as advocates for this truly "silent minority."

The Line in the Sand. 2005. 100 minutes, color. Sun Films, Inc.
This documentary film deals with illegal immigration and the issue of security along the southern border of the United States. It has a segment on the Minutemen Project, whose members practice vigilantism along the border in an attempt to enforce border control when and where they feel the U.S. government is failing in its duty to secure the border.

Precious Knowledge. 2011. 75 minutes, color. Dos Vatos Productions, ITVS.
In this documentary, filmed in Tucson, Arizona, disenfranchised high school seniors become academic warriors and community leaders trying to save their embattled ethnic studies classes when state lawmakers sought to eliminate the program.

Sin Nombre (Without a Name). 2009. 96 minutes, color. Creando Film, Focus Films.
This feature-length film won several awards at the 2009 Sundance Film Festival. It features the life and experiences of a Honduran teenager, Sayra, who reunites with her father and tries to realize her dream of a life in the United States. It is directed by Cary Toji Fukunaga and is in Spanish with English subtitles.

The State of Arizona. 2014. 90 minutes, color. PBS/ITVS, Latino Public Broadcasting Production.

> This riveting documentary covers the turbulent battle over unauthorized immigration in Arizona that came to a head with passage of Arizona Senate Bill 1070. It tracks multiple perspectives of the results of the law's passage as seen from all sides of the issue.

They Come to America: The Cost of Amnesty. 2012. 99 minutes, color. Corinth films.

> This polemical film by Dennis Lynch of FAIR depicts the human and financial costs of undocumented immigration.

Those Who Remain. 2008. 96 minutes, color. Sombre del Guyabo Productions.

> This documentary film is directed by Carlos Hagerman. It tells an intimate and discerning tale depicting the impact of migration on the families and communities left behind by loved ones who have traveled north to find work in the United States.

Under the Same Moon. 2007. 106 minutes, color. Creando Films.

> This documentary won a Sundance Film Festival award. It is directed by Patricia Riggin, in Spanish and English, and follows a young Mexican boy who travels to the United States to find his mother after his grandmother, who was caring for him in Mexico, passes away.

The Undocumented. 2004. 90 minutes, color. ITVS/Two Tone Production.

> The documentary film depicts the tragic tale shared by the approximately 2,000 immigrants who died while trying to cross the Sonoran Desert in search of a better life in the United States. It gives faces to some of the dead and follows their long journey home.

Wetback: The Undocumented Documentary. 2005. 96 minutes, color. IMDb Productions.

> This Canadian documentary film chronicles the struggles and hardships of a handful of Mexicans trying to relocate to the United States.

Videos

The Dream Is Now. 2013. 31 minutes, color. At http://www.thedreamisnow.org/

> This video is a moving and thought-provoking look at the undocumented youth in America commonly known as "the Dreamers." Directed by an award-winning documentary film director, the short video brings the pressing issue to the nation's attention and debate for the viewers to decide for themselves.

Facing Up to Illegal Immigration. 2004. 23 minutes, color. Films Media Group.

> The video discusses whether there is a realistic way to stop unauthorized immigrants at the border. This ABC News special presents a balanced look in addressing issues such as the liability of porous borders in a time of terrorism, the seeming need for illegal workers, and whether or not they really take work away from citizens or are doing work that Americans themselves are unwilling to do.

The Immigration History of the United States. 2014. 21:22 minutes. The Daily Conversation.

> This is a TDC original documentary explaining the history of immigration to America from the "natives" who first populated the land to Mexican migrants coming in huge numbers today.

Immigration: Who Has Access to the American Dream? 2002. 28 minutes, color. Film for the Humanities and Sciences.

> The program reviews how post-9/11 policy affects the survival of new immigrants to the United States. It covers a variety of questions, such as how many should be let in, who should receive preferential treatment, and how illegals should be handled when apprehended. It examines the issue from several perspectives.

INDEX

About the Author

Michael C. LeMay, PhD, is professor emeritus at California State University–San Bernardino, where he served as director of the National Security Studies Program, an interdisciplinary master's degree program, and as chair of the Department of Political Science and assistant dean for student affairs for the College of Social and Behavioral Sciences. He has frequently written and presented papers at professional conferences on the topic of immigration. He has also written numerous journal articles, book chapters, published essays, and book reviews. He is published in the *International Migration Review, In Defense of the Alien,* the *Journal of American Ethnic History,* the *Southwestern Political Science Review, Teaching Political Science,* and the *National Civic Review.* He is the author of 30 academic books, more than a dozen of which are academic volumes dealing with immigration history and policy. His prior books on the subject are: *Homeland Security* (ABC-CLIO, 2018), *Religious Freedom in America* (ABC-CLIO, 2018), *U.S. Immigration Policy, Ethnicity, and Religion in American History* (Praeger, 2018), *Illegal Immigration: A Reference Handbook,* 2nd ed. (ABC-CLIO, 2015 [1st ed., 2007]), *Doctors at the Borders: Immigration and the Rise of Public Health* (Praeger, 2015); editor and contributing author of the three-volume *Transforming America: Perspectives on U.S. Immigration* (ABC-CLIO, 2013), author and/or editor of *Guarding the Gates: Immigration and National Security* (Praeger Security International, 2006), *U.S. Immigration and Naturalization Laws and Issues: A Documentary History* (edited with Elliott Barkan; Greenwood, 1999), *Anatomy of a Public Policy:*

The Reform of Contemporary American Immigration Law (Praeger, 1994), *The Gatekeepers: Comparative Immigration Policy* (Praeger, 1989), *From Open Door to Dutch Door: An Analysis of U.S. Immigration Policy Since 1820* (Praeger, 1987), and *The Struggle for Influence* (1985). Professor LeMay has written two textbooks with considerable material related to these topics: *Public Administration: Clashing Values in the Administration of Public Policy*, 2nd ed. (2006), and *The Perennial Struggle*, 3rd ed. (2009). He frequently lectures on topics related to immigration history and policy. He loves to travel and has lectured around the world, having visited more than 180 cities in 51 countries. His most recent works are *The American Congress* (with Sara Hagedorn; ABC-CLIO, 2019) and *Immigration Reform: A Reference Handbook* (ABC-CLIO, 2019).